Real Things in Nature

REAL THINGS IN NATURE

·The· ⚒ ·Co·

REAL THINGS IN NATURE

A READING BOOK OF SCIENCE
FOR AMERICAN BOYS AND GIRLS.

By

EDWARD S. HOLDEN, Sc. D., LL. D.,

LIBRARIAN OF THE UNITED STATES MILITARY ACADEMY, WEST POINT.

New York:

THE MACMILLAN COMPANY

LONDON: MACMILLAN & CO. LTD.

1903

PRESS OF
THE NEW ERA PRINTING COMPANY
LANCASTER, PA.

TO MY YOUNG FRIEND
KATHARINE TILLMAN

PREFACE.

The immediate object of this volume is to present to young children a view of the world which shall be, in its degree, complete, useful and interesting.

An American lad of a dozen years of age has had training at home and at school; he has observed the world for himself, and has profited more or less by the experience of his fellows. He has ideas upon many subjects; he is forming habits of thought that will be of the greatest consequence to others and to himself in the future. He is just at the time of life when his mind is open to direction, and is eager for explanations of the world in which he lives. He is full of questions. The various parts of this volume give the answers to such questions.

For example: the American school boy is familiar with railways, electric lights, the telegraph, the telephone, etc. He has many questions to ask concerning them, and concerning the machines that he sees in daily use — the lever, the balance, etc. The answers are given in the book on Physics.

Every American boy is interested in the habits of animals and has met in his own experience many instances of their intelligence. He listens with interest to accounts of their social organizations,

and to explanations of their adaptations to environ-
ment and circumstance.

It is not possible to give complete explanations;
but it is not difficult to have the explanations complete so far as they go. He will have nothing to
unlearn in the future; on the foundations here laid
in these and other subjects he can go as far as he
likes.

Certain scientific ideas are entirely too difficult
to be grasped by young minds. It is better to omit
some topics altogether than to present a set of words
which can have no vital meaning. Very much of
chemistry, for example, is above the capacity of
young pupils. All that can be done is to present a
few fundamental ideas, to enforce them by a few
simple and safe experiments and to leave the rest
of the science untouched.

It is the fundamental ideas of science and its
methods that are here insisted upon; its *facts* are
of importance chiefly as illustrating its mode of
thought.   The methods of astronomy, of geology, of chemistry, for example, are very different.
The answers to the questions: How do you know
that the stars are self-luminous? How is it proved
that water is compound? How is the age of the
Earth determined? are reached by very different
paths. It is of the first importance that the pupil
should know how his elders set about to prove such
things. He should carry away from his reading
an intimate conviction that such answers have

really been found, and that, on the whole, he knows *how* it was done, although he may not know all the details of the processes.

The experiments here described are, with very few exceptions, such as can be performed by the teacher in the class-room or by the pupil at home. In general, it is a mere waste of words to describe an experiment that requires complex apparatus which the pupil will never see except in the figures of his text-book. Simple experiments are here suggested and the pupil is reminded of verifications that he himself can make by the words (try it) — which occur very frequently in this text.

The main object is to teach *ideas*. Technical words are avoided so far as possible. At the same time technical terms have been unhesitatingly employed when they are essential to brevity, or when they are such as will be constantly met with hereafter. It is necessary to say *protoplasm*, for instance; there is no royal road round it.

The book is designed to supplement the instruction which the pupil has gained from other text-books and to carry it further, according to a symmetric plan. It is occasionally necessary to treat subjects here that have already been studied by the child in his Geography, History, etc.; but it will be found that the old topics are approached in new ways, so that there is no real loss of energy or time.

Sometimes the same topic has been treated twice, from two different points of view, in two different sections of the book. New relations of familiar things are thus disclosed; and this method would have been followed oftener had the limits of space permitted.

The illustrations have been carefully chosen, usually from books published by the Macmillan Company, especially : Huxley's Physiology, Bailey's Botany and Lessons on Plants, Davenport's Zoölogy, McMurry & Tarr's Geography, Tarr's Geology and Physical Geography, etc., etc. To these and other authorities the writer's obligations are gratefully acknowledged.

The titles to the cuts are usually given in two parts: first, a short title which the pupil will remember; second, a longer explanation which makes the cut complete in itself and saves a reference to the text. The pictures in the book, with their titles, constitute an abstract of the whole work. When the book is used in the class-room the pupil should be instructed to point, with a long pin, at each part of a cut as he reads its explanation in the title.

After a cut in the book is understood the pupil should, in many cases, be required to draw it from memory. If he can reproduce such cuts as those giving the theory of shadows, the connections of an electric bell, the genealogical tree of the mammalia, etc., he understands what he has studied. There is no better test.

There can, of course, be no originality in the subject matter of an elementary book of this sort. The chief merit which can be hoped for is a clear presentation of well-known facts. It is possible to make great subjects interesting to both teacher and pupil, even where they must be treated with extreme conciseness. If, as is hoped, this has been done the volume should be of value. If America is to take and maintain a foremost place in the world, it can only be done through the predominance of certain qualities in its citizens that scientific education fosters to a very important degree. We cannot afford to neglect any means of developing thoroughness and faithfulness in the performance of duty in those who will soon be the responsible governors of our country.

Every year thousands of children leave the public schools to begin life for themselves. Only a small percentage enter high schools, and a very much smaller percentage enter colleges. It is the duty of the common schools to prepare their graduates as fully as possible for the business of life. They must be thoroughly grounded in the elements of knowledge. What more can be done under the circumstances? Some of the workings of the world around them can be explained. They can be made to understand the fundamental notions of government, law, history, science. They can be taught to reflect on what they see and hear.

It is believed that a book like the present volume in the hands of the zealous and intelligent teachers of the country will be a suggestive help in all these matters. Under the most favorable conditions the pupil will have been taught what it contains in his own home. In many cases he must depend upon formal instruction at school. To aid formal instruction of this sort, to systematize it, is the main object of the book. Its ultimate purpose is fully explained in the introduction that follows.

E. S. H.

U. S. Military Academy,
   West Point, New York,
      June 17, 1902.

INTRODUCTION.

(TO BE READ BY THE CHILDREN WHO OWN THIS BOOK.)

THE children who read this book ought to know before they read it what use it is going to be to them. Let us see. The book is owned by an American school boy (or school girl) who was born ten or twelve years ago and who expects to live in this world fifty or sixty years more. Fifty years is a very long time — think of all the things that have happened in the last fifty years — and then think forward what may happen in the next fifty years — things that may happen in the world, in this our country, or to you.

Suppose that we could make things happen by merely wishing them, what would you and I wish for the whole world? We should begin by wishing that there might be peace and plenty—no wars, no famines, plenty of work for all of us, a chance for every one, and a wish in every one to do his best. What we desire for the whole world in general, we particularly wish for our own country. We hope its future will be peaceful, that there will be no quarrels or wars, that every man can always find work to do, that every one of us will wish to work and will do his work faithfully and cheerfully.

Your best friend will wish the same thing for you that we have wished for the country. He will wish that your whole life shall be peaceful and happy, that whenever you need money for yourself or for your family and friends you can find plenty of well-paid work to do and that you will wish to do it faithfully and with all your might, that you will always try to do the right and useful thing cheerfully.

If these wishes come true you will lead a happy life, you will be useful to your country; and if all the school children are like that, your country will be useful to the whole world and honored everywhere. Something depends on you, then; you can be useful to your friends and family and country if you will try; and if you try, you will be happy yourself. If enough of us try we can make the country useful to the whole world. But we must try in the right way; we must know what to do and how to do it.

We must understand things and the reasons of things—what they are and why they are. Not to understand is like trying to work in the dark. The better you understand the reasons, the better work you can do, and the happier you will be in doing it.

For instance, just suppose that one of the boys in a school grows up to be the engineer of a locomotive. All engineers understand their business very well, but some understand it a little better than others. Any engineer can run his engine safely so long as all the machinery works well. Some day, in spite of everything, there is danger of an accident. The man that knows his business best is most likely to take his train safe through. Because he understands he is able to save his train and, it may be, to save people's lives. That is worth doing. It is worth while to understand.

This book teaches every boy something about the locomotive. If he understands what is taught here he can easily go on and learn more. It teaches him about electricity, too, so that he will know how the telephone carries the voice from place to place; why it is possible to telegraph from New York to San Francisco, or under the ocean to London; how it is that electric cars are made to go; and a hundred other things of the same sort.

In a small book like this it is not possible to speak of everything; but the most important machines and inventions are explained. By paying attention you can understand these, and if you thoroughly understand one machine you can easily learn about others. While you are learning you are fitting yourself to be a more useful citizen. The man that understands is the man that everyone trusts. He has the work he wants and is well paid for it. He likes his work. It is a pleasure for him to do it. Many of the chapters in this book speak about just such practical things as the locomotive, the telegraph, etc.

Some of them speak about matters that do not seem to be practical at all, about things that are not immediately useful—about the motions of the Sun, Moon and Stars, for instance. You may say, what earthly good can it be to me to know that the Stars rise and set, as the Sun does; or to know what makes the colors of the rainbow; or.to study about the chemistry of sulphur and carbon and nitre?

Here is an answer to one of these questions; and all of them have answers of the same sort. It is extremely " practical" for ship captains to be able to navigate their vessels safely and quickly from port to port. The navigating of vessels is done by the stars. The first thing for a captain to know is that all the stars rise and set. He has to begin with that. Afterwards he finds out the latitude and the longitude of his ship by measuring the height of the sun and stars above his horizon at certain times every day. If he knows his latitude and longitude he knows where his ship is on the trackless ocean. That is " practical." It would be very unpractical for a ship captain to arrive at Brazil when he meant to go to England. But that is the very kind of thing he might do unless he began by learning what is taught in this book about the stars.

Gunpowder is made by mixing charcoal and sulphur and nitre; and it is made according to the rules of chemistry. It is practical and useful to be able to make good gunpowder, so that rocks can be quarried easily, tunnels hollowed out, cannons fired, and so forth.

Moreover, it is interesting to know such things. Here you are living in a world full of interesting things—sunsets, rainbows, machinery, and so forth. Why not learn about them?

Suppose some one working in a factory saw a steam engine driving the machinery every day and all day, and never took the trouble to ask how it was that a little coal put in a boiler downstairs made a wheel turn round in the fourth story. It would show, in the first place, that he was not very much interested in his work, and in the second place that he was rather stupid not to find out how a coal fire could be used to heat water to make steam; and how steam could be made to turn a wheel on the engine; and finally how belts on this wheel could be made to turn all the wheels in a whole building. Suppose a boy never tried to find out what made the hands of his watch turn round so as to tell the time. It would be stupid for him to call it magic, and not to try to understand.

Now the whole world can be explained. It is not magic. There is a good reason for everything. Some of the reasons are not easy to find out but many of them are. This book explains some of the simplest and most interesting and important things. When you have thoroughly understood these you can understand others either by looking about you and thinking for yourself; or by asking questions

1a

of older people; or by looking in encyclopædias and other books of the sort. When you understand, you can be useful; and when you are useful you will be happy. The business of grown-up men and women is to *do useful things;* the business of children is to *learn how to do them.*

This book is written, then, to help you to understand the world you live in; to put you in the way of being a useful citizen; to help you to be happy. Every intelligent American child, boy or girl, ought to know all that is in this book (and a great deal more). Things that are explained here will help you, every day, to understand the world you live in. It is *your* world (whose else is it?). Why shouldn't you take the pains to understand it? The difference between men and animals is just that men are interested and do understand while animals take everything for granted and do not even try to understand what they see.

The boy that tries to understand turns out to be the most intelligent man; the most intelligent man can be the most useful and the happiest; the nation that has the most intelligent citizens is the most useful nation in the world. You have a share in this work and this book is written to help you to do your part.

CONTENTS.

BOOK I. — ASTRONOMY.

PAGE.

ASTRONOMY: 1
What the Different Sciences Teach 1
The Earth 2
The Axis of the Earth 3
The Earth's Equator 3
Day and Night 3
Sunrise and Sunset 4
The Stars Rise and Set 5
The North Star 5
The Great Dipper 6
The Stars of the Northern Sky 6
The Northern Stars Appear to Circle Round the
    Pole 6
The Southern Stars Appear to Rise in the East and to
    Set in the West like the Sun 9
The Apparent Motion of the Stars from Rising to Set-
    ting is Caused by the Rotation of the Earth on Its
    Axis 10
The Celestial Sphere 11
Astronomical Instruments 11
Telescopes 12
Clocks and Chronometers 12
A Home-made Pendulum 13
Circles 13
The Earth and Planets move Round the Sun . . 13
The Sun and All the Stars Shine by their own
    Light 14

xix

PAGE.

The Moon and Planets Shine by Light Reflected from the
   Sun   14

The Orbits (Paths) of the Planets   15

The Distances of the Planets from the Sun .   .   17

The Minor Planets (Asteroids)   17

The Distance of the Earth from the Sun .   .   .   17

The Sizes of the Planets 18, 20

The Size of the Sun 19, 20

The Planet Mercury   20

The Planet Venus   20

The Planet Mars   20

The Planet Jupiter   21

The Planet Saturn   21

The Planet Uranus   21

The Planet Neptune   21

Could Men Live on Any of the Planets? .   .   .   22

The Moon.   25

The Phases of the Moon   26

The Phases of the Planets Venus and Mercury.   .   28

The Mountains of the Moon   28

Satellites (Moons) of the Different Planets .   .   29

The Revolution of the Earth round the Sun .   .   30

The Seasons   32

Eclipses of the Sun   33

Eclipses of the Moon.   34

The Sun   34

The Sun is a Star   35

The Spots on the Sun   37

The Sun's Corona   35

Meteor-Swarms   36

Comets   37

Shooting-stars (Meteors)   39

The Universe of Stars   40

Constellations   41

Clusters   41

The Nebulæ   41

The Distances of the Stars   42

BOOK II. — Physics.

PAGE.

Physics : 44
    Solids, Liquids and Gases 44
    Air 45
    Ice 45
    Steam 45
    Force of Gravity 46
    Fall of Heavy Bodies 47
    Attraction of the Earth 47
    How Fast do Things Fall ? 48
    Weight 49
    The Vertical Line (Up and Down) . . . 51
    The Pendulum 52
    The Level 52
    Measures of Length 53
    The Metric System 53
    Tools to Measure Lengths 54
    Time (Day, Week. Month, Year, Century) . . 55
Heat : 56
    Thermometers 56
    Melting Points 57
    Boiling Points 57
    Hot Bodies usually Expand 58
    Conduction of Heat 59
    Work can be Turned into Heat 59
    Steam 60
    The Locomotive 61
    The Steam Engine 62
Light : 63
    The Sun and Stars Shine by Light of their Own . 63
    Phases of the Moon 64
    Self-luminous Bodies 66
    All Light-rays Travel in Straight Lines . . 66
    Rays of Light go in all Directions . . . 67
    Shadows 67
    Eclipses 69
    Shadows of an Obelisk 70
    The Sun Dial 71

	PAGE
Reflection of Light by a Mirror.	72
Reflecting Telescopes	72
A Home-made Kaleidoscope	73
Refraction of Light	74
Refraction of Light by a Prism.	74
Refraction of Light by a Lens	75
Microscope	75
Burning Glass	76
Spectacles	76
The Telescope	77
The Solar Spectrum	77
Velocity of Light	78
SOUND:	78
Sound Waves	78
Waves of Water.	79
Sound is Caused by a Vibration	79
Musical Instruments.	80
Singing	81
Sound Travels Through the Air	81
Velocity of Sound	82
ELECTRICITY:	83
Friction	83
Experiments	83
Benjamin Franklin's Experiment (1752)	87
Electricity from Batteries	88
The Electric Battery	88
A Home-Made Battery	89
Currents and Circuits	89
Electric Bells	90
The Electric Telegraph	91
The Telegraph Alphabet	92
The Telephone	92
The Dynamo	93
The Electric Railway	94
Electric Lighting	94
MAGNETISM:	95
Natural Magnets	95
Experiments	96
Magnetism.	96

PAGE.

Artificial Magnets 96
Experiments 97
The Mariner's Compass 99
Electro-magnets. 99
MACHINES: 100
The Pulley 100
The Lever 101
The Inclined Plane 102
The Screw 104
Pumps 105

BOOK III. — METEOROLOGY.

METEOROLOGY 107
The Atmosphere 107
Height of the Atmosphere 108
Air is a Mixture of Oxygen and Nitrogen Gases . 108
Air is Heavy . . . . :08
The Weight of the Atmosphere 109
Experiments 110
The Barometer 110
Measurements of Heights by the Barometer . . 112
The Aneroid Barometer 113
The Barometer is a Weather-glass 114
U. S. Weather Bureau Predictions of Weather . 114
A Weather Map 115
Water Vapor 116
Mists and Fogs 116
Dew 116
Frost 117
Clouds 118
Rain 118
Hail 118
Snow 118
Sleet 118
Snowflakes 119
The Rainfall of the United States 119
The Snow Line 121, 122
The Rainbow 122
Halos 122

BOOK IV. — CHEMISTRY.

PAGE.

CHEMISTRY : 123
    Things Needed for Experiments 123
    Physical Changes 124
    Solutions 124
    Mixtures 124
    Chemical Combination 124
    Making Sulphate of Iron 124
    Making Sulphate of Copper 125
    Making Sulphate of Zinc 125
    Making Carbonate of Lime 125
    Chemical Affinity 126
    Chemical Manufactures 126
    Gunpowder 126
    Composition of Air 127
    Composition of Water 127
    Oxygen Gas 127
    Nitrogen Gas 127
    Hydrogen Gas 129
    Combustion (Burning) 130
    Carbonic Acid Gas 130
    Iron-Rust 130
    Temperature of the Human Body 130
    Combustion in Oxygen 131
    Composition of Water 131
    Balloons 131
    Chemical Elements 132
    Metals 133
    Non-Metals 133
    Chemical Compounds 133
    Chemical Symbols 135

BOOK V. — GEOLOGY.

GEOLOGY : 136
    The Earth's Crust 136
    Running Water Models the Shape of the Hills. . 137
    Ocean Waves Wear away Sea-cliffs . . . 138
    Rivers cut Gorges 139

CONTENTS.   XXV

	PAGE.
Gorge of Niagara River	139
The Cañon of the Colorado River	140
Rivers carry Soil to the Sea	141
Stones are Carried by Streams.	141
Streams Sort out Stones in Sizes	142
Flood Plains	143
Deltas	143
Sediments are Deposited in Layers (Strata)	143
All Sedimentary Rocks are Stratified	144
Glaciers	145
Bowlders	145
Glacier-scratches on Rocks	146
The Glacial Period in the United States	147
Icebergs	149
Pack-Ice	149
Soil is Rock that has been Broken up	150
Different Kinds of Rocks	151
Granite	151
Limestone	151
Sandstone	151
Lava	151
Slate	153
Clay	153
Crystalline Rocks	153
Crystals	153
Precious Stones	153
Snowflakes are Crystals	155
Elevation and Depression of the Land	155
Sea Shells on the Tops of Mountains	156
Seals in Lake Baikal	156
The Temple of Jupiter Serapis	156
The Stratified Rocks	158
Crumpling of the Earth's Crust	158
Mountains	159
The Pressure of the Rocks Within the Earth	159
Fauna and Flora of a Region	160
Fossils	161
The Unstratified Rocks	161
Volcanoes	161

PAGE.

Vesuvius 162
Pompeii 163
Earthquakes 164
The Age of the Earth 164
Geological Ages 165
Age of Invertebrates 168
Age of Reptiles 169
Age of Mammals 169
Life in the Age of Invertebrates . . . 169
The Coal-period. 169
Peat-bogs 169
Life in the Age of Reptiles 171
Flora and Fauna of the Jurassic Period . . . 172
Life since the Age of Coal 172
Ancestors of the Horse 174
Natural Selection 175
The Struggle for Existence 175
Heredity : Adaptation 176
Recent Geological Periods. 177
The Glacial Period 147, 178
Botanical Regions 179
Prehistoric Man 181
The Pyramids of Egypt 181

BOOK VI. — ZoÖLOGY.

ZoÖLOGY : 183
  Kingdom, Class, Order, Family, Genus, Species . 183
  Differences between Plants and Animals . . . 184
  Fossil Animals 185
  Fauna and Flora 185
  The Eight Branches of the Animal Kingdom . . 186
  Cells 187
  Protoplasm 187
  One-celled Animals — the Amœba 187
  The Ooze or Mud at the Bottom of the Ocean . . 189
  Many-celled Animals — Sponges 190
  Jelly-fish 191
  Corals 192
  Coral Islands 192

PAGE.

Hydra 193
Worms 194
Star-fish (Radiates) 195
Oysters 196
Clams 197
Pearls 197
Mother-of-Pearl 197
The Lobster 197
Crabs 199
Insects 199
Butterflies 199
Intelligence of Insects — Ants 202
Bees 202
Spiders 205
Vertebrates 206
The Codfish 210
Electric Fishes 210
Sticklebacks 211
Frogs and Toads 211
Tadpoles 211
Reptiles 213
Turtles 213
Rattlesnakes 213
Alligator 213
Birds' Bills 214
Birds' Feet 215
Birds 216
The Sparrow 216
The Blue Jay 217
Nests 218
Migration of Birds 219
Intelligence of Birds 219
Mammals 220
Horns 220
Hibernation (Winter Sleep) of Animals . . 220
Intelligence of Animals 223
Social Life of Animals 223
Monkeys 232
Man 232

BOOK VII. — BOTANY.

	PAGE.
BOTANY:	235
What is a Plant ?	235
Cells	235
Vegetable Protoplasm	235
Experiments	236
Growing-points.	236
Cells Contain Living Protoplasm	236
Division of the Cell	237
Nuclei	238
Mother cells ; Daughter-cells	238
Size of the Cells.	238
A Plant	238
Growth	238
Color of Plants — Chlorophyll	238
Sunlight does the Work	238
Herbs	239
Shrubs	239
Trees	239
Annuals	239
Biennials	239
Perennials.	239
The Roots of Plants	240
Roots of Trees	240
Root Hairs	241
Work of Roots	241
Circulation of the Sap	241
Roots Grow Downward	241
Experiments	242
Water Rises in the Roots	242
Root-pressure	242
Plant-Food from the Soil	243
Length of Roots	243
Aërial Roots	243
The Stems of Plants	245
Fleshy Stems	245
Woody Stems	245
The Plan of a Plant—Maize	246

	PAGE.
Endogens (Maize, Palm)	246
Exogens (Oaks, Elms)	246
A Tree is like a Colony of Corals	246
Underground Stems	247
Branches	248
Struggle for Existence	248
Winter Buds	249
Fall of the Leaf	249
Evergreens	250
Leaf-scars	250
Buds	250
Experiment	250
Leaves	251
Ribs — Mid-rib	251
Veins — Veinlets	251
The Shapes of Leaves	252
Leaves Love the Sunlight	252
Arrangement of the Leaves on the Shoot . . .	254
Breathing Pores (Holes) in Leaves	255
Leaves Breathe in Carbolic Acid Gas (chiefly) . .	256
Leaves Breathe out Oxygen (chiefly) . . .	256
Pores in the Human Body	257
Leaves Breathe in the Vapor of Water . . .	257
Why the Shade of a Tree is Cool	258
How Plants get their Food	258
Plants Contain much Carbon	258
A Green Plant gets its Carbon from the Air . .	258
The Plant makes Starch for its Food . . .	259
The Plant turns Starch into Sugar	259
The Sap	260
The Life of a Plant	260
Plants that Catch Flies for Food	260
Flowers — Branches	260
Solitary Flowers	261
What Flowers are for	261
Calyx	263
Whorl	263
Corolla	263

	PAGE.
Sepal.	264
Petal.	264
Torus.	264
Stamen	264
Pistil.	264
Anther	265
Pollen is Borne by the Stamens	265
Ovary	265
Style.	265
Stigma	265
The Seeds are Borne by the Pistils	265
Fertilization of Flowers	265
Cross Fertilization	266
Pollen is Carried by the Winds	266
Pollen in Carried by Insects	267
Fruits	267
Berries	267
Stone-Fruits	267
Nuts.	267
Grains	267
Pods.	267
Life in Seeds	267
Mummy-Wheat	268
How Seeds Are Scattered.	268
How Seeds Grow to be Plants	269
The Young Plant is in the Ripened Seed.	269
Plants Sometimes Grow from Buds	270
Fruit Trees Grow from Grafts on the Stems of Other Trees.	271
The Form of Plants.	272
The Habit of a Tree.	273
Trees (and Flowers) Suggest Certain Feelings	273
What Makes a Landscape Beautiful?	274
Age of Trees	275
The Struggle for Existence	275
Colors and Odors of Flowers	276
The Gardener helps Nature to form Varieties of Plants	277

PAGE.

Some of the Uses of Plants 278
   I. To Purify the Air for Animals 278
  II. To Make Food for Animals 278
 III. To Furnish Clothing for Men 278
 IV. To Supply Fuel. 279
  V. To Supply Light 279
 VI: To Give Steam-engines their Power . . . 279
All the Life in the World Depends on Plants and upon
   the Sun 279
Arbor Day. 279
Number of Plants 280
Species 280
Names of Species 280
Oak Trees 280
Acorns 281
Pine Trees 282
Pine Cones 282
Ferns 283
How to Make a Collection of Dried Plants . . 283

BOOK VIII. — THE HUMAN BODY.

THE HUMAN BODY : 285
Physiology 285
Anatomy 285
Hygiene 285
Man is a Vertebrate Animal 286
Man is a Mammal 286
The Human Skeleton 288
The Plan of the Human Body 289
The Chest (Thorax) and Ribs 290
The Abdomen 292
Organs of the Human Body 293
What the Body is made of 293
Chemistry of the Body 294
The Human Skeleton — Bones 294
Cartilage 295
Tissue . . . . : . . . 295
The Backbone 297

	PAGE.
The Skull	298
The Soft Bones of Children	299
Bones of the Hips	300
Bones of the Legs	301
Bones of the Arms	301
The Structure of Bones	302
The Biceps Muscle	303
The Elbow Joint	303
It is Worth While to Keep Our Bodies Healthy .	303
What to do	303
Why to do it	304
Tight Shoes	306
The Teeth	306
Muscles	308
Voluntary Muscles	309
Involuntary Muscles	309
Tendons	310
Muscles can be Educated	310
Contraction of Muscles	310
The Skin	311
The Dermis and Epidermis	311
The Veins and Nerves of the Skin	312
The Organs of Touch	313
Some Parts of the Body are more Sensitive than Others.	313
Sweat-glands	314
Use of the Sweat-glands	314
The Complexion	315
Blushing	315
Finger-nails	315
Hairs	316
Oil-glands	316
Food : how it is Used in the Body	316
Food and Work	317
Gastric Juice	318
Chyme	319
Chyle.	319
Digestion in the Mouth	320

	PAGE.
Saliva	320
Mucous Membrane	320
Gullet	320
Food Passes Down the Gullet Slowly	320
Gastric Juice	320
Digestion in the Stomach	321
Digestion in the Small Intestine	321
Digestion	322
Absorption	322
Lymph Vessels	322
The Circulation of the Blood	322
Arteries	322
Veins	323
Capillaries	323
Oxygenation of the Blood	324
The Human Heart	324
The Course of the Flow of Blood	324
Systemic Circulation	324
Pulmonary Circulation	324
The Cavities of the Heart (Auricles and Ventricles)	325
Experiment	325
Beating of the Heart — the Pulse	325
Experiment	326
The Blood	327
Blood Corpuscles	327
Without Blood we Cannot Live	328
Transfusion of Blood	328
We Speak by Air Forced Through the Glottis	328
The Air-passages	329
The Windpipe	329
Pharynx	329
Larynx	329
Glottis	330
Experiment	330
Breathing (Respiration)	330
Experiment	331
Movements of the Chest in Breathing	332
Plenty of Fresh Air is Necessary	332

2a

PAGE.

Good Ventilation 332
Sneezing and Coughing 333
Breathe Through Your Nose 333
The Brain 333
The Cerebrum 333
The Cerebellum 333
The Medulla 334
The Spinal Cord 336
The Nerves 336
The Nerves Carry Messages to and from the Brain . 336
Paralysis 337
Reflex-Action 339
Nerve-Centers 339
Sleep 339
Death 340
The Elements of the Body Return to the Soil . . 340
The Senses 340
We Know the Outside World Through Our Senses . 341
Personality 341
Stimulus and Reaction 342
Cells 343
Each Cell is Alive 343
Your Body is a Colony of Cells 343
The Human Will Governs the Body 344
Seeing—the Eye 345
Experiments 345
Hearing—the Ear 347
Smelling—the Nose 348
Tasting—the Tongue 348

BOOK IX.—THE EARLY HISTORY OF MANKIND.

ETHNOLOGY : 350
Savages 352
Barbarians 352
Civilized Peoples 353
The Stone Age 353
The Bronze Age 353
The Iron Age 354

		PAGE.
Progress of Mankind.	. . . . . .	356
Origin of Mankind	. . . .	358
So Far as we Know every Tribe in the World was once		
Savage .	. . . .	359
Cannibals .	. . . .	360
How we can Tell the Previous Condition of a People.		360
Excavations	. . . .	363
Pompeii .	. . . .	163, 364
ARCHÆOLOGY : .	. . . .	364
Pre-Historic Men	. . . .	364
How to Measure Time in the Ancient History of Man-		
kind	. . . .	364
Wild Beasts that once Lived in Europe	. . .	365
Cave-Men—Cave-Dwellers	. . . .	365
Pictures of Animals drawn by Pre-Historic Men,		366, 367
Pre-Historic Men	. . . . . .	367
Remains of Ancient Peoples	. . . .	367
ANCIENT EGYPT :	. . . .	367
Early History of the Egyptians	. . . .	368
The Pyramids .	. . . . . .	368
The Sphinx	. . . . . .	368
The Great Wall of China .	, ...	370
Life of the Egyptians	. . . . .	370
Egyptian Painting	. . . . . .	371
Egyptian Writing	. . . . . .	372
Hieroglyphics	. . . . . .	372
The King (Pharaoh).	. . . . .	372
The Priests	. . . .	372
The Scribes	. . . .	372
The Army .	. . . .	373
The People	. . . .	373
Egyptian Commerce .	. . . . .	373
Religion of the Egyptians	. . . .	373
Sacred Animals .	. . . . . .	374
Mummies .	. . . .	374
How we have been Taught by Ancient Nations	.	375
How to Study the History of Mankind	. .	376
Pictures that Show How each Nation Lives	. .	377

		PAGE.
RACES OF MANKIND :	. . . . . .	378
Marks of Race .	. . . . . .	379
The Color of the Skin	. . . . .	379
The Color of the Eyes	. . . . .	379
The Shape of the Skull	. . . . .	380
The Shape of the Nose, Eyes, Lips .	. . .	381
The Hair .	. . . . . .	381
Climate	. . . . . .	383
LANGUAGE :	. . . . . .	386
The Aryan People and Language	. . . .	388
Caste	. . . . . .	391
The Semitic Languages .	. . . .	392
Other Groups of Languages	. . . .	392
Sign-Language.	. . . . .	393
The Language of Animals	. . . .	395
WRITING :	. . . . .	396
Writing of the North American Indians .	. .	396
Writing of the Chinese	. . . .	396
Writing of the Egyptians (hieroglyphics)	. .	397
The Alphabet .	. . . . .	397
Printing .	. . . . .	398
Paper	. . . . . .	398
Counting (Arithmetic)	. . . .	398
Measuring (Mathematics).	. . .	399
Music	. . . . . .	399
Beginnings of the Sciences	. . . .	400
FOOD :	. . . . . .	401
Flocks and Herds	. . . . .	401
Government and Laws	. . . .	402
FIRE :	. . . . . .	402
Flint and Steel .	. . . . .	402
The Fire-Drill .	. . . . .	402
Matches (invented in 1840)	. . .	403
Light	. . . . . .	403
Metal-Working .	. . . . .	403
Pottery	. . . . . .	403
Bricks	. . . . . .	403
The First Books	. . . . .	403
Money	. . . . . .	403

CONTENTS.

	PAGE.
WEAPONS:	405, 406
Clubs	406
Bows and Arrows	406
Stone-Axes	407
Swords, Battle-Axes and Guns	407
Knives and Swords	407
Blow-Guns	408
Poisoned Arrows	408
The Musket	409
DWELLINGS:	409
Tree-Dwellings	409
Huts — Villages	410
Lake-Dwellings	410, 414
Cottages	411
Houses	413
Cliff-Dwellings	415
Persepolis (destroyed B. C. 330)	416
The Colosseum of Rome (built A. D. 72)	416
The Doge's Palace at Venice (XIV. Century)	417
Castles in the Middle Ages (before XV. Century)	418
BOATS:	417
Canoes	419
Oars and Sails—Rudder	420
The Phœnicians	420
Kayak	420
Chinese Junks	421
Modern Sailing Vessels	421
Ships of Columbus (A. D. 1492)	422
Modern Steam Ships	422
SOCIETY:	422
Laws	402, 423
The Family	425
The Clan	426
Totems	426
Marriage	427
Slaves	428
RELIGIOUS IDEAS:	428
The World of Ghosts	428
Fetishes	428

	PAGE
Causes of Sickness	429
Sorcerers	429
Magic	429
The Gods of the Greeks	429
The Gods of the Hindus	430
The Gods of the Aryans	430
The Sky, the Sun, the Moon were once worshipped as Gods	430
Names of the Days of the Week	431
The Gods of the Japanese	432
The Planets	432
Buddha and Buddhism	433
Christian Churches	435
Mohammed and Mohammedanism	435
Chinese Temples	440
Worship of Ancestors	440
PROPERTY:	441
Taxes	442
CONCLUSION:	443

BOOK I: ASTRONOMY.

THE Earth that we live on is the most important *thing* in the whole universe to us; and accordingly, nearly all books that are written relate to the Earth itself; or to the creatures that live on the Earth —men and animals; or to the history of what men have done; or, most important of all, to the thoughts that they are thinking, or have thought.

Geography teaches us about the divisions of the Earth into land and water; why the rivers run as they do; what lands are fertile and what barren; and describes the different countries of the globe. *Meteorology* explains why certain countries have pleasant climates while others are cold and bleak, or too hot to live in with comfort; it describes the atmosphere of air which we breathe; tells us what fogs, mists and clouds are made of; why we have storms, and so forth. *Geology* describes the rocks of which the earth is made; shows how the mountains were lifted up; explains the causes of volcanoes and earthquakes. *Ethnology* tells us about the different races of men; and *History* recounts everything that they have done, and shows why they did as they did. *Natural History*—the history of Nature—is a description of all the living

1   1

beings of the globe—animals, and so forth—and *Botany* is an account of all the plants.

Every *thing* that we know about is a solid, a liquid or a gas. *Physics* is a science that explains how solids, liquids and gases behave when they are heated or cooled; what sound, light, electricity and magnetism are. *Chemistry* explains how two things can be combined so as to make a third thing different from either—how, for example, you can mix two gases together and get a liquid, or how common salt can be separated into a metal and a gas.

All these different sciences are treated in this book. It is so important for us to understand about *Machines* that a chapter has been given to them; and as the *Human Body* is the most important of all machines it also has a chapter to itself.

The present chapter is devoted to *Astronomy*. You know that the Earth is one of the planets and that the Sun has a family of such planets—Venus, Jupiter, the Earth and others beside. Astronomy is the science that explains what the sun and stars really are, how they move in the sky and why they seem to move as they do. It tells the same things about planets and comets, too.

The Earth.—In the first place, you know that the Earth is a globe about 8,000 miles in diameter and that it is about 25,000 miles round the surface from New York back to New York again.

The Axis of the Earth.—An imaginary line joining the north pole of the Earth with its south pole

FIG. 1. We know the Earth is a sphere because men have gone to nearly every part of it, and because surveys have been made of nearly all the continents.

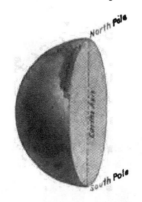

FIG. 2. A picture showing how the Earth would look if it were cut through its center. The diameter of the Earth is about 8,000 miles.

is called the Earth's axis.

The Earth's Equator. — A circle round the Earth midway between the Earth's north pole and south pole is the Earth's equator.

Day and Night.— The Earth turns on its axis once every day. The Sun shines on that

FIG. 3. The Earth's equator —an imaginary circle—passes through Brazil, *Ecuador*, Kongo and Borneo.

half of the Earth which is turned towards him. That half of the Earth has daylight—sunshine; the other half has night.

FIG. 4. A school room experiment to explain just how the sun lights one half and only one half of every globe. (Try it in a darkened room.)

Sunrise and Sunset.—You are on the Earth which is turning round its axis once in every 24 hours, but all the while the Earth seems to you to stand still while the Sun seems to move from rising to setting. It is really the Sun that stands still.

When you are in a railway train that is moving swiftly and smoothly the houses and fences seem to fly past you. In fact the houses stand still and it is you who move—but you know it only by thinking about it. In the same way, you know that it is the Earth that moves, and not the Sun, only by thinking about it.

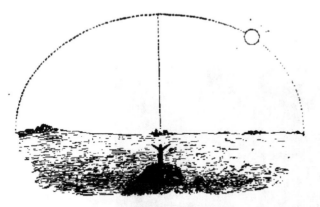

FIG. 5. The sun seems to rise in the east, mount in the sky till it is highest at noon, then sink towards the west till it sets. The picture shows how things look about 3 P. M. (Why about 3 P. M.?) The stars, at night, seem to rise and set also.

The Stars Rise and Set.—You know very well that the Moon rises and sets. All the Stars, too, rise and set, once every twenty-four hours, except some of the northern stars. They turn around *Polaris*[1]—the pole star—once in 24 hours, but they are always above the horizon—always in sight except in the daytime and, even then, they can be seen in telescopes.

The North Star.—A bright star named Polaris, the pole-star, is very near the north pole of the sky. You can always find it in a clear night by first finding the *Great Dipper* (some people call it the *Great Bear*, or, in Latin, *Ursa major*) in the northern part of the sky, then finding the two *Pointers*,

[1] Pronounced Pō-lă′ris.

and then by following the line of the two pointers
to the pole-star.

Fig. 6. The seven stars of the Great Dipper. Four of them, *a*
(*alpha*), β (*beta*), γ (*gamma*), δ (*delta*), make the bowl of the
Dipper and the other three, ε (*epsilon*), ζ (*zeta*), η (*eta*), make the
handle. *a* and β are the Pointers. A line through them points
nearly to Polaris—which is the upper star of the picture. You
can always find Polaris on a clear night. (Try it, not once only,
but every time you go out of doors at night.)

*The Northernmost Stars Appear to Circle
Around the Pole.*—In any clear night you can
easily prove that all the northern stars circle around
the pole. First find the *Dipper*, then the *Pointers*, next, *Polaris*. This bright star is not exactly
at the pole, but happens to be near it. As you
face north the east is on your right hand. Pick
out some group of stars towards the east, and
look at it every quarter of an hour for a couple of
hours. You will see that this group moves around

the pole in the direction of the arrows in Fig. 7. (Try it.)

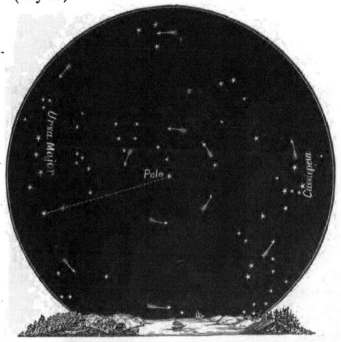

FIG. 7. The stars of the northern sky as they appear to a person in the United States in the early evening at the beginning of August. *Ursa Major* (the Dipper) is towards the west. Its two Pointers mark out the line to the pole-star. The arrows in the picture show the direction in which all the stars appear to move— from east towards west. Watch them some clear night for a couple of hours, and you will see that they do so.

Children who live in the country can easily prove that the northern stars appear to circle round the pole, by watching them. It is not so easy in the city where the electric lights dazzle the eyes and where houses are in the way of a clear view. Still, it can be done, even in the city, by going on the roof of the house, or by finding a place in the street where the northern stars can be seen.

A very good way to prove that the north stars appear to circle round the pole is to photograph them. A camera is pointed to the north pole early

FIG. 8. A photograph of the northern stars that was exposed 12 hours on a long winter's night. The pole is exactly at the center of the plate. Each star as it moved left a *trail* on the plate. These trails are exactly half circles (half of 24 hours is 12 hours). The bright trail nearest the pole was made by Polaris.

in the evening and the plate exposed so soon as the
sky is dark, and left exposed for several hours.
When the plate is developed it will show a picture
like Fig. 8.

All the northern stars, then, appear to circle
round the pole. If you will take pains enough you
can prove it for yourself.

*The Southern Stars Appear to Rise in the East
and to Set in the West, like the Sun.*—By watching

FIG. 9. A photograph of the apparent motions of southern
stars made by exposing a plate to stars of the southern sky. Each
star leaves a *trail*, which is nearly a straight line. This line is a
small part of the circle in which the star appears to move from
rising to setting.

any star in the southern sky you can prove that it appears to rise in the east, moves upward till it is exactly south of you, and then sinks down till it sets in the west. (Try it.) Different stars rise at different points of the eastern horizon, rise to different heights, and set at different points ; but all southern stars rise and set, just as the sun does.

The Apparent Motion of the Stars from Rising to Setting is Caused by the Rotation of the Earth on its Axis.—All the facts that have been described are explained by remembering that the Earth revolves

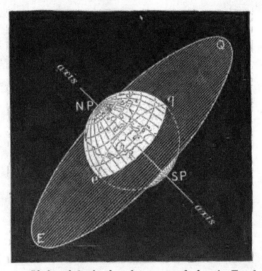

FIG. 10. If the globe in the picture stands for the Earth, N. P. is its north, S. P. its south pole. Its axis extended upward meets the celestial sphere near Polaris. The Earth's equator, extended outwards ($E\mathcal{Q}$) meets the celestial sphere in the celestial equator —the equator of the celestial sphere.

on its axis once in twenty-four hours. If you could extend the axis of the Earth (the line about which it turns, see Fig. 2) up to the stars it would meet the sky at the north pole of the heavens, near the star Polaris.

The Celestial Sphere.—When you look at the sky on a clear night the stars all *seem* to be at the same distance from you. They look like bright shining points fastened to the inside surface of a hollow globe.

The ancients called this globe the *celestial sphere* and they thought there actually was such a solid sphere to which all the stars were really fastened.

Nowadays we know that different stars are at different distances from us and that there is not any one globe to which all of them are fastened; but we speak of the celestial sphere just the same. It

FIG. 11. The largest telescope in the world. It belongs to the University of Chicago.

is a convenient name for the sphere to which the stars *seem* to be (and are not) fastened.

Astronomical Instruments.—The principal astronomical instruments are telescopes, circles and clocks.

Telescopes are described in Book II. of this volume (Light). The smallest telescopes are opera-glasses and spy glasses. If you can get an opera-glass you should use it to look at the stars, the planets and the Moon.

Do not look at the Sun, however: its light is so intense that it will make you blind.

A telescope consists of two lenses held at the right distance apart by a tube. It is usually mounted on a stiff stand. The lens at one end of the tube is large. It collects all the rays of light from the object you are looking at and makes a little picture of them (at the other end of the tube). You can see just such a picture on the ground glass of any photographer's camera. The small eyepiece is nothing but a magnifying-glass that magnifies this picture.

FIG. 12. A good school telescope on a tripod. It is about three feet long.

Clocks and Chronometers.—If you say the Earth turns round in twenty-four hours you ought to be able to prove it; and to prove it you must have some way of measuring time. A foot-rule measures distances; a clock or chronometer measures times.

The Pendulum. — Every boy should make, for himself, a pendulum like the one in the picture. The length of the pendulum can be changed (by winding up the thread on the spool). When the pendulum is short, it swings quickly; when it is long, it swings slowly; when it is $39\frac{1}{10}$ inches long, it beats seconds. (Try it.)

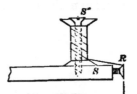

FIG. 13. A home-made pendulum : Screw a spool to a table by the screw (S'); in the edge of the table put a smaller screw (R); fasten a weight (B) to a thread and wind it round the spool; make the distance from R to the middle of the weight (B), $39\frac{1}{10}$ inches and then the pendulum will swing to and fro in exactly one second. It will swing 60 times in 1 minute; 3,600 times in an hour; 86,400 times in a day.

Circles. — Astronomers measure the angle between two stars by telescopes fastened to circles. The circumference of each circle is divided into 360 degrees (360°). See Fig. 14.

The Earth and Planets Move Round the Sun. — The Earth moves round the Sun, in a path that is called its *orbit*, once every year—every $365\frac{1}{4}$ days. There are other planets beside the Earth, and each and every one of them moves round the Sun in an orbit—a path—of its own. The planets

are named *Mercury, Venus, Earth, Mars, Jupiter,
Saturn, Uranus, Neptune.* Venus you know because it is often the bright Evening Star. Jupiter

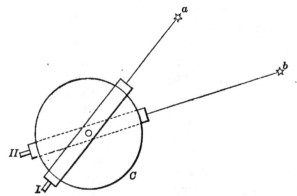

FIG. 14. O is the center of a brass circle whose rim (*C*) is divided into 360°. A telescope moves on a pivot at O and can be
pointed at any star as *a* (the eye will then be placed at *I*), or to
any other star *b* (the eye will then be placed at *II*). The angle
between the two stars (the angle *a*O*b*) is measured by the number
of degrees between the two positions of the telescope (*I* and *II*).

is bright, too. Mars is bright and so is Saturn.
The others are much fainter. All the planets look
exactly like stars, but they are really very different
from stars.

*The Sun and all the Stars Shine by Their Own
Light.*—The Sun and every one of the stars shines
by its own light, just as an electric-light, or a
candle, shines by its own light.

*The Moon and Planets Shine by Light Reflected
From the Sun.*—The planets have no light of their
own. They shine by light sent out from the Sun

and reflected to us, just as a far off mirror has no
light of its own, but is bright because it reflects the
sunlight.   The Moon, too, shines by reflected sunlight.   If you could blow out the Sun as you can
blow out a candle all the stars would keep on shining, but all the planets, and the Moon, would cease
to shine the moment the sunlight was taken away.

The Orbits (Paths) of the Planets.—The Sun is
in the middle of all these orbits—which are nearly

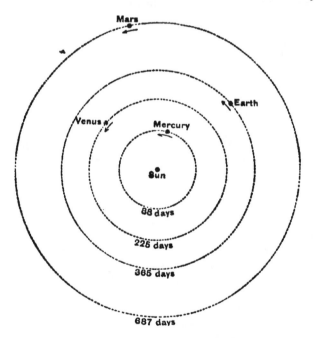

FIG. 15. The orbits of the four planets that are nearest the
Sun. The orbits are drawn in the right proportion. The distance from the Sun to the Earth is 93,000,000 miles.

circles.   Each planet moves in its orbit around the Sun.

The planet Mercury goes once round the Sun in 88 days.
     "   Venus   "   "   "   225 "
     "   Earth   "   "   "   365 "
     "   Mars   "   "   "   687 "

We must make another picture to show the orbits of the four planets that are farthest from the Sun, because the page of this book is not large enough to show them on the same scale as Fig. 15.

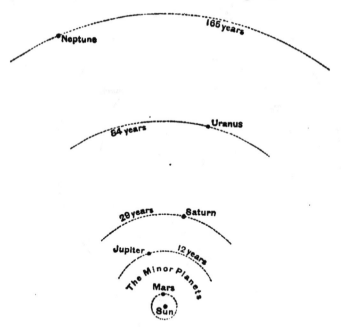

FIG. 16. The orbits of the four planets that are farthest from the Sun. The orbits are drawn in the right proportion. The distance from the Sun to Mars 141,000,000 miles.

The planet Jupiter goes once round the Sun in 12 years.
   "   Saturn   "   "   "   29   "
   "   Uranus   "   "   "   84   "
   "   Neptune   "   "   "   165   "

The Distances of the Planets from the Sun.—

Mercury is 36,000,000 miles from the Sun.
Venus is   67,000,000   "   "   "
Earth is   93,000,000   "   "   "
Mars is   141,000,000   "   "   "

Jupiter is 5 times as far as the Earth.
Saturn is 9   "   "   "   "
Uranus is 19   "   "   "   "
Neptune is 30 "   "   "   "

The Minor Planets.—Between Mars and Jupiter there are several hundred very small planets, none of them more than 200 miles in diameter. (See Fig. 16.)

The Distance of the Earth from the Sun.—The distance round the Earth from New York back to New York again is 25,000 miles. Four times round the Earth is 100,000 miles; forty times round the Earth is 1,000,000 miles; three thousand seven hundred and twenty times round the Earth is 93,000,000 miles. If you were to live long enough to go three thousand times round and round the Earth, still you would not have travelled so far as the distance that separates the Sun from the Earth.

A fast railway train travels forty miles an hour. If such a train could travel to the Sun it would take 363 years to make the journey. A cannon ball

2

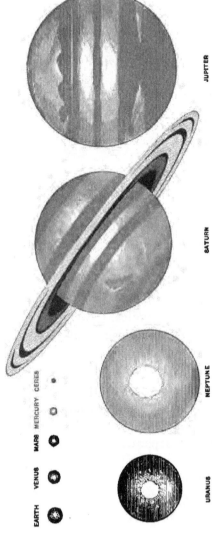

FIG. 17. The comparative sizes of the planets : If the Earth should shrink so as to be of the size of the little circle in the upper left-hand corner, all the other planets would shrink, in the same proportion, to be of the sizes drawn. The Earth, Mercury, Venus, and Mars, are about of the same size. Ceres is one of the largest of the Minor Planets. Jupiter and Saturn are giant planets, and Uranus and Neptune are immensely larger than the Earth. Notice that Saturn is surrounded by rings. You can see the rings in the telescope, but not with the naked eye.

shot from a gun goes about 2,000 feet every second. If such a cannon ball were shot towards the Sun by powder strong enough to carry it all the way it would have to travel for eight whole years to get there.

You can form some idea of the immense, prodigious, distance of the Sun from these examples. Immense as the Earth's distance is, Neptune's is

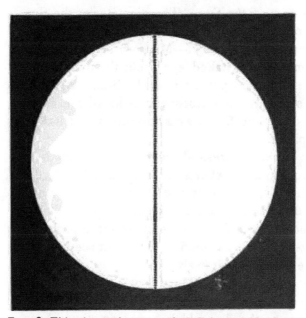

FIG. 18. This picture shows 109 black dots across the diameter of the white circle. If the whole Earth should shrink till it was of the size of one of the black dots, and if the Sun should shrink proportionally, the Sun would be of the size of the white circle. One hundred and nine Earths in a row would just reach from side to side of the Sun's disk.

thirty times greater; and the stars are very much further away than Neptune, even.

The Sizes of the Planets.—The diameters of the planets are:

Mercury, 3,000 miles;	Jupiter,	86,500 miles,
Venus, 7,700 " ;	Saturn (the globe),	73,000 "
Earth, 7,900 " ;	Uranus,	32,000 "
Mars, 4,200 " ;	Neptune,	35,000 "

The Size of the Sun.—The diameter of the Sun is 870,000 miles.

The Planet Mercury.—Mercury can sometimes be seen with the naked eye about the time of our sunrise or sunset, not far from the Sun. Its looks like a star. In the telescope it looks like a small bright disc. So far as we know this planet has no atmosphere.

The Planet Venus.—Venus is often seen near the Sun about sunset or sunrise as the bright Evening Star. In the telescope it looks like a small bright disc; sometimes, a crescent. It probably has an atmosphere and the disc that we see is probably the outer layer of its clouds. We never see the real surface of the planet itself.

The Planet Mars.—Mars looks like a reddish star to the naked eye. In the telescope we see markings on the disc which have sometimes been supposed to be land and water. There is, in all probability, little or no water in Mars and it has little or no atmosphere. The temperature on Mars is so low that no human life could exist there.

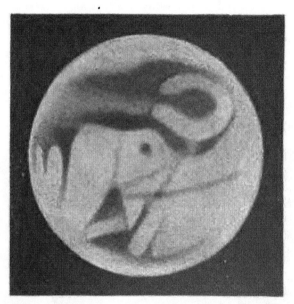

FIG. 19. The planet Mars as seen in a large telescope.

The Planet Jupiter.—Jupiter looks like a bright white star to the naked eye. In the telescope we see whitish clouds on its disk and reddish bands. The temperature on Jupiter is probably so high that no human life could exist there.

The Planet Saturn.—Saturn looks like a dull yellowish star to the naked eye. In the telescope we see nothing but the outer layers of clouds that cover the surface of its globe. The globe is surrounded by two rings, as in the picture, (Fig. 21).

The Planets Uranus and Neptune.—In powerful telescopes these planets look like round disks and

we probably only see the outer layers of their
clouds.

Could Men Live on Any of the Planets ?—Men
live on the Earth, we know. If a man could be
suddenly taken to Mercury it is probable that he
would not find air enough to breathe, and it is
likely that the planet is too hot for men to live on,

FIG. 20. The planet Jupiter as seen in a large telescope.

because Mercury is very much nearer to the Sun
than we are.

Jupiter is too hot for men to exist there, not because it is near the Sun, but because the planet

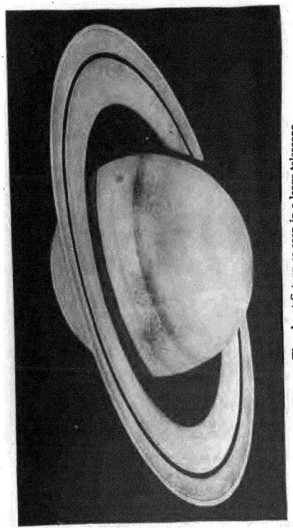

FIG. 21. The planet Saturn as seen in a large telescope.

FIG. 22. The Moon—from a photograph.

itself is hot—red hot. If a man could be suddenly
set down on Mars he would probably not find
enough air to breathe there, and little or no water.

The Moon also has no water and no air. It is possible that we may, by and by, learn that men might possibly live on some one of the planets—on Venus for instance; but so far as we know now we have no reason to believe it. There is probably no human life on the Sun (where it is very much too hot for men to live) or on the planets Mercury, Mars and Jupiter. We know absolutely nothing of what is underneath the clouds on Venus, or Saturn, or Uranus, or Neptune.

The Moon.—The planets revolve about the Sun. They are his family. Some of the planets have moons that revolve about them in circles while

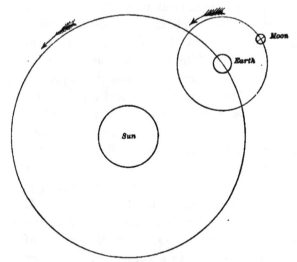

FIG. 23. The orbits of the Earth about the Sun and of the Moon about the Earth. The distance from the Sun to the Earth is 93,-000,000 miles; from the Earth to the Moon is 240,000 miles.

the planet itself is revolving about the Sun. Our Moon revolves about the Earth (once every month) while the Earth is revolving about the Sun (once every year).

The Phases of the Moon.—The Moon's disk has different shapes at different times of the month. You have noticed this, of course. Why is it so?

The half of the Moon that is turned towards the Sun is always lighted; it shines by his reflected light. Suppose, in Fig. 25, we take the candle to stand for the Sun, the boy's head to stand for the Earth, the ball to stand for the Moon. Now the Moon travels round the Earth and the Earth travels about the sun. The boy then must slowly walk around the table and one of his friends must, while he walks, move the ball round his head. (Try this experiment in a darkened room. The boy must turn his eyes towards the ball, of course, wherever it is, just as we on the Earth, turn our eyes toward the Moon.) Half of the ball is always bright. Half of the ball is always turned towards the boy. But these two halves are not always the same. Sometimes the boy will see none, or only a very little, of the bright half of the ball. It is then New Moon (☾). Sometimes he will see all of the bright half (☺). Sometimes he will see less than this. (Try it.) The different shapes shown in Fig. 24 are the *phases* of the Moon. They occur, in a regular order, every month, as you can prove by watching the real Moon in the sky. When the Moon is a thin sickle

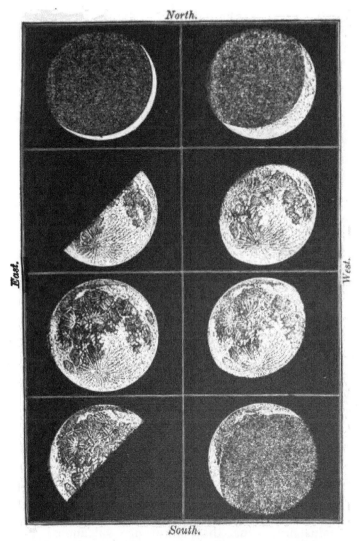

FIG. 24. The phases of the Moon : New Moon is shown in the upper pictures; Full Moon in the fifth; First Quarter in the third; Last Quarter in the seventh. (p. 27)

(in the West, about sunset) we have New Moon. The Moon's bright disk grows until about a week

FIG. 25. To show how the Sun lights one-half of any globe (the globe of the Moon for instance).

later we have First Quarter. Another week and we have Full Moon (in the East, about sunset); and then Last Quarter. About 29 days after one New Moon we have another, and so on forever. It takes the Moon 29 days to revolve once about the Earth.

Venus and Mercury have phases like the Moon, although they revolve about the Sun.

The Mountains of the Moon.—When we look at the Moon with a telescope we see that its surface is covered with mountains. The shape of these mountains proves that they were once volcanoes. There are probably no volcanoes now active on the Moon. If you were looking at mountains on the

Earth you would be able to tell whether their slopes had been worn by water.   The shapes of the mountains on the Moon prove that their slopes have not been worn by water.   There is no water on the

FIG. 26. A small part of the Moon, showing a group of lunar volcanoes (see Fig. 22, also and pick out other groups of volcanic craters—ranges of mountains—long streaks of lava streaming out from craters).

Moon.   In other ways it can be proved that there is no air on the Moon.   There can be no human life there, then; for men cannot exist without air and without water.

Satellites (Moons) of the Different Planets.—

Mercury has no moon ;   Venus has no moon.

The Earth has one moon ; its diameter is 2162 miles.

Mars has two moons; their diameters are about 7 and 5 miles.

Jupiter has five moons; their diameters are 100, 2,500, 2,100, 3,550, 2,960 miles.

Saturn has eight moons, their diameters are 600, 800, 1,100, 1,200, 1,500, 3,500, 500, 2,000 miles.

The rings of Saturn are made of thousands of little satellites very close together revolving round the planet, somewhat as a swarm of May-flies revolves about an electric street-lamp.

Uranus has four moons; their diameters are 500, 400, 1,000, 800 miles. Neptune has one moon; its diameter is 2,000 miles.

Several of the moons of the planets are as large as our own Moon; some of them are as large as the planet Mercury (whose diameter is 3,030 miles) and nearly as large as the planet Mars (4,230 miles).

FIG. 27. The three boys are holding three apples in a darkened room to represent the Earth at three different times in the year.

The Revolution of the Earth Round the Sun.— The light of the Sun shining on the Moon as she revolves in her orbit makes her phases. The light (and heat) of the Sun shining on the Earth as it revolves in its orbit make the seasons—Spring, Summer, Autumn, Winter.

The knitting needles (Fig. 27) stand for the axis of the Earth. They point towards the North Star; and they must be inclined, as in the picture, because the axis of the Earth is not perpendicular to its orbit, but inclined. The upper ends of the needles stand for the north pole, the lower ends for the south pole, of the Earth. The real Earth, in December every year, is where the right-hand apple of the picture is. The real Earth is where the middle apple is, in March every year. The real Earth is where the left-hand apple is, in June every year.

You live in the United States, let us say in latitude 45° north. Stick a pin in each apple anywhere in 45° north latitude. The pin stands for you. Take the right-hand apple and turn it slowly round its axis, just as the earth turns. This pin will be a shorter time in the light than in the dark. Now you see why the days are shorter than the nights in December. The pin in the middle apple is half the time in the light, half in the dark. Now you see why the days and nights are equal in March (the *equi-nox*).[1] The days in June in the United States are longer than the nights. (Try these experiments with the apples several times.)

Suppose you lived at the north pole of the Earth. Your nights would be nearly six months long. If the right-hand boy moves his apple completely round the candle the knitting needle will be in the dark half the time. (Try it.)

[1] If there were a fourth boy in the picture holding an apple just opposite to the middle one his apple would stand for the Earth in September; the days and nights are equal in September, too.

Suppose you lived at the equator of the Earth—in Brazil or Africa. Stick a pin in each apple half way between the poles. As the apple turns this pin is half the time in the light, half the time in the dark. (Try it—and you will see that this explains why the days and nights at the equator are equal—as they are.) Suppose you lived in the southern hemisphere. See if you can find out what would happen there.

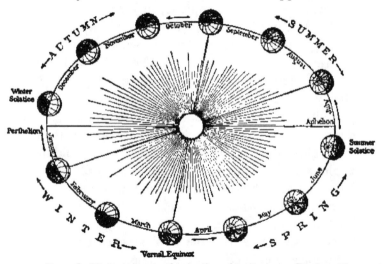

Fig. 28. The seasons in the northern hemisphere : Begin with the picture of the Earth in March and notice the changes of season at the north pole throughout the year.

Perihelion is the point where the Earth is nearest to, *Aphelion* where it is farthest from, the Sun. Vernal Equinox = the Equinox of Spring. The *Solstice* is a point than which the Sun goes no further south (in our winter) or north (in our summer).

The Seasons.—During winter at any part of the Earth the nights are very much longer than the days. During summer the days are very much longer than the nights. The Sun sends out rays of light, but they are rays of heat, too. They make whatever thing they touch *bright;* and they also make it *warm.* In our Spring (March) the days and nights are of equal length. All summer, until the Autumn, the days are longer than the nights. In September the days and nights are equal. All winter, until March, the nights are longer than the days.

This is true for the northern hemisphere of the Earth. In the southern hemisphere winter is in July, summer in January. Prove this from Fig. 27.

Eclipses of the Sun.—The Sun is eclipsed to an observer on the Earth when the Moon moves in between him and the Sun.

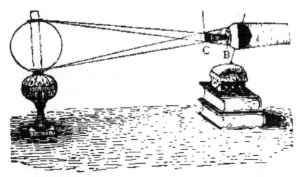

FIG. 29. A school-room experiment to explain an eclipse of the Sun : The room must be darkened. The lamp should have a ground-glass or an opal shade to represent the circle of the Sun's disc. An orange (*B*) fastened to a pincushion stands for the Earth. A small ball (*C*) on a string stands for the Moon. The Moon casts a shadow on part of the Earth. Anyone who lives on that part of the Earth has an eclipse of the Sun until the Moon moves out of the way.

3

Eclipses of the Moon.—The Moon is eclipsed to an observer on the Earth when it is in the Earth's shadow.

The Earth casts a shadow. At times the Moon moves through it. When it does so all its sunlight is cut off. In the last picture if the ball (*C*) were in the shadow of the ball (*B*) the circumstances would be the same as those of an eclipse of the Moon.

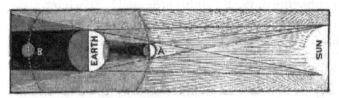

FIG. 30. Eclipses of the Sun and Moon : The reader should use this picture to explain both solar and lunar eclipses. Notice that each shadow is composed of two parts, one very black—the *umbra*, and one lighter—the *penumbra*. Try to explain why the different dotted lines of the picture are drawn as they are.

The Sun.—The Sun is a huge globe nearly 870,000 miles in diameter. It is intensely hot and is made of gases and vapors. All the metals that we know—iron, gold, copper, silver—are in the Sun but they are not solid. They are vapors. The clouds in the Sun are made up of drops of melted iron, gold, silver and so forth, just as our clouds are made up of drops of water. These fiery clouds are inconceivably hot; and they are driven to and fro by terrific hurricanes and winds. If you look into an iron furnace where the white-hot iron is boiling you get a kind of a picture of what the Sun's surface is. The boiling lava in a

volcano is a little like the surface of the Sun, only
not nearly so hot. The Sun is 5,000 times more
brilliant than white-hot boiling iron.

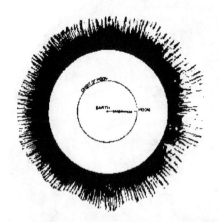

FIG. 31. The Sun is the large white circle. The real Sun is
870,000 miles in diameter. If you could put the Earth at the center
of the Sun the whole orbit of the Moon would be far inside the
Sun's surface. The Moon's distance from the Earth is 240,000
miles. The next time you see the Moon in the sky recollect that
the Sun is large enough to contain the Earth and the Moon's
whole orbit.

The Sun is a Star.—All the Stars are Suns.
They are all made up of boiling metals and white-
hot gases. The Sun is just one of the millions of
Stars.

The Sun's Corona.—Outside of the boiling surface of the Sun with its atmosphere of white-hot
metallic clouds there is another envelope something
like another atmosphere. It is called the *corona*—

the crown—of the Sun. We see it only at the time
of a solar eclipse.

Fig. 32. The Sun's Corona at the eclipse of 1871. The black
circle is the Moon between us and the Sun. (See Fig. 30.) The
bright Sun is hidden behind the Moon, but the bright corona
streams out in all directions beyond it.

Meteor Swarms. — The universe is full of
swarms of meteors—clouds of stones travelling in
orbits of their own. Many such swarms travel in
orbits about the Sun, as the planets do. They are
usually quite invisible. We know they exist,
though, because whenever the Earth passes through

one of these swarms we have showers of shooting-stars.

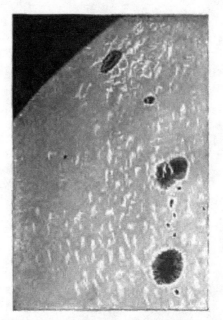

FIG. 33. This picture is part of a photograph of the Sun. (The whole circle of the Sun would be two feet in diameter, and so only part of it can be given.) The edge of the Sun is seen next to the dark sky. Then come different spots. The spots are huge geysers—fountains—in the Sun. Some of them are bigger than the Earth.

Comets.—Comets usually come from the spaces outside our solar system and move round the Sun once and then go off again, never to return.

Comets are crowds of stones moving in a swarm. If you ever see a swarm of May-flies round the

FIG. 34. The bright comet of 1858.

globe of an electric street-lamp, go off a little distance and you will see that the swarm looks like a whitish cloud. The rings of Saturn and comets are swarms of stones. If you go near to the electric-light you can see the separate flies. If you could go near enough to a comet (or to the rings of Saturn) you could see the separate stones. Comets give out light of their own, perhaps due to electricity. The rings of Saturn shine by reflected sunlight.

Shooting-Stars (*Meteors*).—If you will watch the sky, any clear night, patiently you will be sure to see several shooting stars every hour. You will see a little spot of light like a star suddenly appear and move across the sky, often leaving a bright trail of light. Each of these shooting stars (or meteors) is caused by a stone from a meteor swarm which enters the Earth's atmosphere and falls towards the Earth. As it falls (at the rate of about 20 miles a second) it becomes hot and bursts into flame and fire. Even a rifle bullet, which only goes half a mile a second, gets very hot in its passage through the air. A meteor becomes so hot that it burns up completely unless it is very large. Sometimes pieces of large meteors are found and our museums have many such specimens. The heights of meteors have been measured and it appears that they often become visible as much as 75 miles above the Earth's surface. Our atmosphere must be at least 75 miles high,

then, for it is the atmosphere that makes them
burn and become visible.

FIG. 35. A photograph of a very small part of the sky.   Each
dot is a star—a sun.

The Universe of Stars.—All the planets belong
to the family of the Sun.   The comets move in all
directions through space, and we only see a few
of them—namely, those that come near enough to
the Sun to be attracted into our solar system as
visitors.   They usually make one visit and then
leave us forever.   The stars are suns scattered at
immense distances from us and from each other

throughout space.   There are millions of them
visible in the telescope but only about 6,000 visible
to the naked eye.   All of these latter have been
counted and numbered and photographed.

FIG. 36. A cluster of stars.   The Pleiades is a well-known
cluster.

Constellations.—The stars visible to the naked
eye seem to fall into groups like the *Great Bear*
and *Cassiopeia* of Fig. 7.   (Look at it.)   The ancient astronomers gave special Latin names to these
groups—*Aries*, the ram; *Leo*, the lion; *Taurus*,
the bull, etc.

The Nebulæ.—At the same immense distances
from us as the stars there are thousands of whitish
cloudy spots that are called nebulæ.   Some of them
are masses of gas; some of them are huge clusters
of very small stars.

FIG. 37. The great nebula of Andromeda (from a photograph).
Each separate white dot is a star—a sun—and the cloudy mass is
made up of millions and millions of small stars.   Other nebulæ
that look like this one are made of gas.

The Distances of the Stars.—No one of the stars
is nearer to us than 200,000 times 93,000,000 miles
or 18,600,000,000,000,000—say twenty millions of millions of miles.   And the stars in the sky, although
they *look* as if they were close together are really
separated, one from another, by a distance as great
as this, except when they lie in clusters.   Light

travels about 186,000 miles in a single second, as you will by and by learn. It takes a ray of light a little over a second to come to the Earth from the Moon, about eight minutes to come to us from the Sun, and more than four years to come to us from the *nearest* fixed star. The light of *Polaris*—the pole star—takes nearly 50 years to reach us.

If the star Polaris were to be suddenly destroyed—now, this instant—its light would continue to shine for nearly half a century more. The moonlight that you see now left the Moon a second ago. The sunlight that you see now left the Sun eight minutes ago. The starlight that you see now left the stars years ago.

BOOK II: PHYSICS.

Physics.—Several of the sciences deal with living things in Nature: Botany is the science that tells us about living plants, for instance; Natural History the science that tells us about living animals. *Physics* is one of the sciences that deals with things in Nature that are not living. It speaks about solids and liquids, and tells how they differ from each other; about Heat, Light, Sound, Magnetism and Electricity—what they are and what they do. Chemistry and Meteorology are parts of Physics, but they are so important that separate chapters are given to them in this book.

Solids, Liquids and Gases.—A piece of iron, lead, ice or cork is a solid. A solid body (or thing) is one that is rather hard to the touch and that has a shape of its own. If you put a solid in a cup it keeps its own shape.

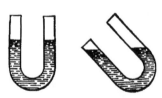

FIG. 38. A liquid takes the shape of the cup that contains it.

Quicksilver, water, kerosene oil, alcohol, are liquids. Liquids have no shape of their own. If you put a liquid in a cup it will take the shape of the cup.

44

The air and the coal-gas that is burned to give light in street-lamps are gases. Gases are usually invisible. You cannot see the coal-gas, but you can hear it rushing out of the opened burner, and when you touch it with a lighted match it burns. You cannot see the air you are breathing but it is there, just the same. The wind is nothing but moving air, and you can feel the wind. Clouds float in the air just as corks float in water. A balloon floats in the visible air.

FIG. 39. A balloon floats in the air somewhat as a cork floats in water.

Ice is a solid; melt it, and it becomes a liquid; the water is just the same thing as the ice—the same thing in a different form. You can freeze the water again, if you like, and have ice, once more. Or you can take the liquid water, heat it in a tea-kettle and boil it all away into steam. *Solid* ice, *liquid* water, *gaseous* steam, are three different forms of the same thing.

Real steam is invisible, as you could tell if you boiled water in a glass tea-kettle, You would see the water and nothing else though the steam would be there, filling the kettle above the water. The little clouds of vapor at the spout of a tea-kettle are not clouds of gaseous steam, but extremely small drops of liquid water. They look white just as the little drops of spray from a fountain look white. Both the fine spray of the fountain and the fine bubbles that make the clouds at the spout of a tea-kettle are water and only water. By pressing and freezing air it can be made liquid and even solid.

Force of Gravity.—If you drop a stone from your hand it falls to the ground. Anything—lead, iron, stone, wood —falls when you let it go, and it keeps on falling till it reaches the ground, or until it is stopped by something—by a table, or something of the sort. Every heavy thing falls as far as it can. And everything that you know of is heavy. Paper is heavy ; it has weight. (The Latin word for weight is *grav-itas* = heaviness.) A newspaper crumpled up into

FIG. 40. The leaning tower of Pisa. This tower was built about A. D. 1200, and is still to be seen, as in the picture.

a ball has the same weight as the same newspaper loose in sheets. If you let the loose newspaper fall from a second-story window it will flutter about and take a long while in falling ; but if you crumple it up tight it will fall to the ground in just the same time as a stone dropped at the same moment. (Try it.)

Fall of Heavy Bodies.—Drop a heavy stone and a lighter one from the second story window at the same time and you will see that both of them reach the ground at the same instant. (Try it.) For thousands of years men thought that a heavy stone would fall quicker than a light one, but Galileo [1] tried this experiment from the leaning tower of Pisa [2] and proved that all things, heavy or light, fall with the same quickness.

FIG. 41. A magnet attracts bits of iron near it. (The experiment should be tried.) There is something about the magnet that attracts iron ; there is something about the Earth that makes things fall. There is a force in the magnet, and a force in the Earth.

Ten pounds of loose feathers float about in the air for a long time. The air blows them about. But if you put them in a tight bag they fall just as fast as ten pounds of ice, or water, or lead ; just as fast, and no faster, than one pound of lead, or ice, or water.

Attraction of the Earth.—Why do these things fall down? Why do they not rise up? The answer is : They fall

[1] Pronounced gal-i-lē′ō, He was born in Italy in 1564, and died in 1642.

[2] Pronounced pē′zä. A city of Italy.

because the Earth attracts them—somewhat as a magnet attracts a piece of iron. (Try it.)

The weight of a horse walking presses on the ground and makes deep footprints. The heavier the horse the deeper the footprints. If you hold a stone by a string as in the picture of the pendulum (Fig. 13) the weight of the stone pulls on the string. The heavier the stone the more it pulls. A large stone pulls twice as much as one half as large. If you fasten the stone to a spring-balance, you can measure how heavy it is—one pound, two pounds and so forth. What you are measuring is how much the Earth is pulling the stone downwards.

If you throw the stone in the air it goes a certain distance upwards but it always falls. The Earth is always attracting the stone; it is always attracting apples downwards from the trees (when they are ripe the stems are weaker and the apples fall); it is always pulling down the mountains by attracting the rocks and making them fall; always, day and night, making the rivers flow down hill. After a stone has fallen as far as it can go and is lying flat on the ground, the Earth still attracts it. Try to pick it up and you will see that the stone still has weight—that the Earth keeps on attracting it, somewhat as a magnet holds fast to the bits of iron it is attracting.

How Fast do Things Fall?—All heavy things fall at the same rate; one falls just as fast as another. By dropping things from high towers and timing their fall by a watch, it has been found that All heavy things fall 16 feet in the first second,

"   "   "   " 64 " " " " two seconds,

"   "   "   " 144 " " " " three seconds,

and so on.

You can prove a part of what has just been said if you can find two windows one 16 and the other 64 feet from the ground. A stone dropped 16 feet takes one second (by a watch) to reach the ground. A stone dropped 64 feet takes two seconds. If you have no watch you can make a pendulum that swings in just one second by taking a string $39\frac{1}{10}$ inches long and tying one end to a nail and the other to a weight (a key will do):

One swing of the pendulum of Fig. 13, from any point back to the same place again takes two seconds. One boy can drop the stones and another can count the swings—the seconds. (Try it.)

Weight.—The government keeps a piece of metal in Washington which is called a *pound* weight; and there is a law that all the pound weights in the whole country from Maine to California shall be alike.

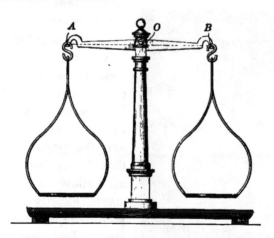

FIG. 42. A balance. If you put two weights that are alike in the two pans, the arm (*AB*) will be level. If one weight weighs more than the other its pan will go down. You can make a weight like another weight, then, by filing it down till the two just balance.

One-sixteenth of a pound is called an *ounce*. All the ounce weights of all the druggists in the whole

4

country are alike. If you have a balance, and the weights that go with it, you can weigh anything you choose. A pound of anything must just balance the pound weight.

Notice that a pound of lead is smaller in size than a pound of iron; *lead is heavier than iron* we say—and we mean that a cubic inch of lead weighs more than a cubic inch of iron. Notice that a pound of soap is bigger than a pound of iron ; *soap is lighter than iron,* we say—and we mean that a cubic inch of soap weighs less than a cubic inch of iron. Your body is a little lighter than water ; and the proof is that if there were a hollow glass statue exactly of your shape and size, filled with water, the water in it would weigh more than you do.

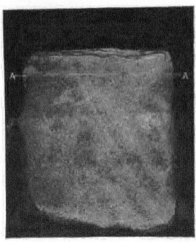

Fig. 43. Photograph of a piece of floating ice. The level of the water is along the line *A*.................*A*.

Another proof is that you can float in water. Your body is lighter than lead ; and the proof is that if there were a lead statue exactly of your shape and size it would weigh much more than you do.

Ice is lighter than water; it floats.

Gold is 19 times heavier than water;
Quicksilver is 13½ times heavier than water;
Lead is 11 times heavier than water;
Copper is 9 times heavier than water;
Iron, Tin, Zinc are 7 times heavier than water;
Common stone is 2½ times heavier than water;
Ice is $\frac{9}{10}$ as heavy as water;
Oak wood is $\frac{7}{10}$ as heavy as water;
Kerosene oil is $\frac{7}{10}$ as heavy as water;
Cork is $\frac{2}{10}$ as heavy as water.

Notice that things that are heavier than water sink when
they are put into it; and that all things that are lighter than
water (ice, wood, cork, etc.) float. Iron will float on Quicksilver. (Try it.) The air is much lighter than water (and so all
air-bubbles rise in a tumbler of water). The air in any box weighs
only one one-thousandth as much as the water that would fill it.

The Vertical Line; Up and Down.—The Earth
attracts all heavy bodies somewhat as a magnet attracts every piece of iron. All heavy bodies fall
down as low as they can. Fasten a string to a nail
and a weight to the other end of the string. The
string points *up and down*, we say. It is a vertical
line. *Up* is towards the nail; *down* is towards the
Earth. Wherever you may be a pendulum at rest
is vertical—is up and down.

Now the Earth is round, and as you travel round
the Earth you will have a vertical line at each city,
but a different vertical line at different cities.

Up then really means away from the center of
the Earth; *down* really means towards the Earth's
center. A vertical line is really the line of that
diameter of the Earth which passes through your

feet. The point in the sky, among the stars, over your head is called your Zenith-point.   The four boys in the picture have four different zenith-points.

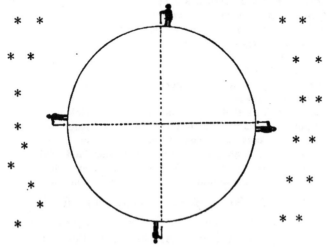

FIG. 44. A pendulum at rest anywhere on the surface of the Earth points to the center of the Earth.

The Sun attracts the Earth and all the planets just as the Earth attracts everything in its neighborhood. Everything on the Earth is held near it by its attraction, just as all the planets are held near the Sun by its attraction.

FIG. 45. A level somewhat like the levels used by carpenters. When the little air-bubble is in the middle of its tube, the straight-edged board is level—is horizontal.

The vertical line is perpendicular to the level surface of the ocean, or to the level surface of still water anywhere (hold a pendulum over a basin of water and see for yourself). Masons use a pendulum swung in a board to get their brick walls verti-cal, and carpenters and surveyors use levels—which are glass tubes almost filled with alcohol—to get their lines horizontal, or level.

Measures of Length—a foot, a yard, a mile.—The government keeps a bar of metal in Washing-ton and the distance between two particular lines on that bar is called a *foot.* Three feet make a *yard;* 5,280 feet make a *mile.* Twelve *inches* make one foot. There is a law that every foot-rule in the whole country, from Maine to California, shall be of one and the same length. Every carpen-ter's foot-rule is just the length of the foot-rule of every other car-penter.

Carpenters measure by feet and inches; machinists file iron by fractions of an inch—as $\frac{1}{32}$ inch, $\frac{1}{64}$ inch; shopkeepers sell cloth and ribbons by the yard; sur-veyors measure roads by the mile.

The Metric System.—In France there is a metal bar kept by the government as

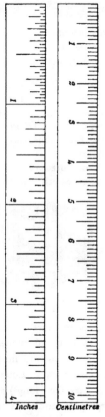

Inches   Centimetres

FIG. 46. Ameri-can inches com-pared with French centimeters.

a standard. The distance between two particular lines on it is called a *metre* (or *meter*). A meter $= 39\frac{37}{100}$ inches; it is about

three inches longer than a yard.

A *kilometer* is 1,000 meters $=$ about $\frac{6}{10}$ of a mile.

A *decimeter* is $\frac{1}{10}$ of a meter $=$ about four inches.

FIG. 47. A carpenter's two-foot rule. It is usually made so as to be only six inches long when folded up.

A *centimeter* is $\frac{1}{100}$ of a meter $=$ about $\frac{4}{10}$ of an inch.

A *millimeter* is $\frac{1}{1000}$ of a meter $=$ about $\frac{4}{100}$ of an inch.

A *gram* is the French measure of weight and it is equal to about $\frac{4}{100}$ of an ounce: a *kilogram* is about 2 pounds.

A *litre* is the French measure for liquids, etc., and it is about equal to our quart.

The French measures are used over nearly all of the continents of Europe and of South America, and the laws of the United

FIG. 48. A tape-measure. Short tapes a yard (3 feet; 36 inches) long are used by salesmen to measure cloth or ribbons. Longer tapes (50 or 100 feet long) are used by carpenters and masons. Tapes made of flexible steel are used by surveyors to measure land, lay out streets and so forth.

FIG. 49. Compasses or dividers. These are used by men who draw plans, by carpenters and machinists, to carry a measure made in one place over to another place; or else to find out how many inches long a piece of wood or iron must be to be of just the same length as a plan of it drawn in an office beforehand.

States allow our merchants to use them also; and that is the reason they are mentioned here.

Time.—The instant when the sun is highest in the sky—half way between sun-rise and sun-set—we call *noon*. Our watches are set so as to mark 12^h 0^m 0^s at the instant of noon, and regulated so as to mark 12^h 0^m 0^s again at the next noon. From Monday noon to Tuesday noon is a day = 24 hours. One hour = 60 minutes; and the minutes are marked on all watch-dials. One minute = 60 seconds; and the seconds are marked on most watch-dials.

To keep account of the days we give them names (Monday, Tuesday, and so forth) because we find it convenient, just as it is convenient to name children (Tom, Agnes, Mary, Jack, and so forth). Monday begins at midnight of Sunday; Tuesday begins at midnight of Monday, and so on. Seven days make a week (the first day of the week is Sunday, the second Monday, and so on). The weeks have no names. It has not been found convenient to name weeks as days are named. But months are named for convenience (January, February, and so forth). Some months have 30 days, some 31 and one has 28. (Name them.)

A year has 12 months and common years are 365 days long. 365¼ days is the time required for the Earth to go once round the Sun. It is the period from one midsummer to the next one, from one Christmas to the next one. Every fourth year we call a leap year and it has 366 days (February has 29 days in a leap year). The number of days in four years is, then, $365 + 365 + 365 + 366 = 1461$. One fourth of 1461 is $365\frac{1}{4}$. The years are numbered. The first year of the twentieth century began January 1, 1901. The next year was 1902 and so on. The count began with the year in which Christ was born (about 1900 years ago). He was born within the first century and the centuries are numbered. It is convenient to say that England was conquered by the Normans in the XI. century; that America was discovered by Columbus in the XV. century; that the Pilgrims came to America in the XVII. century; that our Revolutionary War was fought in the XVIII. century; and so on.

HEAT.

Thermometers.—A thermometer is made of a glass tube partly filled with quicksilver, but with no air in the tube. A scale of degrees is engraved alongside the tube. If you put the thermometer into melting ice (or freezing water) the quicksilver stands at 32° of the scale; "Freezing Point." If you put the bulb of the thermometer into your mouth the mercury will stand at about 98°. That is the temperature of your body. If you stand the thermometer in a kettle of boiling water [1] the mercury will rise to 212°.

[1] Do not put a cold thermometer suddenly into boiling water if you do not want to break it. Warm it at a fire beforehand.

Centigrade Thermometer. — The French and most other nations use a different scale for their thermometer from that used by the Americans and English. Our scale is called Fahrenheit's scale [1] from the German scientific man who invented it about 1714. Theirs is called Centigrade, because there are 100 degrees between the melting point of ice (0°) and the boiling point of water (100°). It is used everywhere by scientific men and in most countries of Europe and South America in commerce.

The "heat" of boiling water is the heat that it has got from the fire. Its "temperature" is 212°. The "heat" of your body is the heat you have got from the food you have eaten. The "temperature" of your body is 98°.

Melting Points; Boiling Points.—The melting point of ice is 32°, the boiling point of ice (or water) is 212°. The melting point of anything is the reading of the thermometer when that thing changes from a solid into a liquid; the boiling point is the reading of the thermometer when that thing changes from a liquid into a gas.

FAHRENHEIT.

FIG. 50. A thermometer with the quicksilver standing at 30°.

FIG. 51. A Centigrade Thermometer. The scale is divided into one hundred degrees. Such thermometers are used in European and South American countries.

[1] Pronounced fä ′ren-hĭt.

The melting point of ice is 32°; it changes into liquid water.

The melting point of quicksilver is −38°; it changes from solid quicksilver into liquid at 38° below zero.

The melting point of solid sulphur is 240°; it becomes liquid.

The melting point of solid lead is 600°; it becomes liquid.

The melting point of solid iron is 2,200°; it becomes liquid.

The boiling point of water is 212°; in changes into steam.

The boiling point of alcohol is 172°; it changes into gas.

Hot Bodies Usually Expand.—The tire of a wagon wheel is larger when it is hot than when it is cold. The blacksmith tries a cold tire and finds that it is too small to fit the wheel. He heats the tire; it expands. He slips it over the wheel and lets it cool. It shrinks and fits tight. The quicksilver column in a thermometer becomes longer as the column gets hotter.

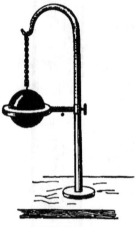

Fig. 52. An iron ball that just fits a ring when it is cold will be too large to slip through it when the ball is red hot. This is a proof that iron expands when heated. The ring remains of its old size. The ball is larger when it is hot. (An apparatus like that in the picture can be made by any ingenious boy.)

Nearly every solid thing is larger when hot than when cold. Very hot cannon balls are larger than the same balls when cold, as can be told by measuring them. Railway rails are longer when hot than when cold and you will notice that they are laid down with a little free space at the end of each rail to allow for expansion. Melted lead takes up more space than cold lead. But there is one important exception to this general rule. Melted ice (water, that is) takes up less space than cold ice. Water gets larger when it freezes, not smaller. This is the reason why our water pipes so often burst when the water freezes. The pipes are full of water at first; when the water freezes it expands and the pipes break.

Conduction of Heat.—Heat is conducted through bodies somewhat as if it were water flowing through pipes. Some bodies (things) let the heat flow fast. A silver spoon, for instance, dipped in boiling water will soon be hot all along its length. (Try it.) A piece of charcoal alongside of the silver will be very hot where it dips into the water, but will remain cool at its upper end. (Try it.)

Silver, iron, copper and other metals are good conductors of heat; charcoal, wood, wool, felt, fur, are poor conductors of heat. We make our winter clothes out of wool and fur because they do not conduct the heat of our bodies away to the cold air. A jacket made of copper would keep the wind away thoroughly, but it would be a very poor garment for cold weather. (Why?)

Work can be Turned into Heat.—If you rub two sticks together both sticks get warmer. Savages light fires by turning a stick of hard wood rapidly in a dent in a piece of soft wood. The hard wood is moved as if it were an auger, boring into the soft wood. By and by the soft wood begins to char and to burn. The movement that you give the stick is turned into heat. If you bore a hole in hard wood with a gimlet both wood and gimlet become warm. If you rub your hands together in cold weather you can warm them. In all these cases work of some sort has been turned into heat. If you place a copper cent on an anvil and pound it with a heavy hammer the coin becomes

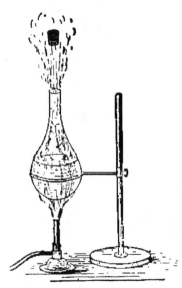

hot. (Try it.) The harder and faster you pound the hotter becomes the coin. A machine could be made to do the pounding so hard and so fast that the coin would become red hot. The work done by the hammer has somehow been taken up by the coin, and given out as heat.

Steam.—When water is boiled in a tea-kettle steam is formed and escapes through the spout and by lifting the lid. If the spout

FIG. 53. Steam from heated water will drive out a tightly fitting cork.

were securely stopped up and the lid soldered down the steam might burst the tea-kettle just as it sometimes bursts boilers. Steam can do work, then. In the steam engine it is made to do useful work.

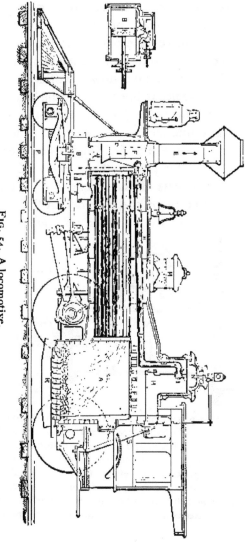

FIG. 54. A locomotive.

The Steam Engine.—The steam engine is a machine that turns heat (of the fire) back into work. The fire makes the wheels of the locomotive turn. You have often seen a locomotive. It is worth while to understand how it works.

A (Fig. 54) is the fire in the *fire-box;* the heat goes through tubes in the *boiler* (*G*) and turns the water round the tubes into steam. The steam is led by a pipe into the *steam-chest* (*H*) and from there it goes through another pipe to the *cylinder* (*B*) just above the front wheels of the locomotive. (There is a separate picture of the cylinder at the top of page 61.) Inside of the cylinder a *piston* (*K*) fits

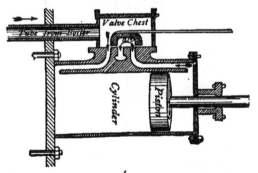

FIG. 55. Another picture of the cylinder of a steam-engine. The steam rushes from the boiler into the *valve-chest* and through the open way into the cylinder and pushes the piston to the right (in the picture). Then the steam is let into the cylinder by another way and pushes the piston to the left (in the picture). The piston-rod keeps moving to and fro. It is fastened to the driving-wheels by a crank, and the wheels keep moving round and round, and the locomotive keeps moving along, dragging the train after itself.

tightly and the *piston-rod* goes out of the cylinder and is fastened to the large *driving wheels* at the rear end of the locomotive.   The machinery is so arranged that the steam is first let into the front end of the cylinder (*B*) and drives the piston backward; then the steam is let into the rear end of the cylinder and drives the piston forward.   The piston keeps moving to and fro, and therefore the wheels keep turning round, and the locomotive keeps going.

The pupil should read this description carefully, pointing with a pin at the different parts of the engine as they are named.

LIGHT.

The Sun and Stars Shine by Light of Their Own.—The Sun and all the stars give out light of their own.   The Moon has no light of its own but shines by reflecting the Sun's light to us.   At times only part of the Moon's face is shined on by the Sun and only part of it, therefore, is seen by us. (See page 26 for an explanation of this.)   A candle, an electric light, a fire-fly, a glowing coal, shines by its own light.   It is *self-luminous*.   Phosphorus is self-luminous, as you can prove by going into a dark closet and rubbing the head of a match gently with your hand.   (Try it.) · The head of the match contains a good deal of phosphorus.

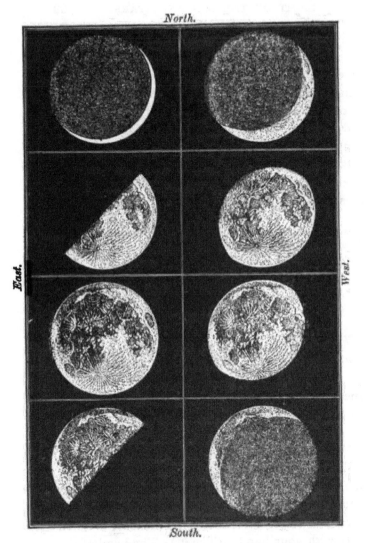

North.

East.

West.

South.

Fig. 56. The Moon as it appears to us at different times of the month. (p. 64)

The upper pictures show the *New Moon*. The third picture shows the Moon half bright, and the others show how the Moon looks at other times. The Sun shines on half the Moon's globe—the half turned towards the Sun —and makes it bright. We 'ook at the Moon and see half of its globe—the half turned towards us. Sometimes the whole of the part turned towards us is lighted, as in the fifth picture. Usually less than this is bright.

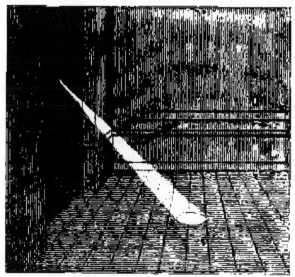

FIG. 57. The Sun shining into a darkened room through a small hole in the wall. The rays of the Sun travel in straight lines. If there is dust or smoke in the room it is easier to trace the course of each ray. Burn a newspaper, then. Notice that the Sun makes a spot on the floor which is an *image* –a picture —of the Sun.

In the daytime all sorts of things shine—a white-washed wall, the windows of a house, a piece of tin, a mirror, a diamond, and so forth. As soon as the Sun goes down they stop shining. They

5

shone, then, by the sun's light.   They were *luminous* (light-giving) but not *self*-luminous.   Most things in the world are seen by the Sun's light which they reflect.   The light comes to them from the distant Sun ; they reflect it somewhat as a mirror reflects ; and the reflected light enters your eye and you see them.   When the Sun goes down you see them no more ; unless, indeed, they are lighted by rays from a lamp.   Daylight is the Sun's light reflected from and scattered by dust in the atmosphere, from clouds, the ground, buildings, streets, and so forth.

All Light-rays Travel in Straight Lines.—The Sun's rays travel in straight lines.   You can prove this by making some room that faces the south very dark and by then letting in a ray of sunlight through a small hole.

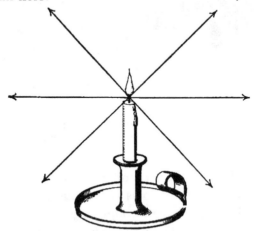

FIG. 58. Rays of light from a candle go in all direction.

Rays of Light go in All *Directions.*—An electric street lamp, for instance, shines towards the north, east, west, south. It shines upwards and down- wards. Its rays of light must, then, go in *all* direc- tions. If you put a candle in a darkened room, the whole of the room is lighted—the ceiling, the walls, the floor. Wherever you place your eye some ray from the candle will enter it. Wherever you are you can see the candle. This proves that the candle's rays go in all possible directions, up, down, sidewise. The Sun shines in every possible direc- tion, too—towards the north, east, south, west.

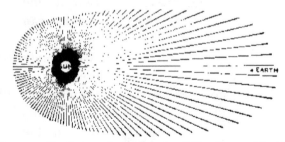

FIG. 59. The Sun sends out rays in *all* directions. The Earth receives only a small part of them.

Shadows.—When the Sun shines on any body (thing) it lights one half of it. The half turned towards the Sun is lighted. The half turned away from the Sun is not lighted. Beyond the body that is shined upon there is the shadow. The shadow of a thing is the space beyond it from which it keeps the light away. Your shadow, properly

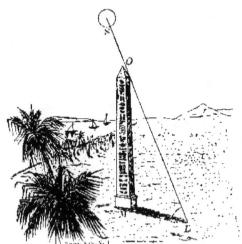

FIG. 62. The shadow of an obelisk when the Sun is high in the heavens.

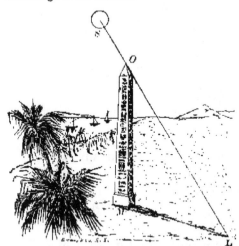

FIG. 63. The shadow of the same obelisk when the Sun is not so high in the heavens.

ground will be short as in Fig. 62. When the Sun is lower, the shadow on the ground will be longer, as in Fig. 63. The height of the Sun in the heavens can be calculated by simply measuring the length of the shadow on the ground—by measuring *LM*. The ancient astronomers of Egypt determined the Sun's height in this way.

The Sun-Dial.—The ancients used to measure the time of day by the movement of the shadow on a sun-dial.

FIG. 64. A Sun-dial. The line through the figure 12 in the picture lies exactly north and south, with 12 at its north end. As the Sun moves the shadow moves. The picture was taken at four o'clock in the afternoon. How do you know it was not taken at four o'clock in the morning ?

Reflection of Light by a Mirror:

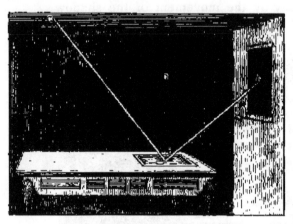

FIG. 65. A beam, or ray, of light is reflected by a mirror, as you know very well; and as can be proved by the experiment shown in the picture.

Let a ray of light into a darkened room through a very small hole and move a mirror till the ray strikes it. The ray will be reflected so that it strikes the ceiling. (Try it.) If you set up a vertical ruler at the point where the ray strikes the mirror the *angle ABD* will *always* be equal to the *angle DBC*.

The teacher should cut a piece of stiff paper so that two of its edges make an angle equal to *ABD*; and by turning the paper prove that it is equal to the angle *DBC*.

Reflecting Telescopes are made by using curved mirrors to collect the rays of light and to direct them to the eye of the observer who uses a magnifying eyepiece.

FIG. 66: *Kaleidoscope.*—Images of a candle made by two mirrors at right angles to each other. There are three images. (Try it.)

If two mirrors *a* and *b* are placed so that they make an angle of 60° with each other like this the reflections will be six-sided. Anyone can try this experiment by I. folding back the lid of an upright piano till the lid and the top make an angle like this . The polished lid and top are mirrors. II. by putting a shawl over the lid so as to make a dark box with the two ends open. III. by placing his eye at one end of the triangular box while a friend moves some bright object like a skein of worsted, a bunch of keys and so forth to and fro at the other end. (Try it.)

Refraction of Light.—A ray of light in the air moves in a straight line. When it moves first in air and then in water the ray is bent just where it enters the water. Take a tumbler half full of water and put a spoon in it. Hold it in front of you at arm's length so that the top of the water is on a level with your eye. (Try it.) The spoon will look as if it were bent out of shape—as if it were broken. The water breaks—refracts—the light.

Refraction of Light by a Prism:

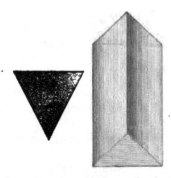

Fig. 67. A triangular prism of glass. Look at it endwise and you see a triangle as in the left-hand picture. The glass pendants to chandeliers are often prisms.

When a ray of light passes through a prism of glass it is also bent out of its course.

Refraction of Light by a Lens.—A *lens* is a piece of glass with curved sides (a burning glass, for instance) which is used to bend rays of light from their first course into a new one.

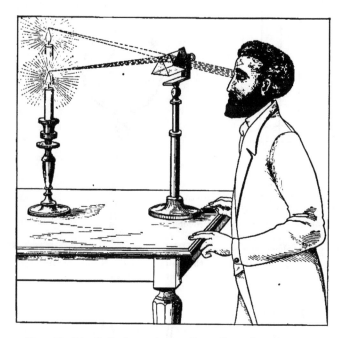

FIG. 68. The light from the candle strikes the prism and is bent down so that the man sees the candle not where it is, but raised in the air. If you have a prism, try it.

Microscope.—If you take a burning glass like that in Fig. 70 and use it to look at this page of your book you will find that it magnifies the letters.

(Try it.)   A microscope is a lens or a set of lenses used to make small things appear larger.

Microscopes are used by geologists to study the structure of rocks ; by physicians to study the bacteria that produce diseases, and so forth.

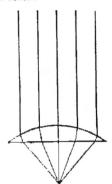

FIG. 69. Hold a burning glass in the sunlight and it will bend the rays of the Sun so that all that fall upon it meet in one point—which is called the *focus*. A burning glass collects the Sun's rays into a small spot of light. All the rays that fall on all the surface of the lens are brought to a single spot.

FIG. 70. A burning glass.

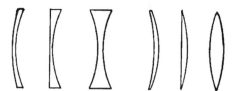

FIG. 71. Glass lenses of different shapes. *Spectacles* are lenses of these kinds.   The different kinds are used for eyes with different sorts of troubles.   Near-sighted eyes need concave glasses, far-sighted need convex glasses.

Telescope.—A telescope is an apparatus used to make far off things seem near (a spy-glass is a small telescope; so is an opera-glass). It is usually made of two, or more, glass lenses. The first lens collects the rays from the distant object at its focus and forms a little picture of the object there. The second lens magnifies the little picture. The two lenses together form a telescope.

In an opera glass, one lens is at the large end; the other (or others) near the small end. It magnifies from 3 to 8 times. It makes things seem 3 to 8 times nearer than they really are.

A large telescope such as astronomers use to look at the stars can be made to magnify about a thousand times. It makes the Moon seem about a thousand times nearer than it really is.

The Solar Spectrum:

You can hold a prism in the sunlight so as to get a band of colored light. (Try it.) There will be seven colors, Violet, Indigo, Blue, Green, Yellow, Orange, Red—VIBGYOR (remember this word and it will recall the order in which the colors come. It is the order of the colors in the rainbow). The prism does two things to the sunlight that falls on it: I. It bends the light into a new course; II. It separates the light into seven colors. Sunlight is made up of seven colors and no more. When they are all together they make what we call *white* light, that is, sunlight. It is just as if every beam of sunlight were made up of seven strands of silk thread —*vibgyor.* When they are all in one bundle they look white. Separate the bundle into parts, and you have seven separate colors—violet, indigo, blue,

green, yellow, orange, red. A few experiments
with a prism will prove this. Looking at the rainbow proves it. The white sunlight going through
the drops of rain (which act somewhat as if they
were prisms) is separated into seven colors.

Velocity of Light.—Light travels from place to place at the
rate of 186,000 miles in one second of time—almost instantaneously.: almost, but not quite. It comes to us from the Moon
in less than two seconds, but it takes eight minutes to come from
the Sun. That is, a ray of light that left the Sun eight minutes
ago arrived at the Earth this very instant. A ray of light just
leaving the Sun now—this instant—will not arrive for eight
minutes. Eight minutes are required to make the journey of
93,000,000 miles. Light goes from any one place on the Earth to
any other place practically instantaneously. You see an electric
street lamp at practically the very instant when it is lighted.
You see the flash of a gun the instant it is fired, though you do
not hear the sound for some seconds.

SOUND.

Sound-waves.—When a church-bell is struck by
a hammer a sound is heard. No matter where you
are—north, south, east, west of the bell—you
hear it. Close to the bell the sound is loud;
two miles away the sound is faint. Anywhere
within two miles you hear it. This proves that
waves of sound travel outwards from the bell, in
every direction, somewhat as waves of water travel
outwards from a stone thrown into a pond. The
waves are more marked where the stone struck the
water; less marked as they go outward. (Try it.)

Finally they die away somewhat as the sound of the bell dies away.

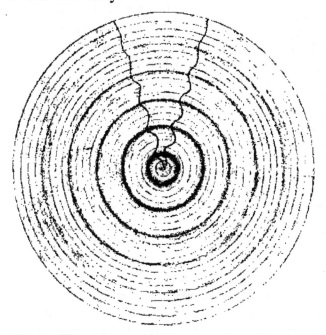

FIG. 72. Waves of water made by a stone thrown into the center of a pool look like the picture. The two wavy lines would not be seen, of course. They are drawn to show the heights of the waves at different distances from the center. The further you go from the center the smaller is the wave.

Sound is Caused by a Vibration.—The hammer strikes the bell and the whole bell trembles—vibrates. If you touch the bell with your finger the vibration can be felt. If you strike a thin tumbler with a spoon there is a sound. If you hold your finger lightly against the glass you can feel it tremble—vibrate. (Try it.) So long as the trembling goes on the sound is heard. Stop the trembling by clasping your fingers round the glass and the sound will stop. (Try it.) To have a sound you must first have vibration of some sort. A vibration is a quick trembling to and fro, like that of a bell when it is struck.

FIG. 73. A wine glass filled with water vibrates when a fiddle bow is drawn across its edge. Touch the glass lightly with your finger and notice that at four places there are no waves. (Try it.)

Musical Instruments. — A drum makes a sound because the parchment drum-head vibrates when it is struck. The air vibrating regularly in an organ-pipe makes a sound. The string of a violin vibrates when the bow is drawn across it, just as the string of a piano vibrates when the hammer strikes it. You can feel the vibrations of the piano strings by putting your finger lightly against them. (Try it.)

The vibrations of all musical instruments are regular—rhythmical—and the sounds are pleasant. Such sounds are called musical. Irregular vibrations, such as are made by beating on a fence with a stick, are unpleasant—we call them noises.

A way has been contrived to count the number of vibrations of the strings of a piano. It is found that the middle C of the piano is made by a string vibrating 256 times in a second; the C next above is made by a string that vibrates 512 times in a second. The shorter the string the more vibrations it makes in a second. The shortest strings in a piano, the ones that give the highest notes, make about 4,000 vibrations in one second; the longest strings, that give the lowest notes, make about 32.

The sounding-board of a piano also vibrates when the string is struck and makes the sound louder; and all the air inside of a fiddle vibrates when the string is plucked. When you are at a concert recollect that all the air inside the concert-hall is set into vibration every time a note is played on the violin. Each stroke of the fiddle-bow sets tons of air into motion.

Singing.—You have in your throat two cords, muscles, called the vocal cords. By making them act you can change the quickness of the vibrations of the air that passes through your throat as you sing. Very deep bass sounds (men's voices) are made by air vibrating about 200 times a second; the very highest notes of a woman's voice are made by air vibrating about 2,000 times in a second. Learning to sing is mainly learning to control the vocal cords.

Sound Travels Through the Air.—Open the window of a room and send a boy to beat on the fence with a stick. You hear the sound which is brought to you by the air. The air cannot go through the window when it is closed. Close it then; and you cannot hear the sound, though you can still see the stick striking the fence.

6

If the fence is very near, and if the boy strikes very hard sometimes you can hear the sound even when the window is shut. That is because the air outside of the window makes the window-glass vibrate, and because the window-glass, in turn, sets the air in the room into vibration. Sounds usually come to us from the sounding body (thing) by vibrations in the air.

But sound travels through solids too. If you hold a watch close against a long plank a boy at the other end of the plank can hear the ticking much plainer than if you hold the watch a foot away from the plank. (Try it.) The ticks of the watch travel through the plank in the first experiment; through the air in the second. If a railroad train is far away, you can hear it better by laying your ear close to the rails than you can by standing up and listening.

Velocity of Sound.—Light travels almost instantaneously from place to place. You see the flash of a distant gun the moment it is fired. But the sound does not come at once. If the gun is 1,100 feet away from you the sound comes one second of time after the flash. If the gun is 2,200 feet away the sound comes two seconds after the flash. Sound travels 1,100 feet (about a fifth of a mile) in one second. It travels a mile in a little less than five seconds.

Any two country boys who own a watch and a gun and who can get a mile apart can prove this. City boys are not allowed to fire guns in the streets but they can recollect that sound travels a distance of about 500 of their steps in each and every second of time.

ELECTRICITY.

Experiments.—Before beginning the experiments you should get

A piece of sealing wax about 4 inches long.

A glass tube or a glass rod about 4 inches long.

A little piece of elder pith with a silk thread run through it so that it can be hung to a long nail in the wall, or to the end of a stick projecting from a shelf (put a heavy book on one end of the stick to keep it steady),

A *little* ball of sealing wax fastened to a silk thread.

A *little* glass bead fastened to a silk thread.

A pound of resin; have it melted and poured into a shallow wooden box to cool. (See Fig. 75.)

A piece of fur—a cat-skin will do very well.

Electricity by Friction.—Now try these experiments one by one:

I. Strew some small bits of paper on the table and hold the sealing-wax, then the glass, near them. Nothing happens.

II. Rub the sealing-wax smartly on the fur or on your sleeve, and then hold it near the bits of paper. It attracts the paper. The little bits of pieces fly to the wax and stick to it.

III. Rub the glass rod smartly on your sleeve and hold it near the bits of paper. It attracts the paper.

Whenever a piece of wax or glass is rubbed it gets a new power. It will attract light bodies such as bits of paper. Before it was rubbed it did not have the power. It is the rubbing—the friction that, somehow, gives the new power to the wax or glass.

The ancients, thousands of years ago, knew that if amber was rubbed it would attract light bodies, such as bits of chopped straw. The Greek name for amber is *Electron*, and from that word we get our name of electricity.

Electricity is the something that gives a piece of glass that has been rubbed the power to attract pieces of paper.

When sealing wax is rubbed you get electricity of one sort; when glass is rubbed you get electricity of another sort, as the following experiments will show:

FIG. 74. A pith-ball hung by a silk string is repelled by an electrified stick of sealing-wax, or glass.

IV. Fasten a little pith ball so that it can swing freely. Hold a piece of sealing-wax near it. Nothing happens if the wax has not been rubbed. Hold a piece of glass near it. Nothing happens if the glass has not been rubbed.

V. Rub the wax and then hold it near the pith-ball. The ball is first attracted and then quickly repelled. The wax repels the ball.

VI. Rub the glass rod and quickly bring it near to the pith-ball. The ball was *repelled* by the rubbed sealing-wax, but it is now *attracted* by the rubbed glass. Wax-electricity seems to be different from glass-electricity.[1] When one repels the pith ball the other attracts it.

VII. Rub the glass first, and it will repel the pith ball; then quickly rub the wax and it will attract the ball. Wax-electricity is certainly different from glass-electricity. You have proved it to be different.

VIII. Rub the little sealing-wax ball with a piece of fur; rub the stick of sealing-wax and bring them close together; they repel each other. If now the glass rod be quickly rubbed it will attract the wax ball.

IX. Rub the glass bead and bring the rubbed glass rod near. They repel each other. The rubbed stick of wax will attract the ball.

All these experiments taken together prove that:

When bodies are charged with *like* electricities, they repel each other [wax repels wax, glass repels glass].

When bodies are charged with *unlike* electricities, they attract each other [wax attracts glass, glass attracts wax].

X. Take the wooden box filled with melted resin and beat or rub it with a piece of fur. Now put

[1] The scientific names are resinous electricity and vitreous electricity; sealing-wax is made of resin.

your knuckle close to the resin and you will feel a little electric shock.   Some of the electricity in the

FIG. 75. Taking a spark from a box of resin which has been electrified by beating it with a piece of fur.

resin has gone into your body. If this is done in the dark you can see a little spark pass; and whenever the spark passes there is a little crackling noise. The spark is just the same thing as *light-ning;* the little noise is thunder. Your knuckle was struck by lightning.

If you break a piece of sugar while you are in the dark you will see a faint light which is caused by electricity. Breaking the sugar is a kind of rubbing of one surface on another. If you rub the fur of a cat with your hand you can electrify the cat and can take sparks from her back or from her nose (much to her surprise!) Rub a dry lamp-chimney with a woolen cloth and you can take sparks from it with your knuckle. In cold dry weather you can scuffle your shoes over the carpet and electrify yourself— so that you can light the gas by a spark between your knuckle and the metal gas-fixture. (Remember these things and try them all when the weather is cool and dry.) Notice that in such weather a rubber comb passed through your hair will attract the hairs and make them rise up.

FIG. 76. Benjamin Franklin bringing lightning from the clouds, 1752.

Until the time of Benjamin Franklin (1752) little more was known of electricity than what you have just learned. Electricity could be made by rubbing wax or glass; and there was lightning during a storm. Franklin electrified a kite by sending it up into a thunder-storm, and from a key tied to the kite-string he got sparks[1]; and he proved that the

[1] You must not try this experiment. It is dangerous, and you might be killed, as men have been, in trying it.

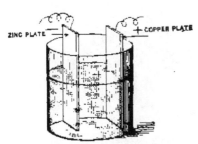

FIG. 77. One cell of an electric battery· The glass jar contains two plates, one of copper, the other of zinc, and a liquid, which is diluted sulphuric acid. A wire is fastened to each plate. The larger the plates the more electricity flows when the two wires are joined.

electricity in the clouds was the same kind of thing as the electricity that he could make, anytime, by experiments.

Electricity from Batteries. — Nowadays electricity is used for sending messages by telegraph; and it is used to light lamps, to drive street cars, automobiles, elevators, etc. The electricity for telegraphs is obtained from batteries; for lighting and power from dynamos.

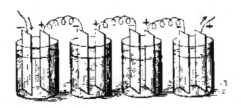

FIG. 78. Several cells of a battery joined together (the zinc plate of one cell to the copper plate of the next one). A strong electric current flows through the wires when they are joined, no matter if the wire is short or long. If the wire extends from Boston to New York a current will flow and if we can make the current work telegraph sounders in the two cities we can telegraph messages.

You can prove that a current of electricity is flowing in a battery by putting one wire above your tongue, and the other below it (both touching the tongue). When you do this you will feel a little current every time you move the wires slightly. A current of electricity flows from the copper slip through the wire to your tongue, through your tongue and back to the zinc slip. The current runs round a circle of wire and such a circle of wire is called an *electric circuit*.

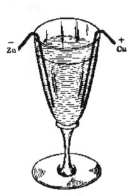

FIG. 79. A home-made electric battery. The glass goblet is filled with weak sulphuric acid and contains two slips of metal, one of Zinc (Zn), the other of Copper(Cu). To use it two pieces of flexible copper wire must be soldered to the two pieces of metal.

The cell that you make is not as strong or as convenient as one that you can buy, and it is worth while to buy what is called a cell of " dry battery,"[1] which is handy and clean to use.

[1] Buy for the school from the Western Electric Company, New York City, its Electric Bell outfit (complete) No. 9429, comprising a bell, one cell of Phenix Dry Battery, one bronze push-button, 75 feet of No. 18 annunciator wire and staples, for $2.75.

Electric Bells:

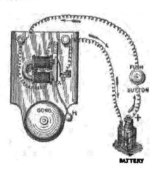

Fig. 80. An electric bell outfit complete—push-button (at the right), one cell of battery, bell and wire.

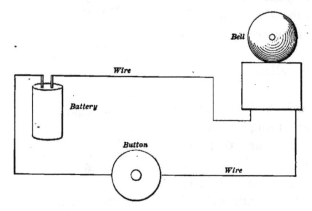

Fig. 81. Plan of the circuit for an electric bell. Touch the push-button and the bell will ring. Touching the push-button connects the two ends of the wire, previously unconnected. When the wire is all in one piece the electricity flows from the battery into the electro-magnet of the bell and makes the bell ring. If the battery were strong enough you could stretch the wires from New York to Boston and make a bell in Boston ring when a button in New York was pushed.

The Electric Telegraph.—Signals can be sent over a long distance by using strong batteries of many cells. Suppose we have a "sounder" in Boston, and a key and battery in New York, and connect all three by telegraph wire strung on posts.

FIG. 82. A telegraph key.

Whenever the key in New York is pressed a current of electricity from the battery runs along the wire and into the coils of the sounder in Boston.

FIG. 83. A Sounder. It is an electromagnet (see p. 99) that is, it is a magnet whenever a current of electricity runs through its coils—whenever a key in the circuit is pressed; and not a magnet when no current is flowing. In the picture one of the coils is shown—a vertical black cylinder.

The sounder becomes a magnet and pulls down the bar above it with a click. Let go of the key in New York and the sounder-magnet lets go of the bar. We can thus make clicks that can be heard in Boston by touching a key in New York. The current of electricity does the work.

The Telegraph Alphabet. — An alphabet has been invented to use in sending telegraphic messages. The shortest touch of the key makes a short click which is called a *dot* . ; a longer touch makes a *dash* —.

To send A make a dot and a dash,   . —;
"   "   B   "   a dash and three dots, — ... ;
"   "   E   "   a dot,   . ;
"   "   M   "   two dashes,   — —;

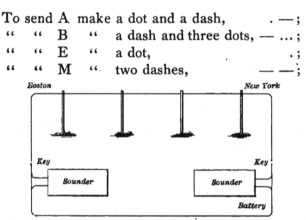

FIG. 84. Plan of a telegraph line between Boston and New York.

and so on for the rest of the letters. In this way any word can be spelled out to the ear in Boston

FIG. 85. Telephone. Each person who speaks has an instrument like this.

by touches of a key in New York. A key (on the same circuit of wire) in Boston when touched will spell out words to the ear in New York. It is in this way that telegraph messages are now sent.

The Telephone.—The telephone is a kind of telegraph. It sends the vibrations of your voice instead of sending the clicks of the telegraph key, and this is done as follows :

I. You call the person you wish to speak to (or the central office) by ringing an electric bell (D).

II. You speak into your " transmitter " (A). This is a box containing a very thin disk of metal. When you speak the vibrations of your voice make this disk vibrate and the vibrations of the disk travel along the wires and reach the telephone which your friend is holding to his ear. In his telephone (and in yours (B) too) there is a little metal disk which vibrates just as your voice vibrates. The air in his telephone vibrates, then, just as your voice did; and it makes the same sounds that you made. It repeats your very words, even your whispers.

The Dynamo.—A dynamo-electric machine is a set of magnets made to revolve rapidly by a steam engine. When they revolve they create a current of electricity. Wires led from the dynamo carry the current wherever you wish. You can use the current to light lamps, or to run elec-

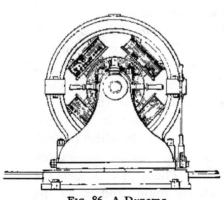

FIG. 86. A Dynamo.

tric cars, or to drive any machine you choose. The more powerful your steam engine, the stronger current you can get and the more work you can do. It is the steam engine that does the work, after all.

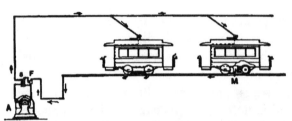

FIG. 87. An Electric Railway. The Dynamo (*A*) in the power-house sends a current of electricity along the wire. Each car takes the electricity it needs by the trolley and motors under-neath the floor of the car drive the wheels.

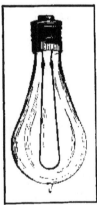

FIG. 88. An elec-tric lamp; a glow-lamp; such as is used in houses. A cur-rent of electricity from a dynamo heats a little strip of bam-boo white-hot, and the glowing of this strip gives the light.

The dynamo simply changes the energy of the steam engine into electricity and the wires carry the electricity to the places where you wish to use it.

The Electric Railway. — A dynamo driven by a steam-engine in a power-house (so-called) is used to send a current of elec-tricity along an overhead wire, and the electricity is led from this wire by a little wheel (a *trol-ley*) to electric motors underneath the car. These motors turn the car-wheels round and make the car move along the track.

Electric Lighting.—A current of electricity is sent out from a power-house by a dynamo driven by a steam-engine. The current is led along wires to light the street lamps (arc lamps, they are called) in cities; and into houses to light the glow-lamps (incandescent lamps, they are sometimes called).

MAGNETISM.

Natural Magnets.—In Magnesia, a district of Greece, the ancients found a kind of iron ore that attracts little pieces of iron filings, tacks, etc., when they are brought near to it. The name "magnet" comes from the name of the place—"Magnesia." Natural magnets are found in many other parts of the world. To try the experiments described in this book it will be best to buy from any toy-shop one of the manufactured magnets shown in the pictures.

FIG. 90. A horse-shoe magnet: it is shaped like a horse-shoe. The piece of steel across the ends is called the *keeper*, or the *arma-ture.*

FIG. 89. A bar magnet dipped in iron filings. It is shaped like a bar. The ends of a magnet are called its poles.

Now take the second needle (call it No. 2 for short) and try these experiments and see what happens.

Touch the eye-end of No. 1 with the point end of No. 2; they attract.

Touch the point-end of No. 1 with the eye-end of No 2; they attract.

Touch the point-end of No 1 with the point-end of No. 2 ; they repel.

Touch the eye-end of No. 1 with the eye-end of No. 2; they repel.

These magnets are just alike ; the eye-end poles (ends) of each are alike, the point-end poles (ends) of each are alike. They were made in the same way and this must be true. But the experiments have shown that the eye-end poles are *not* like the point-end poles ; and the experiments have also shown that *like* poles of two magnets repel each other ; *unlike* poles of two magnets attract each other.

You must try these experiments over and over till you thoroughly understand them.—It is much easier to understand the experiments than to understand a description of them.

If any sewing needle is laid gently on the surface of water the needle will float. (Try it.)

FIG. 92. A magnetized sewing-needle floating on a bowl of water.

If a magnetized needle is laid on water it will turn till it points to the north. It is a compass. (Try it.)

If you take another magnet and bring it near to the floating compass-needle you can easily prove that *like* poles of two magnets repel, *unlike* poles attract each other. (Try it.)

The Mariner's Compass.—If a magnet is suspended by a string (or balanced on a sharp point) or floated on water, so that it can swing freely, it will point to the north. The Chinese knew this centuries ago and used compasses to steer their ships by. Their inven-

FIG. 93. The Mariner's Compass. The needle always points to the north, and therefore sailors can steer by it.

tion was brought to Europe and has been used by our sailors since A.D. 1302.

Columbus (1492) steered west from Spain by the compass and discovered America. If you have a compass see what will happen when you bring a magnet near to one of its ends. (Try it.)

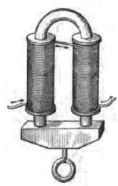

FIG. 94. An electromagnet. It is a piece of iron wrapped with wire. While a current of electricity is flowing through the wire it is a magnet: the instant the current stops flowing it is a magnet no longer.

Electro-Magnets.—You know that a current of electricity from an electric battery flows along a telegraph wire so that messages are sent from Boston to New York. Suppose you took a piece of soft iron and bent it into the shape of a U and wound wire around it, as in the picture and let a current of electricity flow through the wire. You would find that while the current is flowing (and no longer) the iron would be a magnet. Stop the current and the iron is iron and nothing more. You can see an electro-magnet working in any telegraph station. The bell that rings when an electric push button is touched is an electric bell. Its hammer is moved by an electro-magnet. (See page 90.)

MACHINES.

The Pulley.—A pulley like the one in figure 95 is often used to change the direction in which a rope is led. A pull of one pound on the rope will lift one pound and no more.

FIG. 95. A common pulley.

FIG. 96. These two pulleys are rigged so that a pull of one pound on the right-hand rope will raise two pounds attached to the left-hand pulley. (Try it.)

Fɪɢ. 97. A stone raised by a crowbar used as a lever. The point where the crowbar rests on the ground is called the *fulcrum* of the lever—the point about which it turns.

The Lever.—Any stiff bar—a crowbar, for instance—is a lever. By using a lever you can move a stone entirely too heavy to be moved by hand.

Fɪɢ. 98. A little boy on the long end of the see-saw balances a heavier boy on the other end.

A common pair of scales is a lever in which the two arms are equal. One pound in either scale-pan balances one pound in the other. The *fulcrum* of the beam is its middle point.

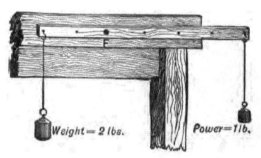

Weight = 2 lbs.   Power = 1 lb.

Fig. 99. A weight of one pound can be made to balance a weight of two pounds if it is hung at the end of a lever twice as long. (Try it by making a stick with holes every six inches, as in the picture, and putting a round iron nail (F) for the stick to move on.) Put the pin in different holes and see what weights will balance each other. The point F is the fulcrum.

Fig. 100. A hammer: A lever with a short arm near the nail—the *fulcrum* is the point where the hammer touches the floor—and a long arm from the floor to where your hand takes hold of the handle.

A hammer is a lever when you use it in pulling out nails. A pair of scissors, of pinchers, of nut-crackers, are levers. The fulcrum of each one is the place where the two parts are joined together. A butcher's steelyard is a lever in which a little weight at the end of a long arm balances a larger weight at the end of a shorter arm.

The Inclined Plane.—A weight too heavy to lift

FIG. 101. A barrel too heavy to lift may be rolled up an inclined plane.

may be rolled or slid up an inclined plane. The work is done a little at a time. A railway can be

FIG. 102. A railway on an inclined plane in the Rocky Mountains. The altitude is conquered gradually.

laid up a mountain by making it curve so that the mountain is climbed a little at a time.

FIG. 103. A screw-press : By turning the screw a great pressure can be put upon the books—a little at a time.

The Screw.—A hole can be bored in a piece of hard wood by a gimlet when you cannot possibly make a hole by a smooth straight brad-awl. The screw is made up of an inclined plane wound round a straight line. It enters the wood gradually—a little at a time.

The Common Suction Pump.—This picture and the three following it explain the way in which the common pump raises water from a well.

In the picture I. the pump is empty. There is no water above the level of the top of the well. We wish to raise the water as high as the nozzle of the pump. How shall we do it? Recollect that the air—the atmosphere—is pressing on the

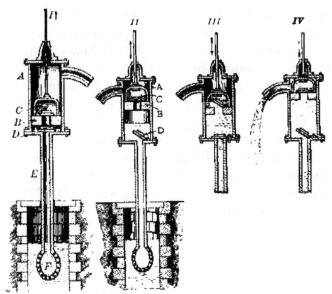

FIG. 104. *I*. A common pump. Its barrel is empty of water but full of air. A *suction pipe* (*E*) with a strainer (*F*) on the end of it leads down to the water in the well. At the top of this pipe is the *suction-valve*—a little door opening upwards (*D*). Above this is the *pump barrel* (*A*) in which the *piston* (*B*) works airtight. The *piston-valve* (*C*) is a little door opening upwards. The piston is moved up and down by the pump handle (not drawn in the picture).

FIG. 105. *II*. A common pump : The piston is moving upwards. When the piston has reached the top the barrel of the pump will be nearly full of water.

The upper valve will be shut, the lower one open.

FIG. 106. *III*. A common pump : The piston is now moving downwards. Its valve is opened and some of the water rises above the piston.

FIG. 107. *IV*. A common pump : The piston is now moving upwards, and some of the water in the barrel has been lifted high enough to flow from the spout.

upper surface of the water in the well and that the
suction-pipe (E) and the whole pump barrel is full
of air pressing down.   Air, like all heavy things,
presses downwards by its weight.   If we can take
this air out, the air over the well will press the well-
water up, just as the quicskilver is pressed up in
the barometer (see page 111).

II. Let us raise the pump piston then.   As this
rises its piston will lift all the air above it.   Below
the piston the barrel will be empty of air and the
water from the well will rush up and fill it.   The
air above the well-water presses it up.

BOOK III : METEOROLOGY.

The Atmosphere.—The Earth that we live on is composed of land and water and surrounded by an atmosphere of air. The land and water we can see, but the air is invisible. We know it is there, however, because clouds float in it just as corks float in water. The winds are nothing but air moving past us.

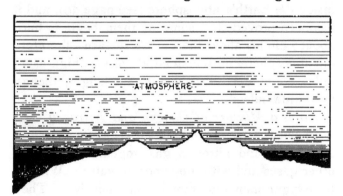

FIG. 108. The atmosphere is an ocean of air lying above the land and sea. We live at the bottom of the ocean of air just as some fishes live at the bottom of the ocean of water.

The higher you go in the atmosphere the less air there is. It is easy to breathe anywhere near the level of the sea. On the top of a mountain a mile high (5,280 feet) you begin to feel that there is not

107

air enough ; on a mountain two miles high you feel
this very distinctly ; on a mountain three miles high
it is very difficult to breathe ; and in the Andes or
Himalaya mountains, where men have gone as
high as four miles, it is hardly possible to breathe
at all. Men have gone somewhat higher than this
in balloons ; and the higher you go the less air
there is. Even birds do not fly more than four
miles high.

Height of the Atmosphere.—Shooting stars do not
begin to burn until they have come from space well
inside the Earth's atmosphere (see page 39), and it
has been proved that some of them begin to burn
about 75 miles above the Earth's surface—therefore
the atmosphere must extend at least as high as 75
miles. There is *some* air at that height, though
very little indeed.

Air is a Mixture of Oxygen and Nitrogen Gas.
—Chemists have proved that air is chiefly a mixture
of oxygen and nitrogen gas, together with some
other gases and with the vapor of water. Without
the oxygen men and animals could not live. They
need it to breathe.

Air is Heavy.—The simplest way to prove that
air has weight is to take a tight box with a stop-
cock and to weigh it when the stop-cock is open
and it is full of air, and then to pump all the air
out of the box and to weigh it after the stop-cock is
closed. A cubic foot of air (that is the air in a box
12 × 12 × 12 inches) weighs a little over an ounce

at the level of the sea. A cubic foot of water weighs about 67 pounds.

The Weight of the Atmosphere.—Each cubic foot weighs something. Near the level of the sea a cubic foot weighs more than an ounce; higher up, it weighs less; higher up still, it weighs less still. Imagine a tall column of air reaching from the ground to the top of the atmosphere (see Fig. 109) and instead of thinking of cubic feet let us think of cubic inches (1728 cubic inches make a cubic foot). The base of the column (*AB*) on the ground will be *one square inch*. On the top of that is a cubic inch of air pressing down by its weight; on the top of that another; and then another; and so on. It will be proved in the next paragraph that the weight of each and every such column of air is about fifteen pounds.

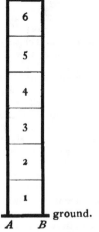

Fig. 109. The atmosphere presses the surface of the ground about 15 pounds on every square inch.

Each and every square inch of the Earth's surface and of the surface of everything up on the Earth is pressed about fifteen pounds. The pressure is not only downwards but sidewise, too, because gases and liquids press equally in all directions.

Fig. 110. Fill a tumbler partly full of water, cover it closely with a piece of writing paper, hold the paper with your hand and turn the tumbler over. Now take your hand away and the paper will stay in place. The weight of the water is pressing it down, but the air outside the tumbler is pressing it up and keeps it in place. (Try it — you may have to try several times in order to get the paper to fit tight enough to keep the air out of the tumbler.)

Fig. 111. Wet a piece of leather tied to a string (a sucker). Press it tight to a piece of wood. You can lift the wood. Why? Because the air presses the sucker with a pressure greater than the weight of the wood. If it did not, the wood would fall.

Fig. 112. Fill the tumbler as in Fig. 110, cover it, turn it over, put it in a basin of water, and carefully draw the paper out. The water in the tumbler will stand above the level of the water in the basin. Why? Because the air is pressing on the water in the basin and *not* on the water inside the tumbler.

The Barometer.—Why does the quicksilver stand in the tube about thirty inches above the quicksilver in the basin? (Fig. 113.) Because the air is pressing down on the basin and forcing the quicksilver upwards. It goes upwards a certain distance (about 30 inches) until the weight of the quicksilver in the tube, pressing downwards, just balances the pressure of the atmosphere upwards. If the glass tube is one square inch in area the quicksilver in it will weigh 15 pounds. Therefore the pressure of the air (which is balanced by this weight) is 15 pounds on a square inch: on this square inch and on every other one near the level of the sea. If you try this experiment on a mountain the quicksilver column

FIG. 113. Fill a tube closed at one end and about 34 inches long completely full of quicksilver; there will be no air in it. Cover the tube with your thumb. *Carefully* and *slowly* turn the tube upside down and put the end of it in a basin of quicksilver. Now take away your thumb. The quicksilver will stand about 30 inches high in the tube.

will not be so high; it will weigh less; because
the pressure of the atmosphere (which it just balances) is less.

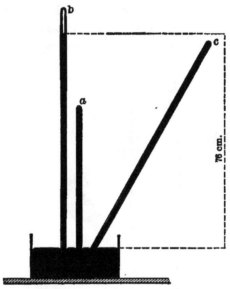

FIG. 114. In order to have an empty space above the quicksilver the barometer tube must be more than 30 inches long and
it must stand upright.

Measurement of Heights by the Barometer.—If
you are at the level of the sea the barometer will
stand at about 30 inches. If you go up in a balloon or ascend a mountain there will be less air
above you and the barometer will stand lower, con-
sequently. On a mountain 7,000 feet high the
barometer will stand at about 24 inches. A balloon
has carried men as high as 31,500 feet (nearly six

miles) and the barometer stood at $7\frac{1}{2}$ inches. There was not air enough to keep the balloonists alive. They breathed oxygen carried up with them in metal boxes. The heights of mountains are usually measured by barometers, not by levelling.

FIG. 115. An Aneroid Barometer, which measures the pressure of the air not by the height of a quicksilver column but by the changes in shape of a metal box (inside the outer case). The box is empty of air, and is sealed tight. As the air presses upon it it changes shape. The needle is arranged so as to mark the changes and to tell the height at which a quicksilver barometer *would* stand (see the inner circle of figures in the picture). The outer circle of figures shows how high above the level of the sea you are when the barometer points at each figure. When you are at the level of the sea the barometer stands at about 30 inches.

At 2,000 feet altitude the barometer stands at about 28.5 inches.
At 4,000 feet altitude the barometer stands at about 27.0 inches.

8

At 6,000 feet altitude the barometer stands at about 25.0 inches.
At 8,000 feet altitude the barometer stands at about 23.0 inches.

The Barometer is a Weather-Glass.—The barometer at the level of the sea usually stands at about 30 inches : in very fine clear weather it often stands higher; in very bad weather it stands between 28 and 29 inches. By watching the barometer you can tell something about the weather you are going to have. If the barometer is rising it is likely that the weather is going to be fine. If the barometer is falling below 29 inches it is likely that you will have rain (see Fig. 115, where the words are written on the dial-plate).

U. S. Weather Bureau Predictions of Weather.—In Washington there is a Government office called the Weather-Bureau. Several times a day this central office receives telegrams from cities all over the country telling the height of the barometer, of the thermometer, the direction and force of the wind, etc., at each and every one of the cities—at San Francisco, Denver, Omaha, Chicago, St. Paul, New Orleans, Mobile, Charleston, New York, Boston, Bangor for instance. Several times a day all these things are marked on a map.

Every few hours a weather map is made and the tracks of storms are drawn. Therefore the Weather Bureau can tell us beforehand when we are likely to have a storm. Farmers can take care of their crops in time; fruit-growers are warned of frosts; railway managers know when to expect

snow; sailors know when dangerous winds are to
be feared. The Weather-Bureau predictions are
useful in a thousand ways.

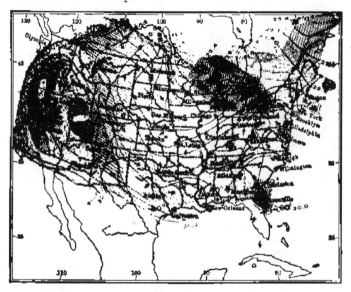

Fig. 116. One of the Washington weather-maps.
The red lines join places where the barometer is the same.
The blue lines join places where the thermometer is the
same.
The reddest regions have the highest barometer.
The bluest regions have the lowest temperature.
The dotted regions are being rained on.
The little arrows fly *with* the wind (point to the place towards
which the wind is blowing).
The red figures give the height of the borometer.
The blue figures give the height of the thermometer.
The long dotted line from Manitoba to St. Paul shows the
track of a storm moving eastwards.

Water-Vapor.—The air contains moisture—
vapor of water—which is invisible, just as steam is
invisible. Most of this moisture comes from the

sea. Invisible vapor rises
from the surface of the
ocean into the air. We
cannot see it, but we can
prove that it is there, in this
way :

We know, in the first
place, that warm air can
hold more water-vapor in
every cubic foot than cold
air can hold. If we cool
any mass of air some of the
water-vapor in it will be

FIG. 117. Drops of water
will condense on the out-
side of a glass of ice-water.
(Try it.) The little drops
on the outside come from
the warm air of the room.

squeezed out by the cold.

If you are in a warm room
on a cold day you will see
that the cold window glass
is covered with moisture.
The air near the glass is cooled and some of its
vapor of water is condensed in drops on the panes.

Mists and Fogs.—If warm air with plenty of
invisible moisture in it is blown by the wind across
a cool valley or lake some of its moisture becomes
visible as mist or fog.

Dew.—Some of the moisture of the air condenses
upon cold solid bodies and we call that visible moisture *dew*. You can see it in the morning before

sunrise covering bricks, the grass, plants, with thousands of little drops of water. When the sun gets high all the air becomes warmer and the visible dew is taken into the air as invisible vapor. A tumbler full of ice-water held in a warm room will soon be covered on the outside with hundreds of fine drops of water (see Fig. 117). Why? These drops do not come *through* the glass from the ice-water; they come from the invisible moisture in the air of the room which is cooled because it is near the cold tumbler. (Try it.)

Frost instead of dew results when the temperature is below the freezing point.

Fig. 118. Clouds along the (cold) face of a cliff in the Yosemite Valley in California.

Clouds are formed just as fogs are formed by the cooling of the air and moisture by the meeting of cold and warm currents, or otherwise. We call them fogs when they are near the surface of the Earth, clouds when they are high above it.

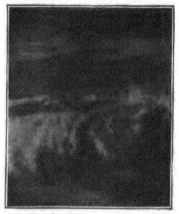

Fig. 119. Cirrus clouds. Such clouds are usually high up in the air—about five to six miles. They are formed of very small crystals of ice—frozen moisture.

Rain.—The very small water drops in a cloud often unite to make larger drops which fall in rain.

Hail.—If they are frozen on their way down we call the frozen rain drops hail.

Snow is frozen water-vapor, not frozen rain drops. If you look at snow flakes with a microscope, or a strong magnifying glass they always have the shape of a six-sided crystal. (Try it.)

Sleet.—If the falling snow flakes are driven about by the wind they lose their shape and they fall as sleet.

FIG. 120. Photograph of snow flakes.

The Rainfall of the United States.—The amount of rain (and melted snow) falling at different cities in the United States is measured in every storm, and the whole amount that falls in any year is the annual rainfall for that year. It varies from year to year at the same place, but not *very* much. At New York, for instance, the annual rainfall is usually more than 40 and less than 50 inches. That is, if all the rain of a year that fell into a barrel were kept it would more than fill a barrel 40 inches high. Study the map (Fig. 121) carefully and see what it means.

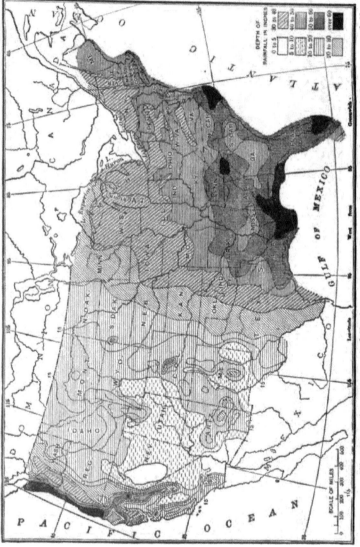

Fig. 121. The annual average rainfall of the United States. Read the legend of the map carefully and compare it with the chart. Such a map is important. Wheat can not be raised on land where the rainfall is less than about 18 inches, unless, indeed, the land is artificially irrigated.

Fig. 122. The snow-line in the Rocky Mountains.

The Snow-line.—On very high mountains the snow never melts even in tropical regions. In the Arctic regions the snow never melts even at the level of the sea. The line above which the snow never melts is called the snow-line. In our Rocky Mountain regions it is about 13,000 feet above sea-level. ..　 ·　—　.

The Rainbow.—A beam of white light that leaves a prism is spread out into the colors of the spectrum (page 77). White sunlight reflected within rain drops makes the rainbow.

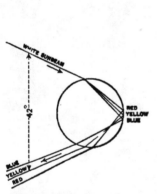

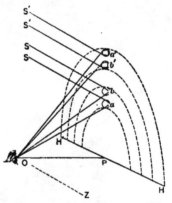

FIG. 123. A sunbeam of white light leaves a rain drop as a beam of colored light.

FIG. 124. The rainbow. It is formed by parallel rays from the Sun (S, S, S', S') refracted by rain drops (a, b, a', b') entering the eye. There are often *two* bows. HH' is the horizon.

Halos.—Most halos are formed by the light of the Sun (or Moon) refracted by crystals of ice in the upper air.

BOOK IV: CHEMISTRY.

CHEMISTRY is the science that tells us what things are made of; and it is useful in all kinds of manufactures. If you want to make gunpowder, or bread, to tan leather, or to make good steel, you must use a receipt that chemists have found out. The best way to understand chemistry is to make a few experiments.

The teacher should prepare the apparatus and try the experiments beforehand, and repeat them before the class. As the subject is not an easy one the experiments chosen are purposely made simple. Here, as elsewhere, it is sought to inculcate principles and to teach methods first of all. Little more than this can be done with children who have had no formal instruction in chemistry.

The following materials are needed. Every bottle should be plainly labeled.

In small glass-stoppered bottles:

Sulphuric Acid, Nitric Acid, Hydrochloric Acid, Acetic Acid.

In cork-stoppered bottles:

Sulphur, iron wire or filings or tacks, copper wire or filings or tacks, zinc wire or filings or tacks, quicklime, chalk crayons, scraps of zinc, scraps of pure lead, gunpowder, oxyd of manganese, sulphur matches, common table salt, phosphorus, fragments of marble, niter.

A pair of scales, a few glass tumblers and dishes, corks, a glass stirring rod, filter paper, a spirit lamp, a pane of window glass, glass jars, will be needed also.

123

Physical Changes: Solutions.—A pinch of common table salt is *dissolved* in a tumbler of water. The salt, which is a solid, becomes invisible in the liquid water. It is invisible, but all of it still remains in the water. If the solution is poured into a flat dish and set on a hot stove, the water will go off in steam and vapor, and will leave the solid salt in the dish. (Try it.)

Mixtures.—Mix powdered sulphur with iron filings by shaking them together in a box. A magnet will attract the iron filings and not the sulphur, and the two things can be separated in this way. (Try it.)

When salt is dissolved in water you can get the salt back again by heating the water; neither salt nor water is lost or changed. And when sulphur and iron are mixed you can separate them by a magnet. Neither is altered.

Combination.—But there are many things which *combine* when they are mixed together. You put in two things and they combine to make a third thing different from either.

Sulphate of Iron.—For instance, take one part (by weight) of iron wire, two parts of strong sulphuric acid in four parts of water and mix them. The acid and the iron will combine, and the iron will disappear.[1] Now filter the fluid and set it on a hot stove in a flat dish. The fluid will evaporate and will leave beautiful green crystals of sulphate

[1] If the mixture is heated the action will be more rapid.

of iron—green vitriol, so called. The acid and the iron have combined to make a third thing—green vitriol—different from either. (Try it.)

Sulphate of Copper.—Or again, take one part, (by weight) of copper wire, with ten parts of strong sulphuric acid (and no water). Mix them and boil the acid over a lamp until gas escapes rapidly. Let the mixture cool and pour off the liquid carefully. Add water to the residue and evaporate the solution over a fire. Beautiful blue crystals of sulphate of copper — blue vitriol — will remain. The acid and the copper have combined to make a third thing—blue vitriol—different from either. (Try it.)

Sulphate of Zinc.—Or again, take two parts (by weight) of zinc scraps and put them with three parts (by weight) of sulphuric acid to which there has been added ten parts of water. (Do not heat it.) When the action ceases you will have a liquid. Evaporate it over a fire and crystals of sulphate of zinc will remain. Two things have combined, and a third thing has been made, different from either of them. (Try it.)

Carbonate of Lime.—A piece of chalk is made up of two things, namely, carbonic acid and lime. Chalk is carbonate of lime. Pour some diluted sulphuric acid on the chalk. The carbonic acid, which is a gas, will be driven off, in bubbles, by the sulphuric acid, and sulphate of lime will remain. (Try it.) It is as if lime were a prisoner and the carbonic acid a soldier holding him. Sulphuric acid is a stronger soldier and takes the prisoner away.

Chemical Affinity.—The sulphuric acid has a stronger *affinity* for (liking for; fondness for) lime than the carbonic acid and always drives it off and takes the lime prisoner in its turn. Vinegar is an acid (acetic acid). It, also, has a stronger *affinity* for lime than carbonic acid has. Pour some strong vinegar on a piece of chalk (carbonate of lime) and the carbonic acid gas will fly away in bubbles and leave acetate of lime. (Try it.) It is just as if lime *liked* to be a prisoner of acetic acid rather than of carbonic acid.

Lime has a greater *affinity* for acetic acid, than for carbonic acid, the chemists say. It is by studying these likes and dislikes of the metals that chemists find out the easiest and the cheapest ways to manufacture them.

Chemical Manufactures.—All sorts of things, gunpowder, glass, soap, cheese, illuminating gas, bread, etc., are made by receipts that the chemists have invented.

Gunpowder is a mixture of charcoal, sulphur and niter.[1] These three things are mixed—they are not combined until the gunpowder is fired off. Then they suddenly combine and make a gas. The gas in the bore of the gun pushes the bullet out quickly. The best gunpowder is that which gives the most gas, and chemists have taught us

[1] Niter is a combination of potassium and nitric acid.

exactly how to make it. A cannon ball can be shot out at a speed of 2,500 feet a second now-a-days; a hundred years ago it was not possible to shoot it out a quarter as fast.

Composition of Air and Water.—Our air—the atmosphere—is a mixture (not a combination) of two invisible gases called oxygen and nitrogen. Water is a combination (not a mixture) of two invisible gases called oxygen and hydrogen.

Oxygen.—Take a piece of oxyd of manganese. It is made up of oxygen gas combined with manganese, which is a metal. Heat it and the oxygen gas will go off in bubbles and can be collected under a jar. (Try it.)

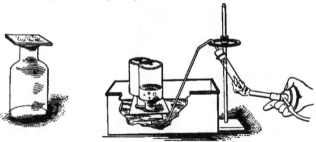

Fig. 125. Preparation of oxygen gas. Heat powdered oxyd of manganese in a tube about one-third full. The oxygen gas will be driven off by the heat and can be collected over water in a jar turned upside down. Afterwards slide a sheet of glass under the jar so as to close it and keep the gas till it is wanted for other experiments.

Nitrogen Gas can be prepared by burning a bit of phosphorus [1] (not bigger than a green pea)

[1] Handle the phosphorus with pincers—forceps; never touch it with the hands as it produces very bad sores.

under a glass jar containing air. Air is oxygen and nitrogen mixed together. The phosphorus burns up the oxygen of the air and all that is left in the jar is nitrogen gas.

Fig. 126. Preparation of nitrogen gas. Float a little phosphorus in a saucer on a small piece of wood in a jar of water. Cover it by a bell-jar. Set the phosphorus on fire. It will burn up all the oxygen in the bell-jar and leave only nitrogen. Slip a pane of glass under the bell-jar while it is in the water and keep the nitrogen gas till it is wanted for use.

In 100 pounds of air, 23 pounds are oxygen and 77 pounds are nitrogen. This is the air we breathe, and it is the oxygen in the air that keeps us alive. If an animal (a mouse for instance) is put into a jar of nitrogen gas it dies. The nitrogen gas does not kill the mouse; it is the lack of oxygen that kills it. A match will not burn in nitrogen. (Try it.)

Preparation of Hydrogen:

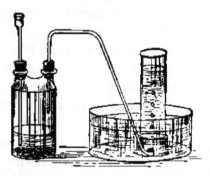

FIG. 127. Preparation of Hydrogen. The left-hand jar con-. tains scraps of zinc in water. Through the straight tube with a cup at the top carefully pour in some strong hydrochloric acid. The liquid will begin to bubble all round the zinc and the bubbles will rise, go over through the bent tube and be caught above the water in the closed jar which has been turned upside down and set on a stand. These bubbles are hydrogen gas.

What has happened is this : the zinc has taken some chlorine from the hydrochloric acid (which is chlorine gas combined with hydrogen gas), and formed chloride of zinc, which stays in the first jar. The hydrogen gas set free has gone over in bubbles, and is collected in the right-hand jar.

N. B. This is a dangerous experiment, because if hydrogen gas mixes with air the mixture may explode. Two things must be carefully attended to : I. The right-hand jar must be *completely* filled with water and then turned upside down so that no air remains at the top of it, above the water. II. The bent tube (which, in the picture, extends too far into the left-hand jar) must not be put under the right-hand jar for some little time after the acid is poured on the zinc—not until it is sure that all the air in the left-hand jar is driven off, and that nothing but pure hydrogen gas is coming through the tube.

Combustion.—Combustion is burning. When a match, or a piece of coal, burns there is combustion. Combustion is usually the combination of something with oxygen. When a match burns, the sulphur on its head combines with the oxygen of the air, and it makes a stifling gas.

FIG. 128. Sulphur burned in oxygen. Fasten a spiral wire to a cork as in the picture. Heat the wire red hot and put it into some powdered sulphur. Light the sulphur with a match and remove the cork that stoppers a bell-jar of oxygen and put the cork with the spiral wire in its place. The sulphur will blaze brilliantly till it is all burned away. (Try it.)

When coal burns the carbon of the coal combines with the oxygen of the air and makes carbonic acid gas. The combustion (burning) is rapid in these cases. When iron rusts some of the iron combines (slowly) with the oxygen of the air and makes the oxyd of iron (iron-rust). When we breathe air into our lungs there is a slow combustion there. Part of our body rusts, as it were; the slow burning of our fat and food keeps the temperature of our body at about 98° Fahrenheit even when the air round us is at zero. The colder the air the more food we must eat to keep warm. That is the reason why the Eskimo eat fat and blubber.

Combustion in Oxygen.—Light a match and let it burn in the air and blow it out. While the end of the match is still glowing red put it into a jar of oxygen gas. The match will instantly burst into flame. (Try it.) Blow out the match and try it again and again.

FIG. 129. Hydrogen burning in air. The bottle contains hydrogen gas. The left-hand tube is stopped up. The right-hand tube leads up inside an empty glass jar. Hydrogen gas will stream up this tube. Light it with a match and it will burn. It will combine with the oxygen of the air. *Hydrogen and Oxygen combined form water.* Notice the drops of water that condense on the inside of the glass. The teacher should try this experiment, using great care.

Hydrogen is the lightest of all gases and is exactly suitable for the filling of balloons. It takes fourteen cubic feet of hydrogen to weigh as much as one cubic foot of air, so that a balloon filled with hydrogen (a little toy balloon for instance) will float in the air.

FIG. 130. A balloon. Hydrogen is expensive and most
balloons are filled with common coal gas (illuminating gas).

Chemical Elements.—When a chemist sees a
substance new to him, a mineral, for instance, the
first thing he tries to find out is whether the substance is a combination of substances that he knows
already. For example, he finds that salt is made
out of chlorine (a gas) and sodium (a very light
metal). Next he tries to separate chlorine into any
other two substances. He cannot do it; or, at any
rate no chemists have succeeded in doing it, so far.
Neither have they separated sodium into any simpler things. Substances that cannot be separated
into any simpler substances are called *elements*.
Here is a list of the most familiar elements.

METALS.

Aluminum	Sodium
Calcium	Quicksilver (a liquid
Copper	metal)
Gold	* Nickel
Iron	Silver
Lead	Tin
Potassium	Zinc.

NON-METALS.

* Arsenic	* Iodine
Carbon	Nitrogen (a gas)
Chlorine (a gas)	Oxygen (a gas)
Hydrogen (a gas)	* Phosphorus
	Sulphur.

There are twenty-two elements named in this list. There are about seventy elements in all, but many of them are very rare. Ninety-nine hundredths of the substances on the Earth are made up of the eighteen elements in this list whose names are *not* marked *.

Every single thing on Earth that you can name is made up of one of these elements, or of a combination of two, three or four of them. And all that we know about the Sun, Planets, Stars and nebulæ leads us to think that they, too, are made up of the same elements.

Chemical Compounds.—Some of the substances that we see and handle on the Earth are elements (gold, silver, iron, etc.), but most of them are compounds—made up of two or more elements (salt, clay, steel, wood, leather, etc., are compound substances).

Clay is silicon, aluminum, oxygen and hydrogen.

Salt is chlorine and sodium.

Steel is iron and carbon and phosphorus and sulphur and nickel.

Wood is chiefly carbon, oxygen, hydrogen and nitrogen.

Leather is chiefly carbon, oxygen, hydrogen and nitrogen (combined in different proportions from wood).

Diamond is pure carbon.

Black-lead, in a pencil, is very nearly pure carbon.

Sugar is carbon, hydrogen and oxygen.

Human hair is carbon, hydrogen, oxygen, nitrogen and sulphur.

Indigo is carbon, hydrogen, nitrogen and oxygen.

Quartz is silicon and oxygen.

Granite is silicon, oxygen, aluminum, potassium or sodium.

Quinine is carbon, hydrogen, nitrogen, oxygen and sulphur.

Air is oxygen and nitrogen (*mixed*).

Water is oxygen and hydrogen (*combined*).

Human flesh—fat is carbon, hydrogen, oxygen; *lean* is carbon, hydrogen, oxygen, nitrogen, sulphur.

Milk is water (oxygen and hydrogen) containing fat (carbon, hydrogen, oxygen, nitrogen, sulphur).

Chemical Symbols.— Instead of writing the word oxygen out in full chemists use the symbol O to stand for it, and in a similar way they use other letters to stand for the other elements. These symbols always stand for *fixed weights* of the elements. O always stands for 16 parts, by weight, of oxygen. H always stands for one part, by weight, of hydrogen. Na stands for 23 parts of sodium, Cl for 35 parts of chlorine, and so on.

Symbols of the Elements.

Calcium is Ca,	Silver is Ag,
Gold is Au,	Zinc is Zn,
Iron is Fe,	etc.
Lead is Pb,	Sodium is Na,
Carbon is C,	Hydrogen is H,
Chlorine is Cl,	Nitrogen is N,
	Oxygen is O.

Chemists write the symbol for water H_2O, which means that in water there are 16 parts, by weight, of oxygen to two parts, by weight, of hydrogen. Sodium combines with chlorine to make common salt. Chemists write the symbol for salt NaCl, which means that it contains 23 parts, by weight, of sodium and 35 parts of chlorine. Sulphuric acid is H_2SO_4; nitric acid is HNO_3; hydrochloric acid is HCl; acetic acid is $C_2H_4O_2$; carbonic acid H_2CO_3.

Green vitriol is $FeSO_4$; blue vitriol is $CuSO_4$; marble is $CaCO_3$; starch is $C_6H_{10}O_5$; cane-sugar is $C_{12}H_{22}O_{11}$; and so on.

This is a short way of writing; and it can be used for describing an experiment and for telling beforehand what third thing is going to be produced when two things are combined. For instance, the experiment on page 125 (to make blue vitriol) can be described in this way:

$$Cu \quad + \quad H_2SO_4 \quad = CuSO_4 \quad + H_2$$

(Copper) (Sulphuric acid) (Sulphate of copper = blue vitriol) and so on for other combinations.

BOOK V: GEOLOGY.

Geology is the science of the rocks. It tells
how rocks were made in the first place, how they
have been raised above the level of the sea, then
crumpled up by earthquakes and pressure to make
mountains, how they have been worn away by
water and ice. The past history of the Earth is
written in the rocks, and Geology tells how to read
the history right. How old is the Earth? How
does it happen to have its present shape? How
long have men lived on it? Such questions as
these cannot be answered without studying the
rocks. We have to begin by studying the way in
which water and ice make changes in the Earth's
surface.

The Earth's Crust.—The crust of the Earth is
the rock and soil of the land and the rock and clay
of the ocean floors. No one knows exactly what
is below the crust. The deepest wells and cañons
are about a mile in depth. The hot lava from volcanoes does not come from very great depths.
The only parts of the Earth that we ever can see or
touch are the rocks of the thin outer crust. Draw
a circle eight inches in diameter, and let it stand
for the Earth. The thin pencil line that bounds it

is wide enough to stand for the crust. Ninety-nine hundredths of the Earth's crust is made up of a dozen of the chemical elements see page 133) as carbon, oxygen, hydrogen, nitrogen, silicon, aluminum, sulphur, iron, etc.

Running Water Models the Shapes of the Hills and Mountains of the Earth's Crust.—If you look at a plowed field after a heavy rain you will see that it is all carved into small ravines and hills. The ground was soft and one rain was enough to do the work. The hard rocks of the mountains have been carved in the same way, only it has taken thousands of years and hundreds of thousands of rains to do the work.

FIG. 131. This map of a river and its branches might be a map of the little rivulets of water in a plowed field after a rain.

The softest rocks of a mountain are quickest worn away and the high peaks usually consist of the hardest rocks.

FIG. 132. A view in the " Bad Lands " of Dakota. The rain has carved all the slopes.

Ocean waves may wear away sea-cliffs several feet every year. There is a church in Kent, England, that was a mile from the shore in the time of King Henry VIII. (1509). In the year 1804 it fell into the sea. In three centuries the ocean had worked its way a mile inland.

FIG. 133. A high peak of hard rock. Deep valleys have been worn all around it by water and widened by glaciers.

Rivers Cut Deep Gorges in Rocks.—Everywhere we see rivers cutting their channels. The Niagara river has cut a deep gorge connecting Lake Erie with Lake Ontario. The river falls over

FIG. 134. A part of the gorge of the Niagara river.

a precipice and wears away the rock over which it falls about three feet every year. It has already cut a deep gorge about seven miles long. To do this work has required at least 12,000 years and probably more time. We can say then that any changes in the rocks that occurred before the

FIG. 135. *The Great Cañon of the Colorado River.*—This cañon is about 300 miles long and its depth is always as much as half a mile, and often as much as a mile. The river used to run on the surface of the ground. It has cut hundreds of miles of the length of its gorge down into and through hard rocks a mile in thickness. Imagine how long a time this work required.

Niagara river began to cut its gorge must have happened at least 10,000 years ago.   It is in this way that time is measured in geology.

Rivers Carry Soil to the Sea.—The Mississippi river, for instance, carries enough solid material to the sea, every year, to make a hill 268 feet high and a mile square.   Five thousand such hills would cover all the land drained by the Mississippi (its drainage-basin) one foot deep with soil.   It will take the Mississippi five thousand years, then, to lower the level of its whole basin one foot.   And, generally, we may say that all the continents have their levels lowered by rivers about one foot every five thousand years.

FIG. 136. A mountain brook.   It can move quite large stones, especially in the spring when the brook is full.

Stones are Carried by Streams.—A stream whose current moves six inches in a second will

carry fine sand along with it; gravel is carried if
the current moves a foot in a second; stones as large
as a hen's egg if the current moves three feet in a
second. (Boys who live in the country can prove
this for themselves.) Very rapid torrents move
large bowlders.

Streams Sort Out Different Sizes of Stones.—A
mountain torrent will carry quite large stones along
with its current. When the stream leaves the hills
and runs more slowly it drops the largest stones.
It will carry gravel a long way, but by and by it
drops the gravel too. As it runs more and more
slowly, in a flat country, it may even drop the sand
it is carrying. The different stones are sorted out,
according to their weight, by the stream. If you
put some sand in a basin full of water you cannot
pour all the sand out with the water unless you give
the basin a swirl to make the water move faster.
Then it will pick up the sand. (Try it.)

Fig. 137. A flood plain.

Flood-Plains.—When rivers are flooded by melting snows or heavy rains, they overflow their banks, and their waters, which carry sand and mud, spread out over the land on each side.   In spreading out they run less swiftly, and drop some of the mud and sand and form a flood-plain.   The mud that is dropped is called *sediment*—that is settlings.

FIG. 138.   The delta of a river.

Deltas.—At the mouth of a river there are often several branches spreading out like the Greek letter *delta* (*Δ*).   Every year much mud and sand is deposited by the river and if the current is strong they are carried out to sea and dropped on the sea bottom, where, in time, they are cemented into rock.

Sediments are Deposited in Layers (*Strata*).— If a river empties into a lake or into the sea it brings great quantities of sand, gravel, etc., and these settle on the bottom of the lake as sediments— settlings.   They lie in layers one above another. The river runs faster in the time of spring floods

than in the dry summer and so layers of gravel
will sometimes lie over layers of sand.   This goes
on for centuries and centuries, and by and by, all
these layers are .cemented together and make a
rock that is called a *sedimentary rock*.   It is sand-
stone if the layers are of sand; limestone if the
layers are made of the shells of dead animals that
live in the ocean.   *All sedimentary rocks are stratified—are in layers; and all rocks that are stratified*
(in layers) *were originally made from materials
sorted out by water.*

FIG. 139. A glacier in the Alps.   From the snow-covered
summits the glacier slowly moves downward like a river of ice.
It carries with it all the rocks that fall on its surface and it
grinds and polishes the face of the rocks in its bed.

Glaciers.—Snow falls on the tops of mountains in the winter and if they are very high it does not melt when the summer comes. Above the snow-line (see Fig. 122) there is perpetual snow. This snow slides downwards on the steep slopes and becomes packed into ice (as a snow ball can be packed, by pressure, into ice) and the ice, like a river, slowly flows downward between walls of rocks towards the valley below. At the lower end of the glacier the ice melts and forms rivers that are usually torrents. Glaciers flow like rivers, only very slowly, a few feet every day. If you drive a row of stakes in a line across a glacier like this:

Rocks . . | . . . . | . . Rocks
Glacier

in a few months the stakes will look like this:

The four stakes on the rocks will not move, of course; the others move as the ice moves; the middle of the glacier moves fastest. (Why?)

Bowlders.—The glacier grinds against its rock walls and carries pieces of rock down with it. Bowlders fall on it and are carried down on its sur-

10

face. Now-a-days we often find great bowlders in places where there used to be glaciers that do not exist any longer. We often can tell just where these bowlders came from because they must have come from ledges of the same kind of rock. This is one proof that glaciers used to exist in that place.

FIG. 140. Boulders on Cape Ann, Massachusetts. They were brought by an ancient glacier that has long since disappeared.

Glacier-Scratches.—The glacial river is heavy and presses hard against its bed and its walls. The stones in the ice are slowly rubbed along the stones of the walls and bed and glacial scratches are made. If you find a rock to-day with such scratches you may be sure they were made by an ancient glacier, although the glacier may have melted away centuries ago.

FIG. 141. Glacier markings on a rock in Iowa.   There are no glaciers in Iowa now-a-days.

A glacier carries a great quantity of rock and dirt with it.   At the lower end of the glacier.much of this dirt remains when the glacier melts.   Some of it is carried away by streams of course, but much remains.   The glacier thus builds up at its lower end a peculiarly-shaped wall.   Wherever you find such walls, now-a-days, was the lower end of an ancient glacier.

The Glacial-Period in the United States.—A great part of the United States was once covered

by glaciers as Greenland now is. This was perhaps a hundred thousand years ago. Since then
the climate has changed and the glaciers have
'melted. The ice sheet was, in parts, nearly a mile
thick. It covered parts of Iowa, nearly all of
Illinois and Ohio, all of New York and New Eng-

FIG. 142. A peculiar shaped hill (*a moraine*) built by a glacier
near Ithaca, N. Y. There are no glaciers in New York now.

land, and all of Canada. (Trace this region out
on the map of the U. S., Fig. 121.) Bowlders,
glacial markings and moraines now to be seen prove
the existence of this ancient ice-sheet. Think what
a different country America then was. Its plants,
animals and men were all driven southwards by this
ice-sheet. Its climate was very different. Nearly
every one of the ponds and lakes in Canada and the

northern United States has been formed by this glacial ice. The valleys of all the rivers were much changed too; though many of the rivers are older than the ice sheet. The ice sheet endured for thousands of years and had time to do much work. The great falls at Niagara were formed by it, probably.

FIG. 143. An Iceberg from the Greenland glaciers. Seven-eighths of its mass are below sea-level.

Icebergs.—When a glacier ends in the sea, as many glaciers in Alaska and Greenland do, huge blocks of ice break off and float away. These icebergs are made of fresh water (why?) and they float so that only about one-eighth part shows.

Pack-Ice.—The salt water in the Arctic regions freezes, too, and makes fields of pack ice so thick that vessels can not penetrate it. It is often so jammed together by winds and currents that its surface is too rough for men to travel on. This is one of the principal reasons why it is so difficult to reach the north pole.

Soil is Rock that Has been Broken Up.—Take up some soil in your hands and you will find that while much of it is soft, it contains little crystals of sand, etc. These crystals are pieces of rock that has decayed and crumbled to pieces. Rub a pane of glass with these crystals and you will find scratches on it.

Fig. 144. A picture to show the soil and what is underneath it. On top is the soil; below that, rock partly decayed; below that again, solid rock. But this last has cracks in it. Water enters these cracks and bursts them apart when it freezes. Rocks are all the while decaying and making soil.

If you go deep down below the soil, anywhere on the Earth, you will find solid rock—below the oceans as well as below the continents.

In the gorges and cañons of rivers, in quarries, tunnels, and railway cuttings you can see the bed-rock, as it is called.

FIG. 145. A mass of stratified rock. The different layers (strata) are of different kinds. This rock was formed under water.

Different Kinds of Rocks.—Granite, lava, sand-stone, limestone, marble, slate and coal are rocks. (Try to get a piece of each kind.) *Granite* rocks have been formed deep down in the interior of the Earth, where it is very hot, and where the pressure is very great. *Lava* is melted rock that has flowed out from a volcano. *Sandstones* are grains of sand that have been cemented together, under water. They are in layers—in *strata*. Most *limestones* have also been cemented together, in layers, under water, from the shells of small sea animals.

Nine-tenths of all the surface of the land is covered with stratified rocks. That proves that the continents were formed under the sea and then slowly lifted up.

Stratified rocks lie under all the oceans.

FIG. 146. A rock made of shells cemented together under water.

Granite is composed of three different minerals, quartz, feldspar and mica. You can see in a piece of freshly broken granite little crystals of hard quartz, and with your knife you can cleave off thin layers of shining mica (isinglass it is sometimes called). Feldspar is there, too, in small flesh-colored crystalline slabs. (Try to find these in a piece of granite.) All the granites were formed deep down in the Earth. The granites that we see have been uncovered by water that has worn away the rocks that once laid above them.

Limestone is made of granules of carbonate of lime cemented together. If you put a drop of sulphuric acid on limestone carbonic acid gas is set free in little bubbles.

Sandstones are grains of sand cemented together. Red sandstones are cemented by a compound of iron, and the air does not affect them. For that reason they make excellent building stones.

Fig. 147. Photograph of two pieces of granite.

Slates are clay in layers each one like the slates that you use in school.

Clay.—When a crystalline rock is broken up into very fine grains and deposited under water we have a clay. The ocean bed, far from land, is, in great part, made of a reddish clay.

Crystalline Rocks and Crystals.—If you break a piece of marble you will see that the rock is made of a multitude of little shining crystals. Sugar, too, is made of crystals.

Precious Stones.—Diamonds (white), rubies (red), emeralds (green), sapphires (blue), topazes (yellow), amethysts (violet)—are all crystals.

FIG. 148. Obsidian—a lava rock like black glass.   Pumice is
another kind of lava.

FIG. 149. A piece of sandstone rock.

FIG. 150. Snowflakes crystallize into six-sided forms.

Dissolve a quantity of salt in water, and then set the water in a metal pan on a stove so that the water evaporates rather slowly. Crystals of salt will form and will gradually grow larger. (Try it.) Every one of these crystals, large or small, is a cube. Salt crystals are all of one form, just as elephants are all of one form, whether they are large or small.

Dissolve a quantity of sugar, or alum, in boiling water and set it away to cool. Hang some threads of string in the solution, and when it cools you will find the string covered with shining crystals. (Try it.) Snow is crystallized water.

Elevation and Depression of the Land. — All stratified rocks, we know, were formed under the ocean. How is it that we find them making the land? Millions of years ago they were formed;

FIG. 151. A crystal of quartz. Quartz crystals usually have a shape like this.

slowly—a layer at a time. It required millions of years to make them. During this long period the crust of the Earth has suffered many changes. Some parts of it have been lifted up; some parts depressed. On mountains, thousands of feet above the ocean, we still find shells of sea-animals bedded in the rock. When the shells were deposited, the tops of those mountains were under water. In Lake Baikal, which is now 1,600 feet above the sea, there are living seals of the same species as those of the Arctic Ocean. Their ancestors came there before the glacial epoch, when Siberia was under water. The interior of the country was then lifted up leaving this lake, and the seals have continued there to this day. They are living evidence of the rise of this country from the ocean. Even now the coasts of Sweden are rising and you find sea beaches there 600 feet above the present sea level. Other coasts are sinking.

There is a temple to Jupiter built by the Romans near the sea-shore about two thousand years ago. Three of its columns are still standing and in them you can still see sea shells which have bored into the marble. When these borings were made the floor of the temple must have been at least twenty feet under water. It was above water when the Romans built it; below water when the sea shells were boring; and it is almost above water now. So that here is a certain proof that the land where the temple stands has been depressed twenty feet and raised again in the last two thousand years. There are many other proofs of the same kind and they all show that in the millions of years during which the Earth has lasted the crust has been elevated and depressed many times, very differently at different places, of course.

All the granites of the Rocky Mountains were formed deep down in the very hot interior of the Earth and have been raised by the crumpling of the crust. All the sandstones and limestones of the country were formed under water and have been raised to their present levels by crumplings of the Earth's crust. Sometimes the lifting was gentle and gradual; sometimes they were raised by violent earthquakes.

FIG. 152. Stratified rocks tilted. Originally the layers were horizontal. During some crumpling of the Earth's crust they were turned on edge.

The Stratified Rocks are About Five Miles Thick.—Few rock walls are more than a mile high. How can we know, then, that the stratified rocks of the Earth's crust are at least five miles thick? In the crumpling of the crust the stratified rocks are sometimes turned on edge, as in Fig. 152. We can then actually measure their thickness.

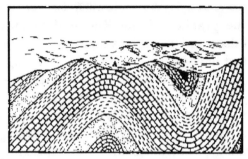

FIG. 153. A series of layers of rocks of different kinds that were originally horizontal and that have been tilted up on edge.

Crumpling of the Earth's Crust:

FIG. 154. A picture to show how mountains are sometimes formed by crumplings of the Earth's crust, and how rivers flow in the valleys. The black stratum is coal. It would never have been found if the layers of rock had not been crumpled.

Mountains are usually formed by the crumpling of the crust of the Earth as it cools. At first the ridge is a huge bulge on the Earth's surface. Afterwards it is sculptured into shape by water. The Appalachian Mountains are 1,000 miles long, 100 miles wide and 3,000 feet high. The Rocky Mountains and the Andes together are 10,000 miles long, 500 to 1,000 miles wide and 10,000 to 20,000 feet high. Water has carved them into shape.

All Nova Scotia and New England and the very places where the cities of New York, Philadelphia, Baltimore, Washington and Richmond now stand were once covered with mountains as high as the Alps. Water has worn them away.

The Pressure of the Rocks within the Earth.— Imagine the pressure on the bottom bricks of a brick wall 100 feet high. If the wall were 1,000 feet high the bottom bricks would be ground to powder. The rocks fifty miles deep in the Earth would be ground to powder, too, if each piece of rock were not packed on every side—from below as well as from above. If a crack opens near such a piece, the rock will *flow* through the crack just as tar would. The motion will produce great heat, just as drawing a rough file over iron produces heat.

The least weakness in the Earth's crust, anywhere, produces crumpling. It may build mountains.

Take a piece of putty or dough and push it sidewise from both sides. The center will rise into the shape of a mountain. (Try it.)

The amount of rock removed by water is enormous, as Fig. 154 shows. Probably five miles of rock has been washed off the top of the Appalachian Mountains and more than a mile from above the present Rocky Mountains. The shapes of the mountains as we see them now are entirely due to water.

Fauna and Flora.—The animals that inhabit any country or region are called its *fauna;* the trees and plants, its *flora.* Some animals (the alligator for instance) are only found in certain regions.

FIG. 155. Characteristic flora and fauna of Australia. The moment you see this picture you know that it was taken in Australia and nowhere else.

Some plants live only in certain places. There were no mammoths or camels in America when Columbus landed (1492), but there used to be thousands of them. Their skeletons are still found by scores.

Fossils.—The stratified rocks were formed in seas, lakes, and in the deltas of rivers. Shells, bones, skeletons, leaves, plants, logs and the like were buried in these layers millions of years ago and some of them have been preserved. They have been turned into stone. We know something about the fauna and flora of past times by the fossils that have been found. We know that the Kangaroo, to-day, belongs to Australia. In the same way we can associate certain fossils with certain layers of rock—with certain ages. If you find a certain kind of fossil fish in Iceland and another of the same kind in Norway you know that the two rocks containing the fish are of about the same age, because that fish lived at one period of the Earth's history and at no other. The animals and plants that first appeared on the Earth are buried in the deepest layers.

The Unstratified Rocks.—Granites and lavas that are not stratified form the greater part of all the mass of the globe. They lie deep down, and we only see them when the rocks above them have been worn away by water or when they have (like lavas) been pushed up by pressure from below.

Volcanoes.—Volcanoes are mountains built up by lava flowing out from the hot interior of the Earth. The lava is forced upwards by pressures in the Earth's interior. Lava is melted rock. Enormous

11

quantities of it flow from some volcanoes. The whole of the Hawaiian Islands have been built from lava flows. In the northwestern parts of the United States (Washington, Idaho) there are lava fields that cover 200,000 square miles, and they are sometimes 3,000 to 4,000 feet thick. Arizona has a lava field covering 25,000 square miles. These immense sheets of lava were not sent out all at one time, but the lava flows were spread over millions of years. Mt. Etna is 11,000 feet high and 90 miles in circumference and is all solid lava; the Hawaiian volcanoes are much larger. There are hundreds of active volcanoes now; and thousands of extinct volcanoes.

The surface of the Moon (see Figs. 22 and 26) is covered with extinct volcanoes.

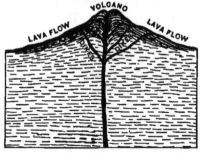

FIG. 156. Lava (colored black in the picture) flows from a hot reservoir deep down in the Earth to the surface and flows out. It builds up first a hill and then a mountain.

Vesuvius.—One of the most famous active volcanoes is Vesuvius, near Naples, in Italy. In the

the year A. D. 79 a terrific eruption took place which buried the cities of Herculaneum and Pompeii[1] under heaps of volcanic mud and ashes.

FIG. 157. A portion of Pompeii with the heaps of ashes removed. Many of the houses remain just as they were twenty centuries ago. Mt. Vesuvius shows in the distance.

Imagine New York to be buried under heaps of ashes and to remain buried for twenty centuries! The people who would uncover it in the year A. D. 4000 would know exactly how we lived, how our houses were built, what clothes we wore, how we worked and how we amused ourselves. The inhabitants of Pompeii rushed from their houses leaving everything behind them. A few who returned to save their money or jewels perished. Everything remained untouched. When the city was uncovered after all those centuries the very bread was found on the counter in the baker's shop! A notice was found *Cave Canem* (Beware of the Dog!) to warn passers-by of a fierce watch-dog.

[1] Pronounced pom-pā′yē.

Volcanoes send out gas, flame, steam, mud, ashes, hot stones and floods of melted lava, or sometimes of hot mud.

The steam causes violent explosions and sometimes tears the mountains to pieces as at Krakatoa, near Java, in 1883, and in Martinique in 1901.

The volcano of Cotopaxi is known to have thrown a rock nine feet square and thirty feet long nine miles away. Instances of the sort give some idea of the immense energy of the explosions.

Earthquakes. — If the underground rocks are moved at all a shock is sent in every direction. Ten million tons of rock moving a hundredth of an inch will make a heavy shock, and if the movement is not too deep underground we shall feel the shock at the surface. The earthquake at Charleston, in 1886, threw down hundreds of houses, opened great cracks in the ground, made new ponds and lakes, and was felt all the way from Wisconsin to Cuba. At the Lisbon earthquake (1755) forty thousand persons perished—many of them by great waves that rolled in from the sea when the level of the ocean-floor was changed. There are earthquakes during every volcanic eruption. It is the earthquakes of millions of years that have crumpled the crust of the Earth.

The Age of the Earth.—No one can tell the age of the Earth exactly, but we can form some idea of it. The sedimentary rocks were all formed by soil washed out to sea. The sedimentary rocks are *certainly* 6,000 feet thick (probably they are more ; see page 158). Rivers bring soil from the land at the rate of about one foot deep of soil every 5,000 years (see page 141) 6,000 times 5,000 = 30,000,000 years. If the rivers of old time worked no faster than the rivers of our time then the Earth must be *at least* 30,000,000 years old.

Suppose that one of your steps—two feet long— stood for a hundred years and that you start out for a walk. Three steps from your house put a stake in the ground to stand for the landing of the Pilgrims, three hundred years ago nearly (1620); four steps from your house put another stake to stand for the landing of Columbus (1492); at eight steps put a stake to stand for the conquest of England by William the Conqueror (1066); at nineteen steps, a stake to stand for the date of the birth of Christ; at sixty steps, another to stand for the building of the Pyramids in Egypt (about 4,000 B.C.). Nearly all the history we know is represented by sixty of your steps. It would take 15,000 such steps (about 6 miles) to mark off a million years of the Earth's history. You would have to walk *at least* 180 miles to represent the age of the Earth.

If the time during which the Earth has endured is represented by 180 *miles* then the whole known history of mankind is represented by not more than a couple of hundred *feet*.

Geological Ages.—We can tell the age of some rocks by noticing what fossils they contain. First of all, there are many rocks (granites, lavas, etc.) that contain no fossils at all. We can tell nothing about them. They are called rocks of the *Archean* age.

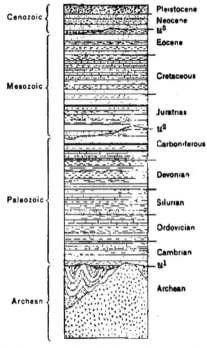

FIG. 158. The succession of the rocks of the Earth's crust. The oldest rocks are at the bottom, the youngest at the top. They were deposited in that order. The *Archean* rocks have no fossils; the *Age of Invertebrates* has few animals with backbones; in the *Age of Reptiles* animals with backbones, especially reptiles, are numerous; in the *Age of Mammals* there are many animals that give suck to their young.

Lying over them are layers of rocks that contain the fossil remains of plants, seaweeds, shellfish, etc.

FIG. 159. Some of the fossils of the age of invertebrates—of
the age when there were few animals with backbones.

This is the *Age of Invertebrates*—of animals without backbones.   There were plenty of fish, though, in this Age.   It is also called the *Paleozoic* Age—the age of ancient life, the name means.

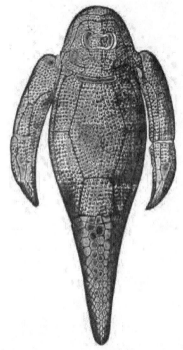

FIG. 160. A fish of the Devonian period.   Its body is covered with scales like that of a reptile—of a lizard, for instance.

Lying over these rocks, again, are others, that are not so old; they lie uppermost; they were deposited later.   The fossils in these rocks are mostly reptiles—lizards, etc., besides fish, plants, trees.

This is called the *Age of Reptiles;* or the *Mesozoic Age*—the middle age of life. And, lying over these rocks, again, are others younger still, that contain the fossils of animals that give suck to their young — mammals (such as foxes, dogs, wolves, lions, horses, cows, elephants, and man). This is called the *Age of Mammals* — the age in which animals that give suck to their young are common. And these great Ages are divided into shorter periods. The *Carboniferous* period is that in which the coal was formed; the *Glacial period* is that when the Earth's surface was largely covered with glaciers, and there are many others.

Life in the Age of Invertebrates.—What life there may have been before this Age we do not know. The earlier rocks have no fossils. The earliest fossils belong to the age of animals without a backbone and to the seaweeds of those times. There were many corals; an incredible number of shell fish, some of them fifteen feet long; fishes of many kinds, some of them almost like reptiles, and so forth.

The Coal-Period.—The coal beds of the world are immense swamps of ancient times in which the trees have rotted and died. During long ages the trees have been gradually turned into coal.

A thick forest makes about a ton of dead leaves, dead branches and trunks on every acre every year. If you spread this evenly over an acre it makes a layer less than a thousandth of an inch thick. In some of the beds of solid coal is over a hundred feet thick, and it must have taken something like a million years ($1,200 \times 1,000 = 1,200,000$) for these beds to be formed.

Fig. 101 A landscape in the coal period. Notice the curious trees, very different from ours. Fossil trees of this kind are found in coal. In fact, coal is nothing but the fossil remains of such trees. Some of the trees were at least 50 feet high and 4 feet in diameter.

Peat-Bogs. — Now-a-days we find in certain countries great marshes or bogs of a thick black mud called *peat*. Ireland has many such bogs — fifty miles long for instance. In the there are many also. The peat is up of decayed trees and plants (carbon, nitrogen, etc.). Plants and trees drop their leaves every year and finally die themselves, and fall. In wet places peat is formed, often rapidly. Coins left by Roman soldiers 2,000 years ago have been found covered by ten feet of peat bog, so that the peat has increased about a foot every two centuries, in that particular place.

There are many single layers where the coal is 50 feet thick and the thickness of the rocks that contain coal is more than two miles. The ancient swamps were of immense extent. In Pennsylvania, Ohio, Virginia, Tennessee, Georgia and Alabama there are more than 60,000 square miles of coal lands, and in North America alone about 200,000 square miles. These were once swamps.

The climate in those times was very different ent from now; it was warm and moist everywhere, even in the arctic regions (where coal is often found and where there must have been forests, of course). There were many corals, land and fresh-water shells, and very many insects, such as dragonflies, spiders, beetles. These insects had organs by which they could make a noise, a note, to call their fellows.

Life in the Age of Reptiles.—Some of the fish of the Age of Invertebrates gradually turned into reptiles—land and sea animals with a backbone—somewhat as a tadpole changes into a frog. That is, the descendants of some of the early fishes became reptiles; the descendants of other fish re-

FIG. 162. Flora and fauna of the Jurassic period. Notice the lizard-like birds with teeth.

mained fish. They breathed through gills and not with lungs. The reptiles lived sometimes on land, sometimes in the sea. After millions of years some of the reptiles grew immensely large as we know by their skeletons found to-day.

FIG. 163. The skeleton of a Brontosaurus. Some of these huge lizard-like animals were 50 feet long and weighed something like 20 tons. They walked ; they did not crawl ; and sometimes they stood upright.

Life Since the Age of Coal.—The plants, trees, fish and animals of the Age of Coal and the ages

FIG. 164. A flying reptile. Some of these reptiles had a spread of wings as much as twenty feet.

before it were very different indeed from those that we know. But they were the ancestors of our plants and animals. Some fishes gradually lost their armored scales and their descendants became our fish. The flying reptiles were the ancestors of

FIG. 165. A landscape of the Chalk period. The trees are not unlike our redwoods and palms.

our birds. Our horses are the descendants of animals of the same sort that lived in these ancient times. Our oak trees, poplars, willows and so forth, were unknown till the Chalk period, but they are the children of old forms of trees, much changed in the course of millions of years. Great lizard-like animals of past times were the ancestors of our crocodiles and alligators.

Ancestors of the Horse.—The fossil remains of horses that lived millions of years ago have been discovered, and their bones are now in our museums. There was the *Eöhippus*, the first horse, the ancestor of all horses. He was no bigger than a fox, and he had five toes on his front feet instead of one toe (a hoof) as our horses have. This horse lived about 4,000,000 years ago. Next came the *Orohippus* (mountain horse), which was about the same size, and which had four toes on his front feet. Next came the *Mesohippus*, a horse about the size of a sheep, having three toes on his front feet. He lived about 2,000,000 years ago. Then came the *Protohippus*, about the size of a donkey, having three toes, only one of which touched the ground. The others were too high to touch it.

Then, about 1,000,000 years ago, came the *Plio-hippus*, a small pony, with hoofs; and finally the horse.

Four million years ago all the horses had five toes and were no larger than foxes. They found good food and grew larger because they found it.

The larger and stronger the horse the more food he could find, the further he could travel to find it. If he lived in stony places, as *Orohippus* did, the horse with the fewest and hardest toes was the most fitted to live in those places. The strongest and biggest horses had the strongest and biggest colts, and they, in their turn had stronger and bigger colts. Finally, in three million years or so, the children of the little *Eohippus* had grown to be real horses. *The fittest survived* and had colts; *the weakest perished* in the struggle for existence.

Natural Selection—The Struggle for Existence. Every animal gets its food and saves its life from enemies by a struggle for existence. The fittest survive; the weaker die. It is the same with plants and trees; with fish and birds. Why, do you suppose, are most wild animals, deer for instance, of the same color on both sides? And why is that color the color of the regions in which the deer live? Because a dun-colored deer is not so easily seen in a desert as a black one. More of the black ones have been killed by lions and tigers; more of the dun-colored have survived. The young deer grow like their parents in color. Deer are the same color on both sides because the deer of different colors are quickest seen and most often killed. Fewer of them live to have young. Lions are the same color on both sides because the lions that were of different colors were more easily seen; they got less food; fewer of them lived to have young. Wild bulls are nearly always of the same color on both sides; farm bulls are often of several colors. It makes no difference in their life on a farm what color they are. But it makes a difference to the wild bulls. Bears that live in forests are brown; polar bears are white to match the snow.

Learn these lines by heart; they were written as a joke, but they are true if they are rightly understood.

The fastest lions caught the most animals,
And the fastest animals got away from the most lions;
So all the slow animals were eaten,
And all the slow lions starved to death!

Heredity: Adaptation.—Young plants or animals are much like their parents. They *inherit* their shape and size from their ancestors. A young tree is always an oak if it grew from an acorn; it never turns out to be a willow or a chestnut. But all the young trees are not equally vigorous. Some of them can stand several dry summers in succession, and some cannot. Trees that can best adapt themselves to their surroundings live the most vigorous lives and have the healthiest acorns. If the climate changes, the weak trees die and the others well adapt themselves to new circumstances. If the climate changes very slowly indeed, the oak tree, in thousands of years may change very much. In California, where there is no winter, the oak trees are evergreen; they do not shed their leaves at all.

Animals change in the same way. Once there were no birds, but there were flying reptiles. Then came a kind of reptile with feathers, and afterwards a bird. Some of the ancient fishes were half reptiles. Some of the great lizards were half whales; others were partly birds, partly mammals.

Every living thing must adapt itself to its surroundings or die. When the surroundings change many animals and plants die, but many others change and become very different from their former selves.

Some kinds of animals and plants (sea-shells and sea-weeds for example) have changed very little in millions of years. Other kinds, trees, horses, men, have changed very much.

Recent Geological Periods.—Any time not more than four or five millions of years ago is recent in Geology. The times that are most interesting to us are the last two or three hundred thousand years; Man appears on the Earth about 200,000 or 300,000 years ago.

If the entire age of the Earth is measured by two hundred *miles* (one of your steps to a century) the time that men have lived on the Earth will be measured by two hundred of your *steps;* the known history of mankind by about thirty steps.

There have been great changes of climate on the Earth in the last million years. Before the Glacial Period Greenland was covered with a rich vegetation like that of our temperate zones. The fossils prove it. The beds of coal found in the Arctic regions prove that the arctic climate was then warm and moist. Fossil trees that need a warm climate (willows and maples) are now found in Greenland

12

under great cliffs of ice.   There were formerly
rhinoceroses, elephants, lions, tigers and hyenas
(animals that live in warm countries) in England.
Their bones are still found in caves together with
stone arrow-heads made by men—our ancestors.

The Glacial Period.—(See page 147.)   For
some reason, not well understood, the climate of
North America grew colder.   Glaciers a mile thick
covered Canada and part of the United States as
far south as Ohio.   At this time our continent was
united with Asia near Alaska and perhaps men
came to America along that road.   The animals of
the country were slowly driven southwards by the
ice in search of food and warmth.   Many trees and
plants were killed by the cold and other more hardy
plants took their places.   Fossils of Arctic plants

FIG. 166. Arctic poppies growing on edge of a snow-bank.

are now found as far south as Pennsylvania. Fossil plants of the temperate zone are found in Old Mexico. The climate again changed, we do not know why, and the glaciers melted after thousands of years and left the country very much as we see it to-day. You can understand the changes that have taken place on our continent as the climate changed, if you will think of what now takes place on a high mountain in the tropics.

Botanical Regions.—A high mountain in Mexico has perpetual snow on its summit. No plants can live there. Then comes a belt of rocks where there are no trees. Below this is a belt where pine trees grow, and then comes a belt of hard-wood trees. Lowest of all is a belt with palm-trees and all kinds of tropical plants. The chief reason for this is, of course, the temperature. Palms can only grow in hot regions. Pine trees can only grow in cold regions. Few plants grow in the snow. If you divide the Earth's surface into zones there are few plants and no trees in the Arctic zone, many pines and hard-wood trees in the Temperature zones; a profusion of palms in the tropics.

Plants are fixed to the soil and cannot travel from place to place as animals do. Plants, then, must stay where the temperature is favorable to them. They cannot live elsewhere. Wild animals like the buffalo used to range over the Western United States from Canada to Texas. But even then they could not live where they found no good

FIG. 167. Zones of Vegetation.

grasses. Animals live in *regions*, too. Each
country has its peculiar fauna and flora. Monkeys,
armadilloes, llamas now belong to South America;
lions, tigers, zebras, hippopotami, etc., to Africa.
They live there because the climate is favorable;
they find good food. When the climate of England was warm and favorable there were hippopotami in English rivers; lions, tigers and hyenas
in English forests. Elephants and mastodons used
to live in North America.

FIG. 168. The pyramids of Egypt and the Sphinx—built six
thousand years ago. The great pyramid was 481 feet high.

Prehistoric Man.—There were men in those
days too—savages, we should call them—but they

are our ancestors.   At first they did not know how
to make a fire and had weapons of bone or chipped
flint (the Stone Age).   They were clothed in skins.
By and by they learned to weave cloth and to make
weapons and tools out of copper (the Bronze Age)
and afterwards of iron (the Iron Age).   At first
they tamed no animal but the dog.   By and by
they tamed cows, sheep, goats, horses.   At first
they lived in caves, then they built huts and afterwards houses.

Ten thousand years ago, in Egypt men were
cultivating wheat, working in metals, living under
a regular government.   Six thousand years ago the
Egyptian pyramids were built; men had learned to
write, to make statues, to live in an orderly way,
in peace and comfort.

BOOK VI: ZOÖLOGY.

Zoölogy is the study of animals; Botany is the study of plants (see Book VII). Biology is the study of all living beings, plants and animals alike.

The Study of Zoölogy.—There are millions upon millions of living things on the Earth—fish in the sea, worms in the ground, birds and insects in the air, animals of all sorts on the land. One of the first things to do is to separate all these animals into classes, so as to get .those that are alike into one class, and then to study each class thoroughly. For instance, the cats form a class—a large family, as it were. The panthers form another class, the leopards another, the tigers another. After each of these classes has been studied by itself, we must see if there is any likeness between the different classes; how the cats, the leopards and the tigers resemble each other and how they differ.

Kingdom, Class, Order, Family, Genus, Species. —In this way animals are separated into groups and companies. All the animals of one group are like those of the same group and differ, in some way, from the animals in all other groups. Take an Angora cat, for instance. It belongs to

The *Kingdom* of animals,

The *Branch* of vertebrates (animals with back-bones),

The *Class* of mammals (animals that suckle their young),

The *Order* of Carnivora (meat-eaters),

The *Family* of Felidæ (the cats, lions, tigers, lynxes, etc., all belong to this family),

The *Genus* Felis (wildcats, cats, but not lynxes, belong to this genus),

The *Species* Domestic Cats (there are several kinds in this species),

The *Variety* Angora (there is only one kind in this variety; but there are other varieties).

A schoolboy—let us call him John Robinson—sometimes addresses a letter to himself this way: Mr. John Robinson, 227 Michigan Avenue, Chicago, Cook County, Illinois, United States, North America, Western Hemisphere, World. The postman can find him in time. The address fully describes him. In the same way the angora cat is fully described by the variety, species, genus, etc., and cannot be *completely* described in fewer words. There are many boys of the *genus* schoolboy, and a number of the *species* Robinson, but not so many of the *variety* John Robinson.

Differences between Plants and Animals.—It is easy to distinguish between the plants and the higher animals. A horse is an animal; an oak-tree is a plant. Most animals can move from place to place, but some animals—corals and sponges, for instance — are fixed to one place; a few plants can move about. Animals can generally see, hear, touch, smell, taste; they digest their food; their blood circulates. Animals usually eat other animals (as the lion does) or they eat plants (as the cow does). Plants usually get their food from the air and from the soil (though there are plants that catch flies and eat them). Animals usually breathe in oxygen and breathe out carbonic acid gas. Plants usually breathe in carbonic acid gas and breathe out oxygen.

Sometimes it is very difficult to tell the lowest kinds of animals from plants. People at the seashore press sea-weeds into albums. Most sea-weeds are plants; but nearly all such albums contain certain animals that look almost exactly like real sea-weed.

Fossil Animals.—Beside the millions of animals now living there are millions of fossil animals (and plants). Usually the living animals are somewhat like their fossil ancestors; they belong to the same family, but not to the same species or variety. The living animals fit the present time and the circumstances in which they live. Their fossil ancestors fitted the very different circumstances of geologic ages long ago. The horse to-day has one toe on each foot; the fossil horses had several toes.

Fauna and Flora.—The animals that live in each country are called its fauna — its animals. The animals of the Arctic regions are the Arctic fauna; those of North America are the North American fauna; of the ocean are the ocean fauna and so forth. Each region has a *flora* too — its plants.

THE EIGHT BRANCHES OF THE ANIMAL KINGDOM.

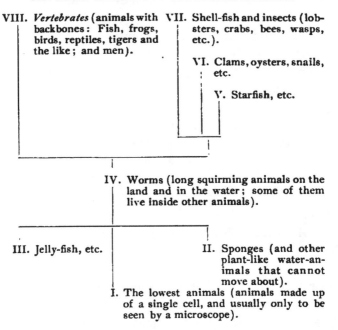

VIII. *Vertebrates* (animals with   VII. Shell-fish and insects (lob-
backbones: Fish, frogs,   sters, crabs, bees, wasps,
birds, reptiles, tigers and   etc.).
the like; and men).

VI. Clams, oysters, snails,
etc.

V. Starfish, etc.

IV. Worms (long squirming animals on the
land and in the water; some of them
live inside other animals).

III. Jelly-fish, etc.   II. Sponges (and other
plant-like water-an-
imals that cannot
move about).

I. The lowest animals (animals made up
of a single cell, and usually only to be
seen by a microscope).

All living and fossil animals belong to one of the
eight branches of the animal kingdom; and in each
branch there are thousands of families, species and
varieties. Zoölogy studies all these animals, all
these species. In this book we shall only describe
a few specimens of each branch, and we shall begin
with the simplest of all animals and go on to the
highest of all—that is, man.

A spade is a machine; a steam engine is a
machine. The steam engine is a higher kind of

machine than a spade not because it is more powerful, but because it is more complicated and because
it can do very many kinds of work while the spade
can only do one kind. The ox is stronger than a
man; but a man is higher because he can do many
kinds of work while the ox is fitted to do only a
few kinds.

Cells. — In the first place it is necessary to say
that the bodies of all animals are made up of *cells*,
so called. The body of a man, for instance, is
made up of thousands and thousands of cells each
one of them being a bit of *protoplasm* (something
like the white of an egg) and all of them being
very small, about $\frac{1}{5000}$ of an inch. When you
wound your hand it heals by new cells forming on
the wounded places and taking the place of the old
ones.

Protoplasm is the glairy mass that makes up
each one of the cells of every animal's body. It is
a chemical compound of carbon, hydrogen, oxygen
and nitrogen. These four things are dead elements
and no one of them, by itself, can be alive. When
they are combined into protoplasm the combination
can be alive. When the body dies it separates into
its elements again.

One-celled Animals — the Amœba. — The very
simplest of all animals are made up of one and only
one cell. They are very small. *Amœba* lives in
pools or ditches of water in the ooze or mud at the
bottom. If you put some of this mud on a plate of

glass under a microscope you will see a very small
moving mass that looks like transparent jelly.   It is
alive.   It moves by swelling out on one side and
then flowing towards that side somewhat as a drop
of honey flows.   It feeds on very small plants
(*diatoms*) by flowing over and around them —
swallowing them, as it were.   If you touch it, its
body shrinks, which proves that it can feel.   It can
move.   It digests its food, using some of it, reject-
ing the rest.   It grows.   It absorbs oxygen, and
gives out carbonic acid gas, which is a kind of

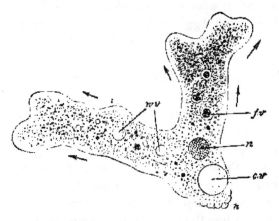

FIG. 169. Amœba, magnified many times.   At *n* is the central
nucleus of the animal; *w* and *v* are water nuclei; *f v* is one of
the food nuclei.   The animal flows outward from the center in
the direction of the arrows.

Scrape the green growth off the outside of a flower-pot and
cover the scrapings with water.   In two or three weeks many of
these animals will be found in the scrapings.   A microscope is
needed to see them.

breathing. It often divides into two masses and each of these masses is alive; and then each of these, again, divides — so that a family is born.

The Amœba has no lungs, and yet breathes; no mouth and yet eats; no fixed shape and yet grows; no nerves and yet feels; it is neither male nor female and yet it has a family.

If a common earth worm (a very much higher creature) is cut into two parts each part lives and becomes a perfect worm. Each half of Amœba is a complete animal. *Bacteria* are small plants, that grow, like Amœba, by dividing into two.

FIG. 170. Globigerina (magnified 100 times). These animals live in the upper layers of the ocean waters by millions. When they die their shells sink to the bottom and are there slowly cemented into limestone rock.

The Ooze or Mud of the Bottom of the Ocean.— Floating on the surface of the ocean there are millions of little creatures that have shells made of lime. Inside the shell is a mass of *protoplasm* (something like the white of egg). The shells are full of little holes and the matter inside them sticks out in spines. All sorts of sea-animals eat them, by thousands, for food. Those that are not eaten die at last and their shells sink slowly to the bottom of the ocean and form the ooze or mud. By and by, in thousands of years, the mud becomes solid chalk. All the great chalk cliffs of England are formed of the shells of such little animals in count-less millions.

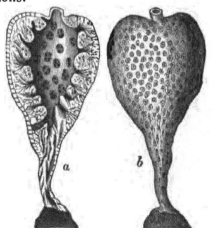

FIG. 171. The right-hand picture shows a sponge with many mouths all over its surface. The left-hand picture shows the same sponge sliced in two. The large central cavity is the stomach.

Many-celled Animals — Sponges. — Sponges are animals made up of cells arranged in layers. The inside of a sponge has many pouches that serve as stomachs and a great many small openings which serve as mouths. The water pours through them and the mouths seize their food (small sea-animals). Inside of the sponge there is a kind of skeleton made of glassy rods and spikes. Young sponges come from eggs formed inside the body of the parent, which is fixed to the rock. The young sponge floats about and, by and by, in its turn, becomes fixed. Some sponges also bud, like flowers, and young sponges are the buds, and are finally separated. You have to remember that even low animals, like sponges, come from eggs. The lowest animals of all divide into parts and each part lives.

Jelly-Fish.—Any one who has been at the sea-shore has noticed jelly-fish floating about on the

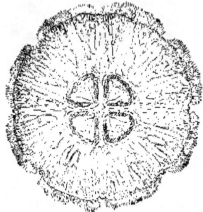

FIG. 172. A jelly-fish seen from the under side—natural size. Some common jelly-fishes grow to be eight or ten inches in diameter.

surface of the water.   There are millions of them
and they make the food of other sea animals.

They can move about by opening and closing
the edge of their flat body as if it were a kind of a
fin.   Water and a kind of fluid circulate through
their veins somewhat as red blood circulates in
ours.   They have eyes to see, and ears to hear,
a stomach, and curious thread-like organs that sting
any animal swimming near by.   The sting para-
lyzes what it touches, and that is the way the jelly-
fish gets its food.   The young of the jelly-fish shown
in Fig. 172 are born from eggs.

FIG. 173. A colony of live coral animals above a rock formed
of the bodies of thousands of dead corals.

Corals are little animals that live in warm sea
water near the surface.   The skeletons of these
little animals are made of carbonate of lime that
they extract from the sea water.   When they die
the skeleton is left and forms a rock.   Corals live
together in colonies.   A coral island is nothing but
the skeletons of millions and millions of dead corals,

and it is usually surrounded by reefs of corals that are living. Branches of red coral are used for jewelry you know.

FIG. 174. An island formed entirely of coral rock.

Hydra.—The hydra is a very small water animal found in fresh-water ponds. It has feelers that

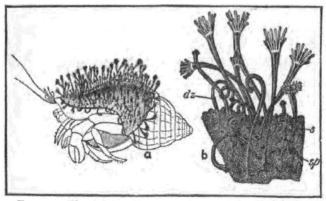

FIG. 175. The left-hand picture shows a colony of hydroids growing on the shell of a hermit-crab. The right-hand picture shows a bit of the colony drawn larger. The hydra forms buds somewhat as plants do. The buds drop off and are small jelly-fish and float away. Some jelly-fishes come from budding; some from eggs.

13

sting like nettles and paralyze other little animals
that it uses for food. Jelly-fishes and coral animals
have the same kind of feelers which they use in the
same way. If a Hydra is cut into slices crosswise,
each slice grows into a complete animal; if it is cut
into strips lengthwise each strip makes a complete
animal.

Worms.—The best way to understand what a
worm is like and how he moves is to dig up a few
earth-worms and to put them on china plates. In
one of the plates put some garden soil and watch the
worm as he burrows into it. We think the worm
is a very low animal, but it has eyes to see, ears
to hear, nerves to feel, a head and a kind of brain
in it, a body made up of separate rings, muscles, a
skin, a mouth and stomach (or, rather, a gizzard in
which the food is ground up) a kind of heart with
white blood in it. It can move about on the
ground or even climb a vertical wall by using rows
of short bristles that are arranged on each side of
its body. The earth-worm burrows by swelling out
its head till it pushes the dirt away on both sides
and also by swallowing some of the dirt and passing it through its body. The thousands of earth-
worms in every field do much good by loosening
the soil, thus allowing the air and rain to reach the
roots of plants. They work the soil over by the
finest kind of gardening, and the layer of blackish
soil at the top of the ground (you can see it almost
everywhere) is their work. Their chief food is

half-decayed leaves. They lay eggs from which the young are hatched; although if a worm be cut into two pieces each of the pieces will grow to be a complete worm. They are like the Amœba (page 188) in this, and like the birds and crocodiles in laying eggs. If two worms are each cut in half the tail of one worm can be made to grow on to the head of the other so as to make a new animal.

Fig. 176. A starfish. This particular kind is blood-red in color and has a skin like leather. It is about four inches in diameter.

Starfish (Radiates).—Children who live near the seashore can catch a starfish any day—for there are thousands of them—and keep it in salt water for study. These animals are built like a

five-pointed star with arms about an inch long.   At
the end of each arm there is an eye—five eyes in
all.   The eyes show the arms which way to crawl,
and underneath each arm are rows of little suckers
by which the crawling is done.   The mouth and
stomach of the animal are at the center of the star.

There is a ring of nerves around the animal's
mouth, other nerves running along each arm, and
little nerves running to each sucker.   The animal
can feel and see, and smell and breathe.   Its young
are hatched from eggs.   Inside of its body are channels through which water and other fluids circulate
somewhat as red blood circulates in our own veins.

If one of the arms is broken off it dies—it does
not grow into a new animal; but a new arm grows
in its place.   Injuries like this are quickly made
whole again in the lower animals.   If your leg
were cut off it would never grow again, of course;
still less would it grow into another boy.   The
starfish can replace a lost leg; and a worm cut
in two grows into two separate worms.   The star-
fishes eat mussels and oysters.   When an oyster is
open (trying to get *its* food) the starfish places
part of its body in the opening and sucks the soft
part of the oyster up into its own mouth.

Oysters have two shells joined by a hinge and
shut by a muscle.   (Look at the two shells of an
oyster and see how the hinge is arranged.   The
muscle is fastened where the purple spot shows on
the inside of the shell.)   The gristly part of the

body of the oyster is the muscle itself and the soft greenish part is the oyster's liver. The layers around part of the body are the oyster's gills by which it breathes. Oysters have a heart somewhat like our hearts and a set of veins and arteries, but no *red* blood, of course.

The young of clams, mussels and oysters come from eggs; and a single oyster may produce a million young. The food of oysters is made up of little sea-animals floating in the water in the oyster's open shell; but they can be fattened on corn-meal, too.

Pearls are formed inside the oyster round some little grain of sand, somewhat as our own flesh might grow around a bullet.

Mother-of-Pearl.—The oyster builds its own shell of layers upon layers of the very same stuff of which pearls are made, adding to them from the inside.

These thin layers one upon another make fine ridges like parallel lines and light shining on the ridges is scattered so as to make the rainbow colors. The colors are due to the ridges, as you can prove by taking an impression of the inside of the shell in wax and noticing that the little ridges in the wax give the same rainbow colors.

The Lobster.—The group of animals to which the lobster, the crab, and all insects belong, has the two sides of the body alike. The legs, jaws and so forth are arranged in pairs. The earth-worm is made up of a number of rings, one ring like another. The arrangement of the starfish is five-fold; it has five arms. Man and the higher animals are built so that the right-hand and left-hand halves of their bodies are alike.

The lobster has a heart which pumps its color-less blood through arteries. It breathes through gills near the roots of its eight walking legs. It has a liver, a stomach, muscles, eyes, ears, feelers. It can smell. It has a memory, too, for lobsters that have been caught, marked, and then set free again, have found their way back to their old home, several miles away. The lobster sometimes has as many as 100,000 eggs. The natural color of its shell is dark green which becomes bright red when the animal is boiled for food. Once a year the lobster *moults* that is, it splits and discards its old shell and appears in a larger and softer shell that has been formed inside of the old one. The new shell soon hardens and the animal lives inside of it for another year.

Fig. 177. The lady-crab (one-third of natural size). This is one of the swimming crabs and is good to eat.

Crabs.—The hermit-crab has no shell of its own but selects an empty sea-shell to live in, backs into it and carries its house about until the house becomes too small, when it chooses another and larger shell. (See the picture, Fig. 175.)

Insects. — Insects have the head well separated from the body. Some insects (the grasshopper for instance) get their food by biting it with their jaws; others (the bee and butterfly) suck their food up through a tube.

FIG. 178. The Regal Moth, natural size. It has olive and red wings with yellow spots.

Insects lay eggs from which the young are hatched, but the egg does not hatch into a complete insect. The butterfly's egg first hatches into a *larva* (the caterpillar for instance); then the *larva* turns into a *pupa* (the caterpillar turns into a chrysalis); and finally the *pupa* turns into the insect (the chrysalis turns into a butterfly).

FIG. 179. Larva of the Regal Moth, one-half of the natural size. Its head is to the left hand.

FIG. 180. The male and female moths of the Tent Caterpillar (the female is the larger). These are very destructive to apple trees.

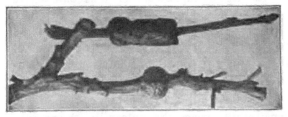

FIG. 181. Masses of the Eggs of the Tent Moth Caterpillar on the branch of a tree. The eggs stay on the tree all winter and hatch out in the spring.

FIG. 182. Nest of the larvæ of the Tent Moth Caterpillar. It looks like a kind of spider web. The larvæ live on it in a colony and each one of them turns into a moth.

Pick up three or four of the common red and black hairy caterpillars and put them in a box with some fresh clover leaves. Before very long you will find one or more hairy cocoons. The caterpillar inside of this in the form of a smooth brown *pupa* or *chrysalis*. A week or so after the cocoon is formed it splits open at one end, and a winged moth—the Isabella Tiger Moth— comes out and flies away.

Intelligence of Insects: Ants.—Insects have a brain and are able to do quite wonderful things. The brain of the ant is pro- portionally larger than that of any other insect. Some of the ants (the rust-red ants that live under large flat stones) make slaves of other ants (black ants). They go out in war-parties, capture the black ants and make them work. The black ants feed their masters and build their nests for them. The agricul- tural ant of Texas clears a space about its ant-hill and allows only one kind of grass to grow there. It harvests the ripe grass seeds and stores them away for winter food. From time to time the seeds are brought out and dried in the sun to prevent their sprouting. The army ants of South Africa live by hunting and migrate from place to place in search of food. The young ants are carried by the older ones. When the army of ants arrives at any place every living thing tries to escape. The ants devour all the other insects, spiders, birds, rats and so forth. When they come to a house the men leave it and in a few hours every- thing that is edible is eaten. If these ants could make a plan and remember it they could drive all the inhabitants of a coun- try out of it. The leaf-cutting ants of South America work in gangs. One gang goes up the tree and cuts the leaves into pieces of a convenient size; another gang picks up the pieces that fall to the ground and carries them to the door of the ant- hill. Another gang stores the leaves away. Some ants keep and feed the *aphis* insects as we keep and feed cows and regularly "milk" them for honey.

Ants Have a Kind of Language.—Two ants continually stroke each other with their *antennæ* (feelers) and can tell each other where to find food; that an enemy is coming, and so forth. They are fond of their comrades, remember them, and show signs of joy when they return after an absence of more than a year.

Bees.—The bumble bees build nests in the ground. All of them except the queen-bee die every autumn. In the spring each queen-bee lays eggs that develop into worker-bees. When the worker-bees are grown they gather and store food in the nest. They live together all summer and only the queen-bees survive the winter. Our honey bees feed their young while they are unable to feed themselves. When a colony of honey-bees gets too large a number of the workers " swarm" and emigrate to a new nest taking a queen-bee with them to lay eggs.

Fig. 183. A swarm of bees.

Honey is derived from the nectar of flowers and is stored into the honeycomb which is made of beeswax.

Intelligence of Honey-Bees.—A hive of bees is a city of 80,000 inhabitants and the wax houses of the city—the cells of the honey-comb—have all been built by the swarm. The city has its laws and its customs, its queen, its royal family, its workers. Its people do different kinds of work—some make wax, some make the wax into cells, some form the cells into the correct shape, some gather honey from the flowers to serve as a store of food for the coming winter, some gather pollen to feed the young

bees. Others go out early in the morning and return to tell the
hive where the best flowers are, others keep the hive ciean,
others guard the door, others feed the young and the queen.
There are more than 60,000 separate cells in a full hive. The
wonderful thing about these cells is their shape. Look at a
honey-comb and you will see that each cell has the shape of a
six-sided lead pencil with a bluntly-pointed end.

Mathematicians can solve by mathematics much too hard for
you to understand now a problem like this one : What is the shape
of a cell that shall have the greatest possible contents and at the
same time the smallest possible surface ? You can see for yourself that it cannot be a sphere, it cannot be a cube. It is in fact
exactly the shape of a bee's cell—a six-sided prism with blunted
ends. The bee has solved this problem all by itself—not by
mathematics but by practice.

In these cells honey is stored and the queen bee lays the eggs
from which new swarms are to be born. When the city gets too
full, and after a new queen bee has been born, the old queen leads
more than half of the inhabitants away in a flight that lasts until
they find a new place to live—usually a new hive that the bee-
keeper provides for them—and a new city is built in the new hive.

Before they leave the old hive they have made about 120
pounds of honey, that is, more than 12 times the weight of the
bees who made it (just as if a city of 80,000 men should make
60,000 tons of provisions). All of this they leave behind them
to keep the old city supplied, and industriously make 120 more
pounds for the new city they have founded. And so each hive
goes on making new hives year after year. Each one of the new
hives is governed like a city—has its queen, its royal family, its
drones or male bees (who do not work), its workers (who are
female bees, but who lay no eggs—all the eggs being laid by the
queen). If too many queen bees are born, the workers kill the
useless queens. If all the queens are dead and there is no
queen to lay eggs for the new city, the workers feed one of the
very young bees on a special kind of food that makes the young
bee turn into a queen. If it had not been so fed, it would have
grown up to be a mere worker.

If you were up above one of our great cities looking down on
it and trying to find out what all its men and women were doing

you would by and by discover that each one was trying to be as happy as possible for himself. Each person is usually trying to be happy *now*, this instant. If you look in the same way at a hive of bees you will find that each bee is working so that the new hive that is going to swarm off by and by shall be as happy as possible *by and by*. Most men work for the present time; most bees seem to work for the future.

Spiders.—The webs of spiders are beautiful pieces of work and show great intelligence. Some spiders make nests in the

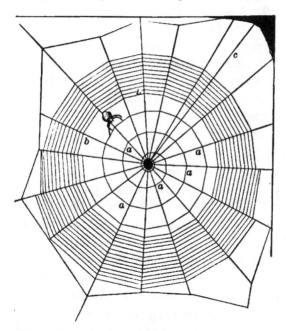

FIG. 184. One kind of spider spinning its web.

ground and close them with a trap door on a hinge. The door is covered with dirt and looks exactly like the ground when it is shut, and this makes it hard for the spider's enemies to find the nest. When an enemy does find it and tries to open the door the spider inside holds it shut with all his force.

Insects are very strong. A fly's wing vibrates 600 times in a second. A flea can jump much further in proportion to its size than any other animal—much further in proportion than even the kangaroo. A bee can pull twenty times its own weight, while a horse can only move about six-sevenths of its own weight.

Insects are both useful and harmful to plants. They are useful in carrying the pollen of one flower to other flowers so that the other flowers can be fertilized. They are harmful too. In four years the Rocky Mountain locusts as they moved eastward did $200,000,000 worth of damage by spoiling the crops in Dakota, etc.

Beetles and other insects are useful to man by eating up or burying offal. Insects are often harmful to man, too. House flies carry the germs that produce typhoid fever. Mosquitoes carry yellow fever germs. The large white ants of the tropics destroy the timbers of houses by eating the fiber of the wood.

Vertebrates are animals with backbones which form part of bony skeletons. They never have more than two pairs of limbs—either two arms and two legs, like men, or four legs like horses. They have a brain-box, or skull; and the mouth, two eyes and two ears are in the skull. All vertebrate animals (fish, frogs, reptiles, birds and mammals — those that suckle their young) have a heart, and birds and mammals have red blood. The fish and the tadpoles breathe by gills, but all the rest have lungs.

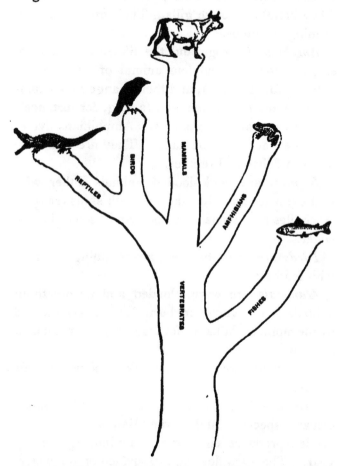

FIG. 185. The vertebrate animals succeed the invertebrates (animals with no backbone). Animals with backbones spread into five branches.

Fishes are cold-blooded animals that live in the water. They are usually covered with scales. They breathe through gills. Their fins are the beginnings of limbs.

Amphibians (frogs and the like)are born from eggs, become a complete animal of one sort (a tadpole, for instance), and then change into a complete animal of another sort (a frog, for instance). The last sort always has legs. Amphibians live in the water and also on land. They are half way between fishes and reptiles.

Reptiles are cold-blooded animals either with shells (turtles and the like), or with skins (snakes, crocodiles). Some live on land, some in the water.

Birds are warm-blooded, air-breathing animals, with feathers.

Mammals are warm-blooded and air-breathing animals. The young are born alive and are suckled by the mother. Whales, for instance, are mammals, not fish.

In what follows we shall speak of some animals of each sort.

Fishes.—The codfish lives in the North Atlantic Ocean, especially on the Grand Banks. The female codfish produces eight or nine million eggs every year. The eggs float on the surface of the water. The mother pays no attention to them and in about twenty days they develop into young fish. Some fishes have a pouch in which they carry the eggs and young fish about till the young are large enough to take care of themselves.

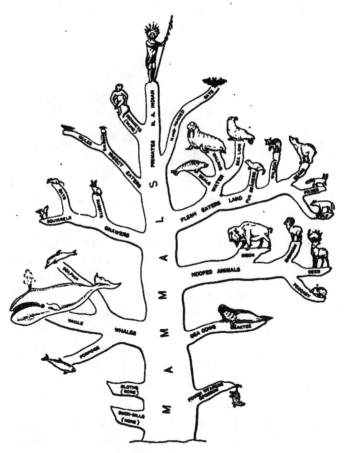

Fig. 186. The Mammals of North America—the highest towards the top. This picture fits at the very top of Fig. 185.

14

The Dace, a small fresh-water fish, lays its eggs
in a running brook, then covers them with a lot of
pebbles, then lays more eggs and brings more
pebbles, and so on till a little heap of pebbles is
formed, in which the young fish are hatched.

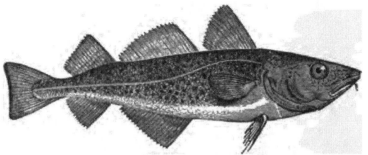

FIG. 187. The Codfish. The real fish is about seven times as
long as the picture.

Some fish can fly; their fins are like wings and
they make long leaps out of the water and back
again. A few fish make sounds to call each other.
Most fish have eyes, but those in the Mammoth
Cave in Kentucky are blind.   Eyes are of no use
in the dark, and these fish, whose ancestors could
see, have lost the use of their eyes, just as the horse
has lost the toes which are of no use to him.

Some fish (the torpedo, the electric eel) have an
electric apparatus in their body so that they can
give an electric shock to anything that touches
them. A fish in the East Indies sometimes travels
over land from one pond to another, and is even
said to climb trees by means of its spiny fins.

Fish show fear, anger, affection, parental feeling, jealousy, playfulness and curiosity; some of them can be tamed.

FIG. 188. Sticklebacks. The male fish (the upper one in the picture) builds the nest under water. Several females lay their eggs in it and then the male guards the nest to keep enemies away till the young hatch out.

Frogs are born from eggs. The eggs become tadpoles, that is, *fish;* they breathe through gills, live in the water, and have tails. The tadpoles

develop into frogs, which live both on land and in
the water (*amphibians*) breathe with lungs, and
have no tails.   Some toads live in trees and their

FIG. 189. The Toad: notice how well his color and spots
match the color and spots of the ground.   The toads that do not
match the ground are seen and eaten by their enemies (snakes,
birds).   Those that do match it live and have young which resemble their parents.

skins change in color to match the green leaves or
the gray bark.   They escape their enemies in this
way.

Reptiles—Lizards, Snakes, Turtles, Crocodiles.

FIG. 190. Head of an alligator of the Mississippi River. Alligators are often a dozen feet in length.

FIG. 191. The three-clawed turtle of the Mississippi Valley (this turtle is often more than 12 inches long).

FIG. 192. A rattlesnake about to strike. The rattlesnake has teeth that leave a poison in the wound; and a rattle on its tail to warn other animals not to attack it.

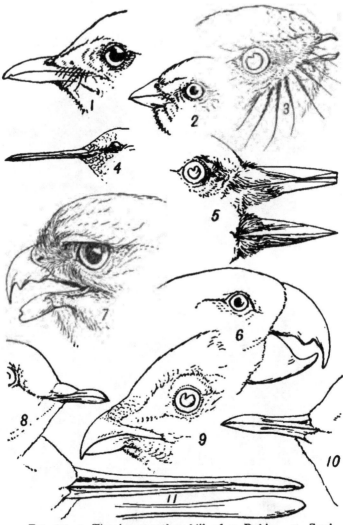

FIG. 193. 1. The insect-eating bill of a Robin. 2. Seed-crushing bill of a Sparrow. 3. Snapping bill of a Whippoor-will. 4. Needle-bill of a Humming Bird. 5. Two views of the chisel-bill of a Woodpecker. 6. Climbing-bill of a Parokeet. 7. Tearing-bill of a falcon. 8. Drinking-bill of a Dove. 9. Gleaning-bill of a Ruffed Grouse. 10. Wedge-bill of a Plover. 11. Two views of the probing-bill of a Snipe. (p. 214)

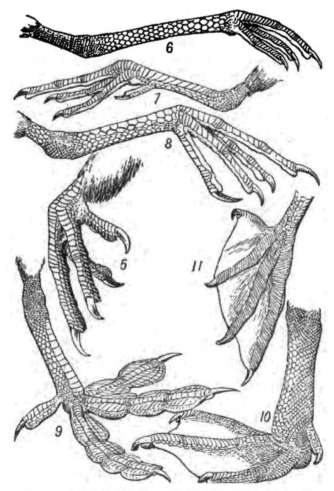

Fig. 194. 5. Scratching-foot of a Ruffed Grouse. 6. Wading-foot of a Plover (only three toes). 7. Wading-foot of a Snipe (one short toe). 8. Wading-foot of a Green Heron. 9. Swimming-foot of a Coot (wide toes). 10. Swimming foot of a Canada Goose (three toes webbed). 11. Swimming-foot of a cormorant (four toes webbed). (p. 215)

Birds are clothed with feathers; have no teeth (though some fossil birds had teeth), have warm, red blood; hollow bones filled with air; a very flexible backbone (they can turn their heads so as to look directly backwards); wing-bones that are like the arm bones of a man; very sharp sight, hearing and smell. They build nests, lay only a few eggs, and the young birds have to be cared for by the parents. Some birds have beautiful plumage and some have beautiful songs. Both plumage and song are used to attract their mates. Doves and other birds are very affectionate to each other and mourn the loss of a mate. Parrots can be taught to speak.

The Sparrow.—The history of the spread of the common sparrow is interesting. Two thousand years ago it lived only in middle Europe. Since then it has covered all Europe and entered Siberia; crossed the Mediterranean Sea and invaded Africa. It was brought to New York in 1850 by persons who thought it would be a useful scavenger. By 1870 it had spread all over the Eastern States; by 1886 it had reached Kansas and it is now abundant all over the United States and in Canada. In fifty years it has covered the whole continent. Other birds were here before it. Why has the sparrow succeeded when they have barely held their own? The reasons are that the sparrow is bold, hardy, crafty; it will eat anything, live anywhere; it has several broods a year. It is like some of the weeds among plants, like the rat among mammals. It fits the conditions in which it lives ; it survives because it is the fittest to survive in those conditions.

A female sparrow has five or six broods each year with four to six young in each brood. If we suppose that twenty-four young sparrows are produced each year, that the young sparrows breed when they are a year old, and that all live—and if all this keeps on for ten years—then one pair of sparrows will produce 138,000,000,000 young ones in ten years! Of course many sparrows are killed, and many die of disease, and some do not have twenty-four young in a year. But the increase is enormous.

FIG. 195. Blue Jay : It belongs to the same family as the crow.

Nests.—Most birds build nests, and sometimes show the greatest skill and patience in building. The tailor-bird sews leaves together with a cotton thread that it makes, and pierces the necessary holes in the leaves with its bill.   Some observers say that it makes a kind of a knot in the end of the thread. The cuckoo lays its eggs in the nests of other birds and allows them to be hatched there to save itself the trouble.

FIG. 196. The Sharp-shinned Hawk.   Its food is poultry and other birds. Hawks and English sparrows are the two birds that can best be spared. No other birds should be killed.

Female birds usually sit on the eggs and hatch them and male birds usually feed the female and the young. The male ostrich, however, sits on the nest.

Migration of Birds.—Some birds live in the same region all the year round. Most birds, however, migrate (travel) from northern regions to southern in the autumn and back again in the spring. The journey is made in search of food and of warm weather.

Fig. 197. Ruby-throated Humming Birds. They feed on insects and on the nectar of flowers. They build their nests in trees and lay only two white eggs.

Intelligence of Birds.—Gulls and crows open shellfish by dropping them on rocks from high up in the air. Woodpeckers store acorns for winter

use. They feed on the grubs fattened by the
acorns. Turkey-buzzards tell each other where
food is by a high flight into the air which calls
other buzzards from a distance. The Frigate Bird
will not fish for itself but it follows the Booby-bird
and takes the fish that it has caught. The nests
of birds are constructed with great intelligence and
are often changed in form when new circumstances
arise.

Mammals. — The young of mammals are born
alive, and are suckled with milk by the mother.
Opossums and kangaroos carry the young in a
pouch till they can take care of themselves. Mammals have four limbs whose bones are alike. Seals
and whales have fins and flippers, dogs and cats
four legs, monkeys and man two arms and two
legs. All are mammals. Man is the only animal
who habitually walks upright and has his arms free.

Horns. — Deer, rhinoceroses, etc., have horns.
Deer shed their horns every year. Most mammals
do not.

Many mammals have good voices : the gibbon ape
can sing eight notes—an octave—correctly. Their
voices are used to call their mates, to give alarms,
etc. Many animals (the bear for instance) *hiber-
nate*—that is sleep—for a large part of the winter.
Most wild animals have a color to match the landscape they live in (see page 175). Arctic animals
are usually white. A red polar bear would starve.
Why?

FIG. 198. Horns: 1, of the Woodland Caribou; 2, of the
Moose; 3, of the Elk.   (p. 221)

FIG. 200. The American Bison (the Buffalo). This animal
used, only lately, to roam the country by millions. It is now
nearly extinct.

FIG. 201. The Red Fox. Rabbit hunting.

FIG. 202. The Wolf. Deer hunting (notice that the deer is driven by another wolf). (p. 226)

FIG. 203. The Puma. Elk hunting. (p. 227)

FIG. 204. The Grizzly Bear. Hunting the Big Horn Sheep.
(p. 228)

FIG. 205. Some Tropical Animals. (p. 229)

FIG. 206. Some Northern and Arctic Animals.

(p. 230)

FIG. 207. Some Animals of the Northeastern United States and of Canada.   (p. 231)

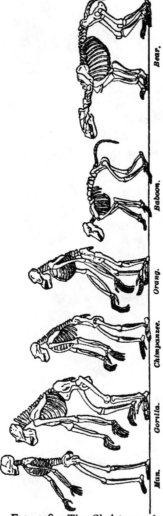

Monkeys are the nearest to man in intelligence. They are, however, far inferior to even the lowest savages. No monkey ever made a fire, or used a bow and arrow. Monkeys have a skeleton made up of the same 200 bones arranged in the same order as in our skeletons. Their 300 muscles are the same as ours, and their teeth are the same. Their hearts are like ours and so with many other organs.

Man.—The body of a man is, then, in a great many ways, like the bodies of the higher animals. The higher animals resemble the lower animals (fossil or living species) in many ways. One of the man-like monkeys is more like a man than

FIG. 208. The Skeletons of Man and Quadrupeds compared.

it is like the lower forms of monkeys. The great difference between man and other animals is in the size and structure of his brain. The brain of a man is more than twice as large as that of any monkey, and very much more complex; and there is also a great difference between the size of the brains of savage and civilized men. It is not at all unlikely that men are descended from ancestors who were very much lower than even the lowest savage of to-day; just as the horse is descended from *Eohippus*, the little five-toed horse of long ago.

FIG. 208a.   Beech Trees, Burnham Woods.

BOOK VII: BOTANY.

BOTANY is the science that tells about plants—about vegetables, shrubs, trees.[1] Suppose you see a cherry tree in full blossom. You know that, by and by, it will bear fruit. It will bear cherries—not peaches, not apples. The tree will grow larger, too, as years go on. Botany teaches us how the roots of the tree find food in the soil, and how the food is carried through the stem to all parts of the tree to keep them alive and growing. It tells what the leaves are and what work they do; what the flowers are for and how the fruit comes; why the leaves fall off in the winter when the tree goes to sleep, as it were; how the whole tree wakes up in the spring-time.

To understand all this we must begin at the beginning and learn one thing at a time. And the beginning of plants, like the beginning of animals, is in small parts called *cells*.

Cells.—All parts of plants are made up of very small cells, or cavities; filled up with living vegetable protoplasm.

---

[1] A tree is a plant; a shrub is a plant; a vegetable is a plant. When we say "plants" we mean all kinds of plants—trees as well as shrubs and grasses.

You have seen a honey comb?   It is full of large cavities bounded by walls.   Every part of every plant — the stem, the leaves, the fruit—is made up of very small cells, and each cell is filled, usually, with vegetable protoplasm, somewhat as the cells of the honeycomb are filled with honey.

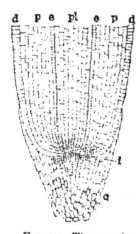

If you take the petal of a flower, or a thin transparent bit of seaweed and hold it up between your eye and the light, you can often see little separate cells that make up the tissue—the woven web—of the petal or the seaweed. (Try it.)

Or, you can take the delicate rootlet of any seedling plant, cut it into thin slices, and then examine the slices with a magnifying glass or with a microscope. (Try it.)

Fig. 209. The growing point of a root of Indian corn (maize) sliced up and down. It is made up of cells. The cells are huddled together in the *growing point* (*i*) where the root is most alive; the very end of the root is protected by a hard cap, the *root cap* (*c*) which bores into the ground like a gimlet; the whole of the root is made up of a tissue of cells, and is covered by a *skin* (*d, d*).

Every part of a plant or tree is made up of such separate cells.   They are usually separated by walls. If you cut a grape into two parts all the liquid inside of it does not escape because most of it is kept in place by the walls of the little cells that have not been cut.

The Cells Contain Protoplasm that is Alive. — No one knows exactly what *life* is ; but a plant that

is growing is certainly alive. Each cell of such a
plant contains a slimy kind of matter (protoplasm)
not so very different from the animal called Amœba.
(See page 188.)

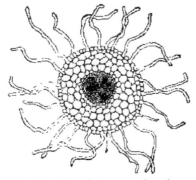

FIG. 210. View of a slice of the root of a plant cut crosswise.
It is very much magnified so as to show the cells. The hairs on
the root stream out in all directions.

The Amœba sometimes divides into two parts
and each part becomes a separate animal. In the
same way the cell of a plant often divides into two
parts and each part becomes a perfect cell. Plants
grow in this way. Where one cell was, you later
on find two, then four, then eight, and so on.

Through canals running lengthwise of the cell the protoplasm
of one cell is connected with the protoplasm of others on all
sides of it. Sometimes the cell-walls become like cork and make
the bark of trees. Sometimes the cell-walls become like wood
and make the stem. Sometimes the walls become like mucilage,
as in the seeds of a quince. Remember that the cells are very
small indeed. The largest are about a thirtieth of an inch in
diameter; the smallest are less than a thousandth of an inch.
There would be 1,000,000,000 of these smallest cells in a cubic
inch.

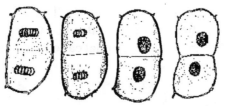

FIG. 211. Four steps in the division of a cell. The left-hand picture shows the mother-cell, very much magnified. There are two nuclei in it, like two yolks in an egg. In the next picture, which was taken a little later in time, a little wall is beginning to grow across the cell. In the third picture the wall has spread all across and has grown thicker. In the last picture there are shown two daughter-cells. By and by each of these will divide and grow, too. In this way each mother-cell will become the parent of hundreds of daughter-cells. The plant grows by the multiplication of its cells.

A plant is made up of thousands of cells just as a wall is made of thousands of bricks, only the cells of growing plants usually have empty spaces between them. In a fine spring day some plants grow three or four inches in length. Millions of new cells must be formed, then, in twenty-four hours. The cells form the *tissues* of the plant; wood-tissue, skin-tissue and so forth.

Color of Plants — Chlorophyll. — The walls of very young cells are usually transparent and colorless. When a plant is growing in the sunlight the cell-walls are stained with a green stain called *chlorophyll.*

Sunlight, acting on the protoplasm of the cell, makes a green coloring stain somewhat as sunlight acting on a photographic plate makes a dark stain.

When an onion grows in a dark cellar its shoots
have a sickly pale yellow color. Bring it out into
the light and in a short while they will become
green. (Try it, if you can.)

Herbs, Shrubs and Trees.—*Herbs* are soft plants
with very little wood in their stems (the catnip, for
example). *Shrubs* are plants with woody stems
that do not grow above twenty or thirty feet high.
Currant bushes are shrubs, and so are lilacs.
Trees are woody plants taller than shrubs.

Annuals, Biennials, Perennials.—All shrubs and
trees are perennials ; they live on year after year.
Some herbs are annuals (the morning-glory, maize,
oats, etc., for example). They grow from the seed,
blossom, and die all in the same season. Plants of

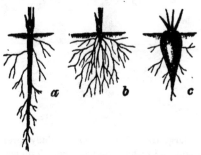

Fig. 212. Different kinds of roots. (*a*) the tap-root of a plant
(like the young oak tree); (*b*) a root made up of fibers, with no
tap-root (like the roots of grass or of the Dahlia); (*c*) a thick
tap-root (like the carrot root).

this kind have fibrous roots. Some herbs are biennials — they live for two seasons (turnips, car-

rots, beets, etc., for instance). They do not blossom at all in the first season but grow leaves and a thick root. The second season they bear flowers and form seeds and then die. Some herbs are also perennials (the peony, dahlia, sweet potato, the iris, etc.).

FIG. 213. A large tree with its roots. They spread out to get food from the soil and to hold up the tree. You see that a good part of the tree is under ground.

The Roots of Plants.—Generally the root strikes downward from the seed into the ground. Its business is to hold the plant up and to get the necessary food and water from the soil. The larger and heavier the plant the firmer its roots must be fixed in the ground. The main body of the root is covered with many fine branches—*root-hairs*—little tubes whose business is to suck water up into the stem and to give it to the leaves. The more leaves there are on a tree the more water they need, and therefore the greater the number of the root-hairs.

Plant a common bean and wait till it has grown a few leaves. Then carefully lift the plant with the soil round its roots and wash away the soil in a wash-basin. Hold the roots up against the light and you can see the fine root-hairs growing from the roots. Each root-hair is a little tube that sucks water up from the soil to feed the plant.

Work of Roots.—The water and some of the solid parts of the soil are sucked in by the root-hairs and passed to the interior of the root, from the root to the stem, from the stem to the branches, and from the branches to the leaves, flowers or fruit.

FIG. 214. A plant with a fibrous root. It has no tap-root and it dies every winter, and is therefore called an *annual*—it lives only a year.

The food of the plant comes from the soil; it is turned into sap and circulates in the plant somewhat as blood circulates in your veins. A tree without sap is dead. No matter how a tree is planted its roots will (generally) grow downward, and its stem upward, even in the dark.

16

Fig. 217. A mangrove swamp. The roots of the trees are more than half out of the ground. They hold up the tree as a mast is held up by ropes.

The Stems of Plants. — Plants are made up of
two kinds of material — *cell-tissue* and *wood*. The
stems of herbs contain little wood and much tissue;
they are sòft and fleshy. The stems of trees are
nearly all woody. There are two kinds of stems.
In the first kind the growth is from the inside outwards. Plants with this kind of stems are *endogens*.
The stem of a sunflower or a cornstalk is a good
example.

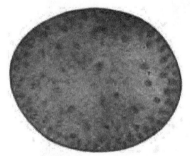

Fig. 219. A corn stalk cut across so as to show the bundles of
fibers. (The pupil should cut and split a corn stalk and see for
himself.)

Our common trees grow in a different way.
Every year they add a ring or layer of wood on the
outside of the stem (but inside of the bark). If
you count the number of rings you can tell how old
the tree is. The thickening of the tree is all on
the outside, so that the oldest wood — the *heart* of
the tree — is on the inside, and the youngest — the
sap-wood — is just underneath the bark. The
heart-wood is dead; the sap-wood alive. (The

pupil should examine a slice of the trunk of a tree
and count the rings and notice the way the bark
grows around the fresh sap-wood.)

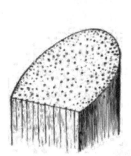

Fig. 220. The stem of palm
tree several years old. It grows
from the inside outwards. It
is, like the corn stalk, endoge-
nous. It grows by adding new
material on the inside. The
new fibers are mixed in among
the old.

Fig. 221. The plan on which Indian corn (maize) is built.
The stalk has here been cut into pieces. Each piece is on the
same plan. Every tree and every plant is built on a certain plan.
The plant keeps on carrying out this plan over and over again.

A coral island is, in many ways, like a tree.
The coral near the surface of the water is full of
life—like the sap-wood and the leaves of a growing
tree. The coral deeper down was once alive and
is now dead — like the heart-wood of the tree. In
the coral island, as in the tree, a colony of live

growing cells is built on a foundation of cells once alive and now quite dead.

The stem of a plant bears leaves and buds; the root of a plant has no buds. This is a general rule, and is the way to tell a stem from a root. A few plants have underground stems just as a few plants have roots in the air. The Irish potato we call, in common language, a root; but it is really an underground stem.

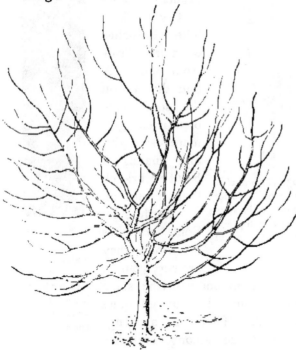

FIG. 222. The branches of a sour-cherry tree. Notice that in this tree the stem is lost in the branches. Maples, oaks, elms and other trees have stems of this sort.

Branches.—All the branches of the same oak tree are somewhat alike, and no two of them are exactly alike. The branches of all white oak trees are somewhat alike. You would know them anywhere for white oak branches, but it would be hard to find, in the whole country, two branches exactly alike. The branches of a tree grow from buds. A bud that is on the south side of a tree gets more sunlight, and makes a better branch than a bud on the north side. Some branches die when they are very young;

FIG. 223. The branches of a pine tree. Notice that in this tree the stem goes to the very top and the branches stream out from it.

FIG. 224. A mullein stalk, which does not have branches. The buds grow close to the stem.

some live but do not flourish; some have enough sunlight, but not quite enough food. There is a struggle for existence among branches as there is among animals. The branch or the leaf that gets the most food and the most sun-

light grows best and lives the longest and healthiest life.

Winter Buds. — A plant gets its food from the
soil through the roots and when the spring comes
it begins to grow quickly after its winter sleep.
During the warm weather the tree or plant is full
of leaves. If you look at the branch of a tree just
where the stalk of a leaf joins the branch, you will
find a little bud—a winter bud, so called. (Try it.)

FIG. 225. Maple leaves. Notice the winter buds at the foot
of the stalk of each leaf next the branch. There are winter buds
at the end of the shoot also.

Fall of the Leaf.—In most of our trees the leaves
fall in autumn (called " the fall "). Their work is
done. They are ripe and die, even before the frost
kills them. The stem falls off with the leaf and
leaves a *scar*.

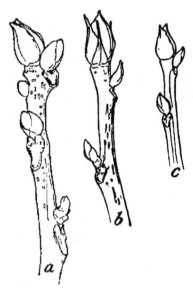

F<small>IG</small>. 226. Leaf-scars of hickory trees. Above each scar you can see the winter bud. The bud becomes a growing point next spring.

Evergreens are trees and shrubs in which the leaves do not fall in the winter.

Buds.—In the growing season the buds are small and many persons do not notice them. In the winter the bud is tightly wrapped up, but it is easy to see because the leaf is out of the way. In the spring the buds grow to be branches, and new leaves grow on the new branches or shoots.

It is easy to make the bud swell in a room in winter-time, even. Cut some branches two or three feet long—from a red maple tree, a lilac bush, a peach tree, an apple tree, etc.—in the winter. Put them into jars or vases of water just as if they were flowers. Renew the water every day or two and cut off the bottoms of the branches once a week so as to give a fresh surface there. In a week or two the buds will begin to swell. In two or three weeks, flowers will appear. Such branches flower best in a room that is not lighted with gas. They flower more quickly if the vases are set in the sunshine for a few hours every day.

Leaves.—A complete leaf has three parts — the blade, the foot-stalk that fastens the leaf to the branch, and the *stipules* (which are often green and leaf-like themselves).

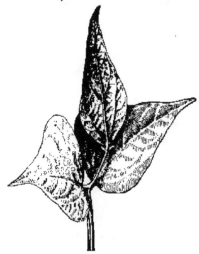

Fig. 227. Three complete leaves of a bean-plant. Notice the leaf whose blade is upright; it has a foot-stalk and stipules.

The pupil should gather several different kinds of leaves and examine them carefully. The blade of the leaf is made up of green pulp covered with a thin skin. It is supported by a kind of framework of thick pieces—the *ribs*. Usually there is a rib in the middle—the *mid-rib*—and other smaller ones called *veins* and *veinlets*. Hold a leaf up against the light and you will see how it is covered by a network of veins. If you press leaves in the summer-time, you can have plenty of specimens to examine in the winter.

The Shapes of Leaves.—Leaves are of all kinds of shapes and each shape has a particular name. The names are given here so that when you read the description of a plant, you will know what shape is meant. For instance, the leaves of a willow or peach-tree are lanceolate like the fourth figure below.

FIG. 228. Linear, oblong, elliptic, lanceolate, spatulate, ovate, obovate, orbicular, reniform, leaves.

Leaves Love the Sunlight.—The more sunlight a leaf gets the larger it grows. Leaves are arranged on a tree so that, on the whole, each leaf gets its share of sunlight and air.

Fig. 229. Leaves of the Norway Maple. Notice that the
leaves that have had the most light are the largest.

Fig. 230. Leaves and flowers looking for sunlight.

(p. 253)

Arrangement of the Leaves on the Shoot.—The leaves (and the buds from which next year's leaves

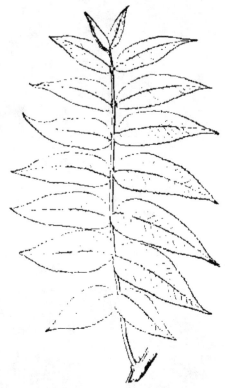

Fig. 231. The leaves of the black Walnut tree are arranged in pairs; each leaf of the pair is *opposite* the other.

are to spring) are arranged on the shoot in two ways.   Either the buds are *opposite* each other, or they are *alternate*.

FIG. 232. The leaves of a Mulberry shoot are *alternate.* The
leaves are not arranged in pairs, but one by one.

Breathing-pores (or Holes) in Leaves. — Every
leaf has a framework of ribs and veins that hold it
together like the ribs of an umbrella. The blade of
the leaf is very thin, but when it is looked at under
a microscope it is seen to have thousands of little
pores, or breathing holes.

On the lower surface of each leaf of a lilac bush
there are more than 150,000 breathing holes to

Fig. 233. The leaf of Poison-Ivy. Notice the ribs and veins. (Be careful not to handle it.)

every square inch! Each leaf has several hundred thousand pores, and the whole bush has millions and millions. The breathing holes take in air and carbonic acid gas. Plants need the oxygen of the air as animals do, only they do not need so much of it. Plants also need carbonic acid gas. They breathe it in. When animals breathe, they breathe carbonic acid

Fig. 234. Part of the thickness of an ivy leaf, very much magnified. The bottom of the picture shows part of the bottom of the leaf. The breathing holes are on the under side of the leaf. One of them is shown in the picture surrounded by cells that make up the leaf itself. The leaf takes in air and carbonic acid gas through thousands of pores of the sort. The leaf breathes in this way.

out; if they breathe it in they die. This is one of the chief differences between animals and plants. Remember that animals have pores in their bodies. Perspiration comes from pores in the skin. A man's body has over 2,000,000 pores.

FIG. 235. Plants give off water-vapor from their leaves.

Leaves Give off the Vapor of Water from their Surfaces. — The water taken in by the roots of a plant rises through the whole plant and a great deal of it is given back to the air from the leaves as invisible vapor.

17

You can prove this as follows : Cut off a green shoot of any plant (rhubarb, for instance) and put the end of the shoot through a hole in a cork and stand the shoot in a bottle of water. Put a tumbler upside down over the shoot and its leaves, and notice that a mist soon shows on the inside of the glass. The green shoot sucks up the water. The leaves use all they need for food. What they do not need they give off as invisible water-vapor, and this vapor soon fills the inside of the tumbler. The cold tumbler condenses the invisible water-vapor into visible drops (just as the invisible water-vapor of your breath is condensed when you breathe against a cold window-pane.) (Try it.)

Why the Shade of a Tree is Cool.—The shade of a tree is cool in the first place, because the leaves keep off the direct sunshine. It is also cool because the water-vapor given off by the leaves is always evaporating—and whenever water evaporates, becomes vapor, it uses up heat to do it, and leaves the space round about much cooler. Tie a wet towel round your head. The water will evaporate and leave the towel nearly dry. As it does this your forehead will become cooler.

How Plants Get their Food.—A green plant gets its food *first*, from the soil, through its roots ; *second*, from the air, through its leaves.

Dry a green plant thoroughly in an oven. Water will pass off. *All this water came from the soil.* Burn the dried plant in a fire. Gas will pass off and ashes will remain. *All the elements that come from the air were in the gas. All the ash came from the soil.*

Plants contain much carbon; and you know this because by burning a mass of plants or trees you can make charcoal—which is nearly pure carbon. About half of a dried dead tree is carbon.

A Green Plant gets its Carbon from the Air.—The plant breathes in air (air is a mixture of nitrogen and oxygen gases, with a small amount of carbonic acid gas), and sucks the carbonic acid gas into the little cells inside the plant. If you put a piece of *caustic potash* into a mixture of several different kinds of gases the potash will absorb all the carbonic acid gas out of the mixture and leave the rest. We know that it does so, although we may not know exactly why. In somewhat the same way the leaf absorbs all the carbonic acid gas out of the air and leaves the nitrogen. We do not know exactly why, but we know that it does so.

During sunlight carbonic acid gas is breathed in by the green leaf and some oxygen gas is breathed out.

A tree needs all or nearly all of its leaves in order to make food enough to live. If you strip half the leaves from a tree it will die.

The Plant Makes Starch for Its Food.—Starch (like our common starch) is made out of carbon, hydrogen and oxygen ; $C_6H_{10}O_5$. The plant makes starch out of carbonic acid gas (CO_2) and water (OH_2). All green leaves in the

Fig. 236. A green leaf of a waterplant placed in a tumbler of water will give off bubbles. Some of these bubbles are air but most of them are oxygen gas.

sunlight can and do make starch. It is the sunlight that does the work. Leaves kept in the dark cannot make starch and therefore can not make food enough for the tree.

The Plant Changes its Starch into Sugar.—Starch is $C_6H_{10}O_5$. Sugar is $C_{12}H_{22}O_{11}$. The starch cannot be dissolved in water and therefore is not fit for plant-food, because plant-food must be able to be dissolved by the water that comes from the roots and thus to run all through the body of the plant. Plants turn their starch into sugar somewhat as starchy foods are turned to sugary foods by the saliva of one's mouth. Sugar *can* be dissolved in water and therefore the sugary water can and does run throughout the plant as *sap*. The sugar-maple has a great deal of very sweet sap which, when boiled, makes maple-sugar.

The Sap. — The sap flows everywhere in the plant somewhat as blood flows in our veins. Some of it flows from the roots to the leaves; some of it flows from the leaves to the root. The sap from the roots takes up food from the soil; the leaf sends down its sap; the two together manufacture new vegetable protoplasm. Exactly how this is done no one knows yet; but it is done. The life of a plant goes on somewhat like the life of an animal.[1] It takes in food, digests it, sends it to all parts of its body, manufactures cells of protoplasm. These cells multiply and the plant grows. When the protoplasm in the cells dies, the plant (or the animal) dies.

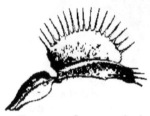

FIG. 237. Leaves of the Venus' Fly-Trap.

Plants that Catch Flies for Food.—There is a plant in America called Venus' Fly Trap that catches flies and eats them ! Three hairs on each leaf are very sensitive like the whiskers of a cat. When a fly touches one of these hairs the leaf closes up with a snap and holds the fly fast. If the fly is alive the leaf keeps closed and sucks the fly dry and then opens. If it is dead the leaf opens almost at once. Somehow the leaf is able to tell that a dead fly is not the food it wants. Blue-bottle flies, spiders, caterpillars and even bits of raw meat are greedily taken by this plant as food.

Flower-branches.—The branches on which flowers grow are born from the winter-buds. Some-

[1] The life of a *tree* is more like the life of the colony of animals that make up a coral bank (see page 246).

times the flowers grow directly on the stem as in the mullein-plant. (See Fig. 224.)

Solitary flowers often grow on the end of the main shoot as in the common white-weed (ox-eye daisy) of our fields.

What Flowers Are For. — The plant bears flowers in order that they may produce seeds and in order that the seeds may produce other plants of the same sort. A single elm-tree might live its own life out without producing seed, but if no elms produced seed there would soon come a time when no more elms would be found on the earth. If none of the Smith or Jones families had children the very names would soon die out.

FIG. 238. Hyacinth flowers grow from buds on the stem of the plant; as does mignonette, etc.

We are apt to think that the beauty and scent of the flowers are made for us — for men. We certainly get the benefit of them. We shall, however, soon see that the flower is a wonderful arrangement for producing seed, for protecting it when it is produced, and for making it fruitful. The color and scent and honey of the flowers are for birds and bees, not for us; but we can enjoy them, all the same.

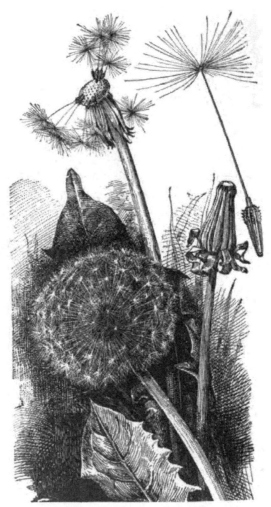

Fig. 239. The dandelion bears a solitary flower at the end of
the stalk.

FIG. 240. The flowers of the Bridal Wreath (Spiréa) are borne in clusters, many clusters on a branch.

The *calyx* of a flower is the outer and lower green cover. You can see it in the picture of the buttercup sliced in two. (Fig. 242.) Let us call this cover a *whorl* (that is a whirl—a circle—that makes a part of the flower). The next whorl is called the *corolla*. It is made up of the five bright yellow

FIG. 241. A buttercup flower.

FIG. 242. A buttercup flower sliced in two.

leaves of the buttercup flower. Double roses have many leaves in their corollas.

A calyx often has several leaves; each one of them is called a *sepal*.

A corolla usually has several leaves; each one of them is called a *petal*.

A flower is borne on the thickened end of the flower-stalk; this end is called a *torus*.

Look at the last pictures again. Inside of the petals of the buttercup you will see: *first*, the *stamens* of the flower (that is the little rods that stand up highest, each rod having a thickened end); and, *second*, the *pistils* (that is the little clump inside of the ring of the *stamens*). The pistil is the seed-bearing part of the flower. You must examine all sorts of flowers and find the *stamens*

FIG. 243. A hollyhock flower sliced into two. The fine little hairs with thickened ends are the *stamens* (point them out). The clump in the middle of the flower is made up of *pistils* (point to it).

and *pistils* in each one, if you can. They are differently arranged in different flowers. Notice that the ends of the stamens are always thickened. The thickened end of a stamen is called its *anther*. (Point out the *anther* in the last three pictures — and find them in real flowers.)

Pollen is Borne by the Stamens.—Pollen is the dust-like grains on the anther. The violet produces about a hundred grains of pollen in each blossom, while the poppy produces more than three million grains, and some flowers (orchids for instance) many millions.

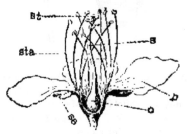

Fig. 244. A plum blossom sliced in two to show: *se*, the sepals; *p*, the petals; *sta*, the stamens. The pistil occupies the middle of the blossom and consists of three parts: *o*, the ovary; *s*, the style; *st*, the stigma.

The Seeds are Borne by the Pistils.—The ovary (*o*) ripens into the fruit. The anthers of the stamens (*sta* — not *s*, not *st*) are tipped with pollen.

Fertilization of Flowers.—Flowers will not produce seeds unless the egg-cells in the ovary (*o*) are fertilized (made fertile, made productive) by pollen-cells from the anthers.

A grain of pollen falls on the stigma (*st* in the last picture). There it absorbs the juices of the stigma and grows a fine hair-like tube. This tube grows downward through the style (*s* in Fig. 244) and reaches the ovary (*o*). When the pollen-cell meets an egg-cell in the ovary, the two join and the egg-cell ripens into a seed.

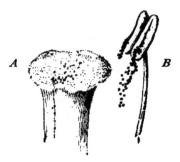

FIG. 245. In the right-hand part (*B*) you see the pollen of a plum blossom escaping from the anther. It falls on the stigma (*A*). It sends out fine shoots that are carried down the style to the ovary. There they meet with and fertilize the egg-cells. Each fertile egg-cell grows into a seed.

Fertilization of Flowers. — A flower may be fertilized by its own pollen; but the seeds grow best if they are fertilized by the pollen from other flowers.

Cross-fertilization is the fertilization of the egg-cells of one flower by the pollen from another flower.

Pollen is carried by the winds from flower to flower.

Pollen is also carried by insects and bees from flower to flower.

Plants that depend upon the wind for bringing pollen to them usually have small flowers with little odor. They do not need to attract the bees by their odor. Flowers that are fertilized by pollen carried by bees usually have large gay flowers with a strong odor. Grasses are fertilized by pollen borne by the wind and so are oak trees, birches, elm trees, poplars and pine trees. The flowers of such trees do not close at night. They must always be ready to catch what pollen the wind brings. Flowers that close at night are usually fertilized by pollen carried by bees. The bees do not fly by night.

FIG. 246. The pollen of this flower is dusted over the back of the busy bee who enters the flower to get its nectar, its honey. When he enters another flower of the same sort he leaves pollen there, and thus the second flower is cross-fertilized. Strawberry plants, for instance, are fertilized entirely by bees.

If all the bees in the world should suddenly die, more than 100,000 species of flowers would perish, too. The bees can not live without the flowers, the flowers cannot live without the bees, and mankind would find it very inconvenient to live without the fruits which the bees help to fertilize when they are flowers.

Fruits.—The ovary filled with seeds ripens into the fruit. It may be a berry, a stone-fruit, a nut, a grain, or a pod. Hickory nuts, chestnuts, acorns, are fruits just the same as peaches, apples, etc. Beans and peas bear pods as fruit. Think of all the fruits you know; and say where the seeds are in each kind.

Life in Seeds.—A seed is alive—the protoplasm in it is alive—but it does not begin to grow until

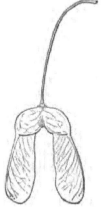

FIG. 247. The fruit of the black maple. Fruits of this shape are called key-fruits.

the spring comes. Seeds in a dry place will keep alive for several years — some for more than fifty years. But the stories about " Mummy-wheat " grown from seeds found in the coffins of Egyptian mummies where they had been for thousands of years are not true.

How Seeds are Scattered. — When the fruit is ripe the seeds are ready for planting. Usually the tree has to do its own planting. The tree that bears the most seeds and scatters them furthest abroad has the best chance of producing new trees of its own kind. Such trees are, then, most numerous.

The seeds of the dandelion and thistle are carried by the wind. Some seed-vessels burst when they are ripe and scatter the seeds in this way. Birds eat fruits and digest the pulp but excrete the seeds, and thus scatter them. Fruits with burs cling to the fur of animals and are thus scattered far and wide. Nuts are buried by squirrels; some of them

FIG. 248. The seed-pod of the balsam plant explodes and scatters the seeds.

are not eaten but grow to be trees.   Finally, men plant the seeds of the plants they value and take care of the young plants.   The plants cared for by men have, accordingly, a great advantage in the struggle for existence.

How Seeds Grow to be Plants. — Each seed contains a young plant all ready to grow.

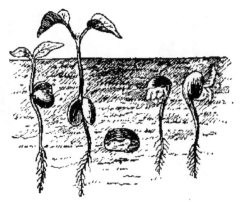

FIG. 249. A seed in the ground (the middle one in the picture) grows a root, and a stem, and leaves, and becomes a complete plant.   The original seed contained a young plant all ready to grow.

Take an almond out of its shell.   Soak it a little in water and pull off the thin brown outer coat.   At one end of the meat you will find a little plant, or bud (called the *plumule*), all ready to grow. (Try it.)   The meat inside a cherry seed is like an almond and you can find the plumule there too. (Try it.)   Open a fresh morning-glory seed; or a dried one that has been well soaked in hot water and see what you'll find. (Try it.)

Plants Sometimes Grow from Buds.—Cut up a potato leaving a bud or "eye" in each piece and plant the pieces. A plant will grow from each piece. (Try it.)

Plants Sometimes Grow from Cuttings.—A bit of rose, or geranium or carnation stem may grow if it is stuck in the ground.

FIG. 251. Cion of Apple. The Cion Inserted. The parts must be well waxed to keep out the air.

FIG. 250. A geranium grown from a cutting. The short cutting is tied to a wooden toothpick to keep it upright.

(Try it.) The tips of strong upright shoots make the best cuttings. Each cutting should have a joint near its lower end. They should be planted in a box about five inches deep filled with loose sandy soil. In about a month roots will form and new leaves will come at the tips. Then they may be transplanted.

Fruit Trees Grow from Grafts on the Stems of Other Trees.
—The *cions* (slips from the tree) are often grafted into the stems
or branches of other trees.

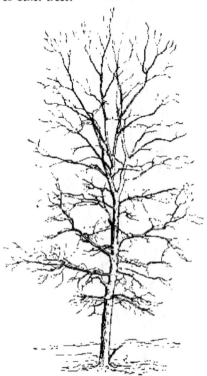

FIG. 252. The small-fruited shagbark hickory in the winter time.

Such grafting is done in the spring, using cions cut in the
winter. Pears grafted on quince trees grow well; but quinces
grafted on pears do not grow so well. Tomato plants grafted on
potato plants and also potato plants grafted on tomato plants
grow well. When the potato is the root, both tomatoes and
potatoes may be produced. When the tomato is the root, neither
tomatoes nor potatoes are produced. Chestnuts can be made to

grow on some kinds of oak trees but not on others. The reasons for these things are not well understood. We have to find out what a graft will do by trying the experiment.

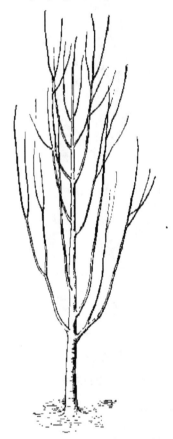

FIG. 253. The sweet cherry in the winter time.

The Forms of Plants. —There are differences in the leaves on the same oak tree, differences in the stems and branches of different white-oak trees and yet, in a general way all white-oaks look alike. All red-woods look alike; all elms look alike. *Each tree and each kind of plant has its own habit of growing.* Oak trees have a habit of growing in a certain form just as tigers or sheep grow in a certain form. New branches grow in the same form every year because they grow from buds which are arranged always on the same plan in each tree.

FIG. 254. A live oak tree in Florida, with Spanish moss hanging down from its branches.

Trees Suggest Certain Feelings.—The oak-tree is strong and sturdy; the lady-birch is slender and graceful; the cypress is gloomy; the pine is solemn; the red-wood is majestic. When we look at any of these trees they give us feelings of pleasure or, it may be, of gloominess or pain. To be in a red-wood grove is like being in a grand church.

18

That is because the light of the sky comes to you from far over-head in such a grove, just as it does in a great cathedral.   In the same way we have special feelings about the modest violet, the lovely wild rose, the formal dahlia, the pure white-lily, the flaunting peony, the stately oleander, the gay phlox.

FIG. 255. A giant cactus on the Arizona desert.

If you look at any landscape and find it beauti-ful, you will find that there are three things that make up nearly all of your enjoyment: *First*, the shapes of the hills and valleys, *second*, the shapes of the clouds, and *third*, the colors and shapes of the trees and plants.   If you imagine any one of these three things to be different either in shape or color your feeling about the landscape will change.

Think of any fine view and imagine all its trees and all its grass to be dead. Your pleasure would go if they were to change. You owe them thanks for being what they are.

Age of Trees.—Some trees like the red-wood and the "big tree" (*Sequoia*) of California grow to a great height and are, no doubt, more than a thousand years old.

Olives, fig trees, yew trees live for many centuries. Oak trees may last for 1,500 years, cedars of Lebanon about half as long.

There is a cypress in Lombardy, 120 feet high and 23 feet in girth, that is nearly 2,000 years old. Francis the First, King of France, who died in 1547, drove his sword into it in despair after he had been defeated in a battle, and Napoleon I, Emperor of France, altered the road he was building across the Alps so as to spare it in 1800.

FIG. 256. Two of the "big trees" of California. Notice the man standing at the base of the nearest tree.

The Struggle for Existence Among Plants, Trees, Leaves, Branches, etc.

The Earth is filled with plants. The strongest and fittest survive; the weaker perish. Plants struggle for room to grow in ; for food and moisture in the soil; and for sunlight.

FIG. 257. The pine trees used up all the food and moisture in the soil and left none for other plants until man took a hand in the struggle and cut down some of the pines. Then, and not before, other plants grew in the open spaces and along the road-way.

Cacti will grow in deserts; eucalyptus trees where there is little water; mosses on rocks. They fit their surroundings. Live-oaks and willows and geraniums would die in such spots.

Colors and Odors of Flowers.—In 4,180 flowers of all kinds : 1,200 were *white*, 950 *yellow*, 920 *red*, 590 *blue*, 300 *violet*, 150 *green*, 50 *orange*, 20 *brown*. It is an advantage to a flower, then,

to be white, yellow or red. More bees and birds see it and come
to carry its pollen to other flowers of the same sort.

Of the 1,200 white flowers 187 had a smell.
"   "   950 yellow   "   75   "   "   "
"   "   920 red   "   85   "   "   "
"   "   590 blue   "   31   "   "   "
"   "   300 violet   "   23   "   "   "
"   "   150 green   "   12   "   "   "
.   "   "   50 orange   "   3   "   "   "
"   "   20 brown   "   1   "   "   "

It is probable that bees and birds and insects are attracted by
the smell of a flower even more than by its color.

*The Gardener Helps Nature to Form Varieties
of Plants.* — Nature selects the best and strongest
plants by making it difficult for the weak ones to
live. Those plants that survive in the struggle for
existence are very apt to be what we call weeds.
But man wants wheat, barley, rye, grass, etc., and
he helps these useful plants to grow by planting
and cultivating them and by killing off the weeds.
Moreover, the gardener saves the seeds of the
strongest and best plants and sows them, but not the
seeds of the poorer sort. The next year he again
selects and sows the best seeds, and so on. Every
plant inherits something from the seed which was
its parent. So, finally, the gardener improves the
plants he selects. His wheat is improved so as to
give the greatest product of grain; his grasses to
give the most hay; his apples to be the largest and
best flavored; his flowers to be the largest, of the
brightest colors and of the finest odors. He helps
Nature to form the very varieties that he wants.

Varieties of animals are produced by the same kind of selection. A good trotting horse is the son of a long line of trotting horses. A good milch cow is the descendant of many generations of good milkers. In every generation man selected the best cows. The others were killed, perhaps, for beef.

Some of the Uses of Plants:

I. *Plants Purify the Air so that Animals can Breathe It.* — Animals breathe in air and use its oxygen in their lungs and breathe out carbonic acid gas. This poisonous gas (which no animal can breathe and live) is being constantly poured into the air by the breathing of animals. Plants breathe it in and use it for food, and they also breathe out oxygen. Plants keep the air pure for animals to breathe.

II. *Plants Make All the Food that Animals Live Upon.*---Some animals eat plants only (cows, sheep, rabbits, etc.). Without plants they could not live. Some animals feed upon smaller animals (lions and tigers do this). Some animals live on animal food and on plant food at the same time (men do this, for instance; they eat meat and vegetables and grain). Without plants there could be no animal life on the earth. Plants could live if there were no animals, but no animals could live if there were no plants.

III. *Plants Furnish Clothing for Men.* — Cotton and linen are made directly from plants; silk is spun by the silkworm that feeds on leaves; wool comes from sheep who are kept alive by grass.

IV. *Plants Supply all the Fuel in the World.*—
Fire-wood and charcoal are made from trees. All
the coal in the world is made from trees and plants
of long-past ages.

V. *Plants Give Us the Artificial Light that Men
Use.*—Gas for burning is made from coal-fossil
plants; kerosene is coal-oil; electric lighting is
done by dynamos that are usually run by steam
engines (a few dynamos are run by water-power,
but even here, their lamps have carbons (coal) for
making the light).

VI. *All Steam-engines Get Their Energy From
Plants.*—The coal, or wood, or petroleum used as
fuel by steam engines is the product of plants, so
that everything in the world that is made by a
steam-engine, or driven by a steam-engine, depends
directly upon plants. Cotton cloth, for instance,
is woven by steam-driven machinery, and it is
carried from Boston to San Francisco and from
San Francisco to Manila by locomotives and
steam-ships.

*All the Life in the World, Then, Depends Upon
Plants.*—But plants cannot grow without sunshine,
so that, finally, we may say that *all* the life on the
earth and in the solar system depends upon the
sun. When the sun stops shining all the solar
system will die.

Arbor-Day.—Americans, especially in the far
West, have learned the value of trees and in many

states there is a holiday in the spring on which
school-children and others plant trees in places
where they are needed. Millions of trees are now
growing on land that was once treeless.

Number of Plants.—There are at least 125,000
known species of seed-bearing plants. We do not
yet know half the plants of Africa, South America
and China.

Species.—Each kind of plant forms a species.
The white oaks form one species, the red oaks
another, and so on.

Names of Species.—Since Linnæus, the father
of modern botany, published his book on the species
of plants (*Species Plantarum*) in 1753 all species
are known by two Latin names. Thus the white
oak is called *Quercus* (oak) *alba* (white). *Quercus*
is the name for all the oaks ; *alba* is the particular
name for the white species. (We say *Quercus alba*
just as one might say " Smith—John.")

Oak Trees.—To show you how different species
in the same *family* differ and how they resemble
each other some of the oaks and some of the cone-
bearing trees (pine trees, etc.) are here described.
A complete botany would give descriptions like
these for every known species of tree and shrub,
and plant and herb.

Cone-Bearing Trees.—*The White Pine* is a large forest tree
much used for lumber. Its leaves are long and soft, light green,
arranged in groups of five. *The Pitch Pine* is a medium-sized
tree. Its leaves are arranged in threes.

FIG. 258. The acorn of the White-Oak.

FIG. 259. The acorn of the Red-Oak.

FIG. 260. The acorn of the Black-Oak.

FIG. 261. The acorn of the Bur Oak.

FIG. 262. The acorn of the Chestnut-Oak.

FIG. 263. The acorn of the Swamp White-Oak.

FIG. 264. The acorn of the Scarlet-Oak.

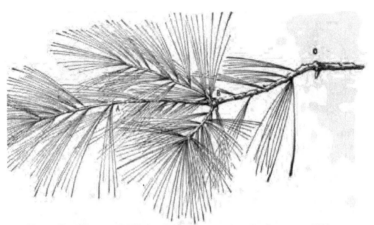

FIG. 265. Shoot of White Pine, one-third as large as life. From the tip of the branch to *A* is the last season's growth; from *A* to *B* it is two years old; from *B* to *C* it is three years old.

FIG. 266. The Pitch Pine. An old open cone is shown on the left hand side of the picture.

FIG. 267. The cone and foliage of the Black Spruce.

FIG. 268. The cone of the Norway Spruce, a common evergreen in the United States.

FIG. 269. The cone and foliage of the Hemlock.

FIG. 270. The cone and foliage of the Arbor-vitæ (used in evergreen hedges).

Make a Collection of Dried Plants.—Plants can be preserved by drying and pressing them between blotting paper cut into sheets 12 x 18 inches. For each species there should-be at least one specimen of the stem, foliage, flower, root and fruit, properly and neatly labeled. After the plants are thoroughly dry they can be fastened (gummed down by strips of paper) to strong white writing paper.

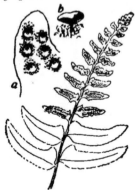

FIG. 271. The Christmas Fern, which remains green all winter.

FIG. 272. The underside of the leaves of the Christmas Fern are covered with little brown spots. Each of these spots (shown magnified at *a*) is covered with a little shield (*b*) and contains fine brown dust. From this dust new ferns will grow. It is not a seed, because it did not come from a flower.

Put Only One Species on a Sheet.—The label of each sheet should give : The name of the collector ; the place where the plant was found ; the date when found ; remarks as to the height, color, etc., of the plant, the nature of the soil, etc., and finally the English and Latin name of the plant.   Consult any large illustrated dictionary or encyclopædia, or work on botany, for help in finding the names ; or ask some one who knows.

Ferns, Mosses, Mushrooms.—All the plants that we have so far studied bear flowers and produce seeds. Their seeds, in turn, produce new plants. There is another kind of plants (ferns, mosses and mushrooms) that do not flower and have no seeds.

There is not room in this little book to say more about this class of plants, or to say anything about *fossil plants* or *bacteria.*

BOOK VIII: THE HUMAN BODY.[1]

Physiology is the science that teaches us the uses of all the parts of the body of an animal and explains the ways in which they do their work. This book will describe the uses of the parts of the human body, and there is only room to describe the most important parts.

Ana'tomy describes the form and uses of the bones, tissues, muscles, etc.

Hygiene (pronounced hī'ji-ēn) tells how the body may be kept healthy.

[1] Note to Teachers:—The subject treated in this chapter is so important, and at the same time, so difficult, that a number of fundamental matters are insisted upon, in various places and in different manners, in order that the pupil may not fail to note their significance. Space is used in these repetitions that it is possible might better have been bestowed upon other topics which are passed over with slight mention, or omitted entirely. It is believed that the method adopted will prove itself to be the wise one, however. It is far better that the pupil should have a firm grasp on a few things, than a merely superficial acquaintance with many. The application of the principles here explained to the art of healthy living is hygiene. The exposition of the laws of hygiene is here left, to a very great degree, to the teacher, who should not fail to point out the injurious effects of stimulants and of tobacco upon the separate organs, upon the general health, and upon the morale.

Man is a Vertebrate Animal. — Human beings
are *vertebrates*, that is animals with backbones.
The vertebrate animals are man, beasts, birds,
reptiles and fishes.

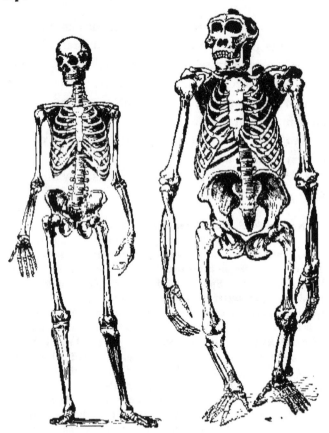

FIG. 273. Skeletons of a man and of a gorilla. They are alike,
bone for bone.

The highest classes of vertebrate animals are men, monkeys and four-footed beasts. They are called *Mammalia* because their young are suckled at the breast (Mamma is the Latin for breast). All the mammals have red warm blood.

The Human Skeleton seen sidewise (see Fig. 274).

Na. = the bones of the Nose,
Fr. = the Frontal bone,
Pa. = the Pari'etal bones,
Oc. = the Occip'ital bone,
Mn. = the Man'dible (lower jaw).

} These bones are in the SKULL.

St. = the Sternum (breast-bone),
R. = the Ribs,
R'. = the Car'tilages of the ribs.

} These form the cavity of the THORAX.

S. = the Sa'crum.
Cx. = the Coccyx.
Scp. = the Sca'pula (shoulder-blade).
Cl. = the Cla'vicle (collar-bone).
H. = the Hu'merus (upper arm bone),
Ra. = the Ra'dius lower arm bone),
U. = the Ul'na (lower arm bone),
Mc. = the Metacar'pus (hand bone),
D. = the Digits (fingers),

} These are in the ARM and in the HAND.

Il. = the Ilium,
Pb. = the Pubis,
Is. = the Ischium.

} These, together, form the HIP-BONE.

F. = the Femur (upper leg bone) (thigh bone),
Tb. = the Tibia (lower leg bone),
Fb. = the Fibula (lower leg bone),
T. = the Tarsus (ankle bones),
Mt. = the Metatarsus (foot bones),
D. = the Digits (toes).

} These are in the LEG and in the FOOT.

The names are Latin names, because early scientific books were written in Latin.

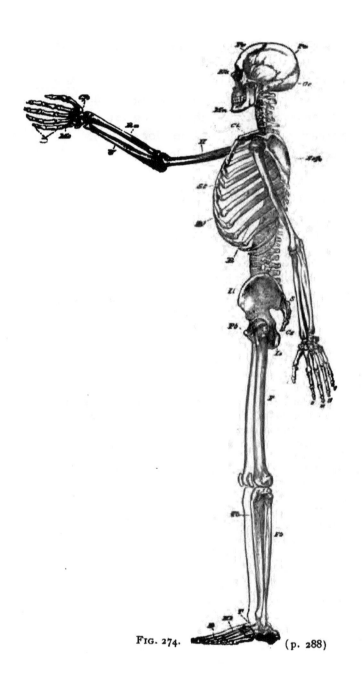

FIG. 274.   (p. 288)

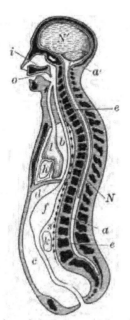

FIG. 275. The plan of the human body. If a dead body were
to be frozen and then cut in two down the middle it would show
somewhat as in the picture. The blackest parts of the picture
stand for bones. *N'* is the cavity of the skull in which the *brain*
lies. The brain is connected with the spinal-marrow or *spinal
cord* (*N*) in the hollow part of the backbone (*ee*). The brain
and spinal cord fill up a space that is called the *dorsal cavity*
(*dorsal* means back). In front of the backbone is the *ventral
cavity* (*ventral* means stomach) *i* is the cavity of the *nose*; *o*, the
cavity of the *mouth*; *l* is the *lungs* (connected with the mouth by
the *windpipe*); *h* is the *heart*; *f* is the *stomach*; the tube leading
from the mouth to the stomach is the *gullet*; the tube from the
stomach to the lower end of the body is the *intes'tine*; *k* is a *kid-
ney*; *d* is a partition called the *di''aphragm.*

The Human Body is Built on a Plan. —The
stems and branches of a tree are built on a plan,
and just in the same way the bodies of men and

19

animals are built on a plan. All vertebrate animals
have a backbone and contain two main cavites—the

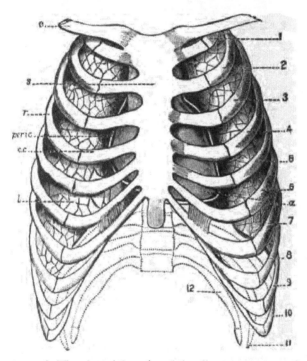

FIG. 276. The chest (*thorax*) and the ribs. 1, 2, 3, 4, 5, 6, 7,
8, 9, 10, 11, 12 are the ribs; *s* is the breast-bone (*sternum*); *c* is
the collar-bone (*clavicle*). You can feel on your own body where
these bones are. Inside them are the lungs *l* (on both sides of
your body—a right lung and a left lung); and also the heart (*a*)
enclosed in a bag called the *pericardium* (*peric.* in the picture).
Breathe deeply and you will know where your lungs are. Put
your hand on the upper left side of your chest and you will feel
your heart beat.

dorsal and the ventral cavities (NN′ is the dorsal, (*b*, *c*) is the ventral cavity in Fig. 275). All *mammals* have the ventral cavity divided into two parts, the *chest* (*b*) and the *ab′domen* (*c*) by a *diaphragm* or partition (*d*).

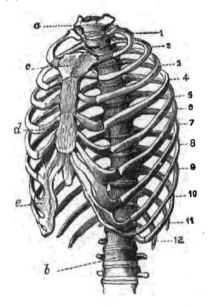

FIG. 277. The bony walls of the chest (*thorax*) and part of the backbone (*a b*). *c* is the breastbone (*sternum*). The ribs are joined to the breastbone by *cartilages* as at *d*.

The chest or thorax (*b* in Fig. 275) contains the heart (*h*) and lungs (*l*) and the windpipe that connects the mouth and nose with the lungs. The breath goes through the windpipe,[1] or *tra′chea*.

[1] The pupil should point out the different parts of the picture with a pin.

The abdomen contains the **stomach** (which is connected with the mouth by the **gullet**), **liver**, intestines or bowels, etc.

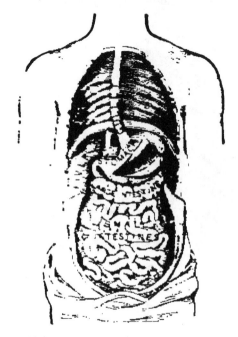

FIG. 278. The contents of the lower part of the ventral cavity
—the abdomen.

Put your finger at the bottom of your neck and move it downwards, feeling for bones. When you feel no more bones you have reached the bottom of the chest (or thorax). Below that is the ab'domen. The food we eat passes through the gullet to the stomach, is there digested, and the useless remainder is got rid of through the intestine.

Organs of the Human Body.—The organs of the body are its separate parts that do special kinds of work. The heart is the organ that pumps blood through the body; the lung is the organ that breathes; the stomach is the organ that digests food; the ear is the organ by which we hear, and so on.

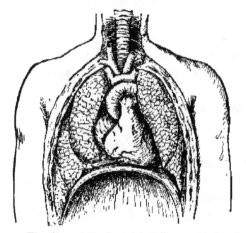

Fig. 279 The human body opened from the front so as to show the contents of the upper part of the ventral cavity. The windpipe comes down from the mouth to the lungs, which lie on both sides of the body. The heart is shown like a bag near the center. The upper part of the ventral cavity is separated from the lower part by the diaphragm, which is a stout membrane, or skin.

What the Body is Made Of.—The outside of the body is covered with skin. If the skin were taken off we should find *fat* below it. Under the fat, in the ball of the thumb, for instance, we should find red flesh, like the *lean* part of beef. This red flesh is *muscle*. The *skeleton* of hard *bones* (see Fig. 274) holds the body together and keeps it upright. Where the ends of joints come together, as in the fingers, for instance, we should find gristle, or *cartilage*. Besides all these things there are various kinds of tissues—stringy networks of fibers.

Connective tissue is tough and binds the different parts of the body together; *muscle tissue* is tough and strong and makes the muscles; *cartilage tissue* makes the gristle; *bony tissue* is stiffer and makes the bones. *Saliva*, or spittle, is in the mouth, *blood* in the arteries and veins, etc.

Chemistry of the Body. — If the trunk of a tree be burned part goes off in gases and part remains as ashes. If a human body be burned part goes off as gas and part remains as solid ash. Chemists have examined all the substances in the human body and have found that its principal *elements* are Carbon (C), Hydrogen (H), Oxygen (O), Nitrogen (N), Sulphur (S), Lime (Ca). These are combined into chemical compounds. Much of the body (of the blood, for instance) consists of water (OH_2); a good part of the bones is lime (Ca), etc.

The Human Skeleton: Bones. — A very young baby has a skeleton but its bones are soft like gristle. As it gets older the bones grow to be stiffer and stronger. Between the joints cartilage is found, and the bones are joined together by connective tissue. There are 206 different bones in the human skeleton. The most important are named in Fig. 274.

The pupil should turn to this page and point out, with a pin, on the picture, the principal bones of the body.

Cartilage.—The end of your nose is cartilage and can be bent. It is elastic. The upper part is bone and cannot be bent. (Try it.)

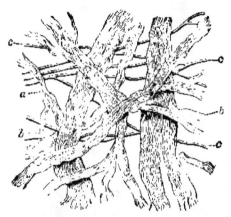

FIG. 280. Bundles of connective tissue such as bind the skin to the body. The tissues that bind the bones together and those between the muscles are of pretty much the same kind.

Connective Tissue.—If you watch the cook cut up a piece of suet you will see all through the mass a lot of tough strong fibers. She takes it out because it will not melt in cooking. Connective tissue in the body sometimes forms *ligaments* to bind the bones together, sometimes *membranes* (a kind of skin) that wraps and supports different parts.

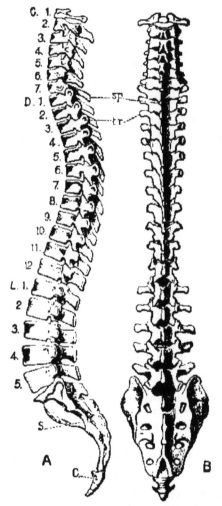

FIG. 281. Side view (A) and back view (B) of a man's back-bone. He has seven vertebræ in his neck (C 1, 2, 3, 4, 5, 6, 7); twelve in his back (D 1, 2, 3, 4, 5, 6, 7, 8, 9, 10, 11, 12); five in his loins (L 1, 2, 3, 4, 5); S is the *sacrum*, C, the *coccyx* (like the beginning of a tail). Notice how each piece in the back view (B) matches a piece in the side view (A). You can feel the different pieces in your own body. (p. 296)

The Backbone (vertebral column).

Figure 281 shows the way the bones stand in a human backbone.   Between each pair of *vertebræ* there is a little elastic cushion of gristle.   If there

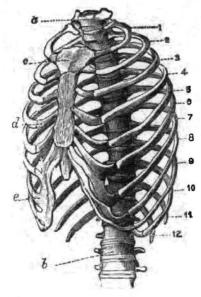

'FIG. 282. The way the 24 ribs are joined to the backbone. The bony ends of 20 ribs are joined to the breastbone by cartilages like gristle.

were no gristle, if your backbone were stiff, you could not bend your body at all.   Throughout the column runs the spinal cord, like the marrow in a bone, and it joins on to the bottom part of the brain in the skull.

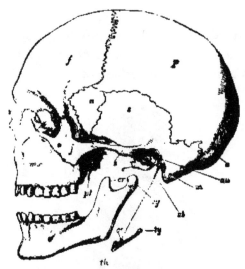

FIG. 283. A side view of a human skull. *f* is the *frontal* bone; *p*, the *pari'etal* bone; *o.* the *occi'pital* bone; *au* is the opening to the ear; *cr* is the place where the muscles of the lower jaw are fastened. The crinkled lines between the bones of the upper skull are called *sutures*. They are dove-tailed so as to be strong. Carpenters make the ends of bureau drawers in the same way for the same reason.

The skull is shaped like a dome so as to be strong to protect the brain. Try to crush an egg-shell between your fingers. Although it is so thin and brittle, its dome-like shape makes it strong. The brain is the most delicate part of an animal's body. If it is injured, its mind will not work. And that is the reason why it is a great advantage to any animal to have its brain well protected.

A bone in the human body is covered closely with a kind of skin or tissue. The tissue or cover-

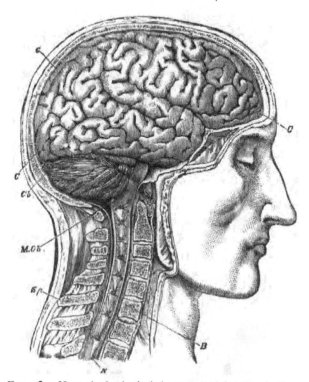

FIG. 284. How the brain (*cc*) is protected by the skull; and how it is joined to the spinal cord (*N*). Notice how far up into the head the backbone goes to support it.

ing is full of blood, and this blood feeds the bone and keeps it alive. If, by an accident, the covering is stripped off the bone it will not grow any more.

The Soft Bones of Children are Easily Bent out of Shape. — The bones of babies are like gristle; the bones of children are much softer than those of grown-up people. It is therefore important that

children should be taught to stand erect, to walk
properly, to sit correctly, and that they should not
wear too tight-fitting clothes or shoes.

A very young child that is allowed to walk before its legs
are strong enough may become bow-legged: a school-child that
sits on a bench so high that its feet cannot touch the floor may
have the bones of the upper leg permanently curved: children
who loll at their desks may get a bad curve to their backbones:
children who wear tight shoes will get crooked feet. A girl that
wears stays that are too tight compresses the lower ribs so that
there is not room enough for healthy organs and they will become more unhealthy as she grows older.

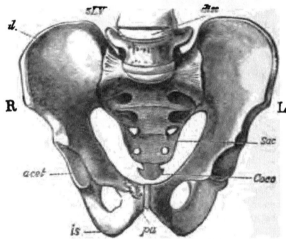

FIG. 285. Front view of the bones of the hips. The lower
end of the backbone is at the top of the picture. Then comes a
cushion of gristle marked *disc*, then the lowest of the vertebræ
of the back (5 *L. V.*), then the sacrum (*sac*) and the coccyx
(*cocc*) (compare this picture with Fig. 281). The upper bone of
the leg fits into the place marked *acet*—there is one such place for
each leg. *R* is the person's right hand side, *L* the left hand.
All these bones together make a ring which is called the pelvis.

FIG. 286. Front view of a man's left leg (*A*) and left arm (*B*).
Take the arm first (*B*): *cl* is the collar-bone (*clavicle*); *scap* is
the shoulder-blade
(*scapula*); *hum* is
the bone of the up-
per arm (*humerus*);
rad and *uln* are the
two bones of the
lower arm (*radius*
and *ulna*); *car* is
the place of eight
bones of the wrist
(*carpal bones*);
metac is the place of
five bones of the
hand (*metacarpal
bones*); *phl* are the
finger-bones (*pha-
langes*). Take the
leg next (*A*): *inn* in
this picture is the
same as the hip-
bone marked *L* in
the last picture
(compare the two):
fem is the bone of
the upper leg (*fe-
mur*); *pat* is the
knee-cap (*patella*);
tib and *fib* are the
two bones of the
lower leg (*tibia* and
fibula); *tar* is the
place of the seven
bones of the ankle
and heel (*tarsal
bones*); *metat* is the
place of the five
bones of the foot
(*metatarsal bones*);
phl are the toe-
bones (*phalanges*). 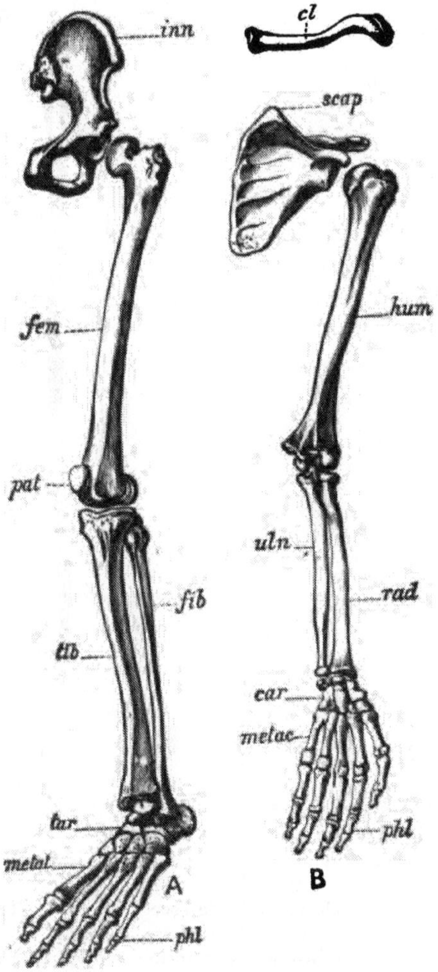
You can easily discover many of these bones in yourself by feel-
ing your own arm and leg. (Try it.)

FIG. 287. The upper bone of
the right arm as it is: and as it
would look if sawed down the
middle. The upper end of the
humerus fits into the shoulder-blade (see Fig. 286). The lower
end forms part of the elbow. The joints are oiled with a fluid
like oil. The bone is hollow and the hollow is filled with marrow.
Round this is the spongy bone *b* and *c*; and outside is the hard
bone. At the ends are two pieces of gristle *a, a*. Split the bone
of a chicken's leg and you will see how bones are built. (Try it.)

The Bones of the Arm, with the Biceps Muscle.

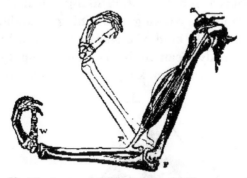

FIG. 288. The bones of the arm, with the biceps muscle. By comparing this picture with Fig. 286 you can see how the muscle of your upper arm is fastened to the shoulder-blade by two *tendons* at (*a*). The lower end of the biceps muscle is fastened to the radius bone of the lower arm at *P*. *F* is the elbow. By willing to do so, you can make the biceps swell up and shorten (the thin lines show its outline then) and thus raise your hand to the place shown in the middle of the picture. Put one hand on your biceps and raise your lower arm as in the picture, and you can feel the biceps grow larger and shorten. Muscles move the bones they are fastened to when they shorten. Muscles shorten when you *will* that they should do so.

It is Worth While to Keep Our Bodies Healthy. —Children usually feel pretty well and think very little about good health or bad health. But if they will look around them they will see that the world is full of older people who are not well. Every one of those people is less strong, less useful, and less happy than he or she ought to be. How would *you* like to be ill and in pain for half of your life? By eating the right kind of food in the right way,

by not eating the wrong kind of food at all, by not
smoking tobacco and by not drinking alcoholic
drinks, by standing, walking and sitting straight,
by wearing the right kind of clothes and shoes, by
keeping your body clean by baths, and strong by
regular exercise, you can keep yourself healthy.

FIG. 289. The elbow-joint—separated. Projections on the
bone of the upper arm (*humerus*) fit into cups at the upper ends
of the two bones of the lower arm (*ulna, radius*). The bones
are joined by ligaments (two of them are shown cut apart in the
picture). Hold your arm straight out and turn your lower arm
round so that the back of your hand is first up, and then down.

If your body is healthy and your mind is healthy
too, you will be able to live a useful and a happy
life. This is worth while. Think about it. At
least half the misery in the world comes because

children have neglected the very simple laws of health during the years when their bodies were growing and developing. Begin *now* to form good habits which will keep you healthy and happy all your life.

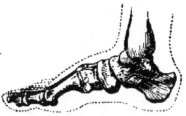

<small>FIG. 290. The bones of the right foot. Notice that the foot rests on two points; on the heel and on the ball of the foot. Between those points there is an arch (the instep) which is elastic. That is why you walk with a springy step. If there were no elastic arch you would feel a jar in your brain every time you planted your foot in walking.</small>

Moreover, if you will look about you, you will see that many older persons who seem, on the whole, healthy enough, are yet not very useful, not very successful, and on the whole not very happy. In very many cases they are less useful and less successful because in the struggle for life they are handicapped and hindered by a poor digestion, headaches, nervousness or something of the kind. Our opportunities for usefulness or success come unexpectedly and do not wait upon our convenience. They come suddenly and do not wait long. The man who is in good health can seize them as they fly. The man who has headaches, who is too fat,

20

or too tired, lets the fortunate moment pass. He
does not succeed; he is not useful. Many battles
have been lost because the Generals were not in
perfectly good condition and health. They could
not think quickly and correctly. Life is, in some
ways, like a battle. The soldier who keeps his

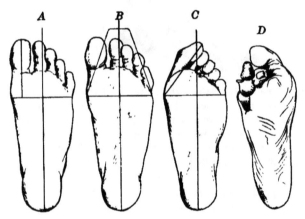

FIG. 291. The human foot is naturally like *A* or *B* in the picture. A narrow-toed shoe, of the shape of the outline in *B*, will
cramp the toes as in *C* or *D*.

body and mind in good health is the one who
succeeds. Healthy minds usually live in healthy
bodies.

The Teeth.—Babies begin to cut their *milk-teeth*
when they are about six months old, and by their
second year they have twenty teeth. The *perma-
nent teeth* begin to grow when the child is six years
old. They take the places of the milk-teeth. The

last teeth (four " wisdom-teeth ") are cut at about twenty-two years. By that time a person is expected to know something. If a tooth of the second set is lost, by being broken, or decayed, no new tooth will come to take its place. Therefore, *be careful of your teeth.*

Go to a dentist at least twice a year and have your teeth examined. Do not abuse them by cracking nuts with them, or by drinking very sour (acid) drinks, or by eating very hot foods. Brush your teeth twice daily with a moderately stiff brush using white castile soap and powdered chalk. Use a quill or a wooden toothpick frequently to remove particles of food lying between the teeth. Never use metal toothpicks like needles, pins, etc.

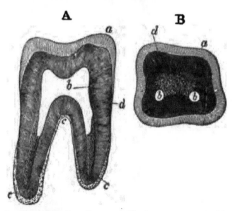

Fig. 292. The left-hand cut (*A*) shows a tooth sliced in two up and down; (*B*) shows the same tooth sliced crosswise. Both pictures are just three times as large as life. In both pictures *a* is the very hard *enamel* of the outside of the tooth, *d* is the hard *dentine* or bone, *b* is the space filled by the *pulp*. The pulp is a soft, red, very sensitive core, full of blood and nerves, and is the part of the tooth that is most alive. Through its blood the rest of the tooth is fed. (It is often called *the nerve*.)

Muscles.—The muscles of our body make it possible for us to move, to walk or to stand erect; for

Fig. 293. The outer muscles of the body. If the skin of a man were transparent you would see his muscles as in the picture. Beneath the muscles shown here there are hundreds of others. The picture shows only the outer layer. Compare this picture with the next one and trace out, with a pin, the muscles of the shin, the thigh, the abdomen, the back, the neck, the arm.

our heart to keep beating, for our lungs to breathe, for our stomachs to digest our food.

We breathe and our hearts beat whether we *will* to have it so, or not. The muscles that do this sort of work are called *involuntary muscles* (that is muscles that work independently of our wills). You cannot make your heart stop beating. (Try it.) You can hold your breath a long time, but not forever. (Try it.) We move our arms and legs by another kind of muscles which do their work when we *will* them to do it — voluntary muscles. You *will* to move your arm first; and then your arm moves.

When a gorilla—whose skeleton is very much like that of a man (see Fig. 273)—is walking, he rests his fists on the ground and goes on all fours nearly all the time. A man walks upright and his two hands are free. Thus a man, even if you think of him as an animal and nothing else, has a great advantage over any other animal. Man is the only "tool-using animal" partly because his two hands are free to use the tools ; partly because his intelligence is sharp enough to invent the tools in the first place.

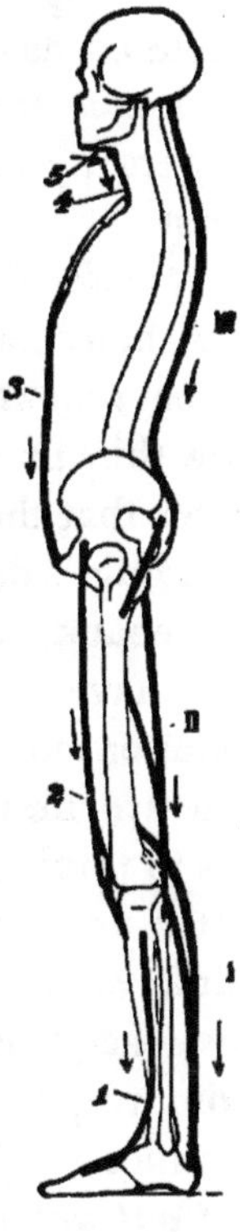

FIG. 294. A sketch to show where some of the most important muscles are : (I.) the muscles of the calf of the leg ; (II.) the muscles of the back of the thigh ; (III.) the muscles of the backbone (these keep the body from falling forward) ; (1) the muscles of the front of the leg ; (2) those of the front of the thigh ; (3) those of the abdomen ; (4, 5) those of the neck. When you are standing still all these muscles are at work to keep you upright. The pull, the force, acts along each muscle in the direction of the arrows.

Tendons.—The middle of a muscle is usually a red soft swollen part (like the biceps of your upper arm — Fig. 288) connected by tendons — tough white cords — with the parts that are to be moved. You can easily find the tendons that bend your fingers by feeling for them on the inside of your wrist.

Muscles Can be Educated and Can Get Habits. —A baby has to *learn* to stand. Each muscle has to be *taught*. By and by the muscles learn just how they must act and each muscle acquires a *habit*. After that the child can stand without thinking how standing is done. Swimming, bicycling, riding on horseback, have to be *learned*. The proper muscles have to acquire *habits*. After that, we can swim or ride on bicycles without thinking. When you are first learning to ride a wheel your brain has to think every minute about what you are doing. After you have learned, you can ride along and think about something else. All your muscles have acquired their habits, and your brain is free from responsibility. Your breathing is done, for instance, without any thought of yours.

Contraction of Muscles.—A muscle does its work by contracting — by getting shorter. If the biceps muscle in your upper arm were a stout rubber band that would get shorter whenever you said " Now " and longer when you said " Enough " such a rubber band would do the work that is wanted. A rubber band would not get tired, but muscles do get tired in time. Then they must rest until enough new blood has been poured into them. They are like willing laborers; but every now and then a laborer must stop for food and for rest.

The Skin.—The skin is the tough outer covering of the whole body. It is like an India-rubber bag fitting loosely over the fat and muscles underneath. You can see that it is not tightly fixed to them by pinching up a fold of skin on the back of your hand and rolling it to and fro. Directly underneath the skin is a layer of fat, and under the fat are the muscles.

The Dermis and Epidermis.—The skin is made in two layers very close together. The outer layer, the one that you see, is the *epidermis* (sometimes called the *cuticle*). The inner layer is the *dermis* or the true skin. The outer skin is thin, horny, almost transparent, without blood-vessels or nerves, and is a protection to the sensitive skin underneath. If there were no outer layer to protect the inner skin, the whole body would feel like the " raw " skin at the bottom of a blister.

You can run a needle under the skin on the palm of your hand without hurting yourself, or without bringing blood, if you are careful not to go too deep (try it). The moment the needle enters the true skin underneath it touches a little vein, and blood flows; and it touches a nerve and you feel pain. Nerves are connected with the brain and telegraph a message there the moment they are touched. The *dermis* is alive and is all the while fed by the blood; the outer horny skin is, in great part, dead, and is all the while being worn off. After a hot bath a great deal of the outer skin can be rubbed off with a towel. A sunburned nose loses its outer covering of skin which peels off. The same thing happens after scarlet fever or measles. The outer skin peels off.

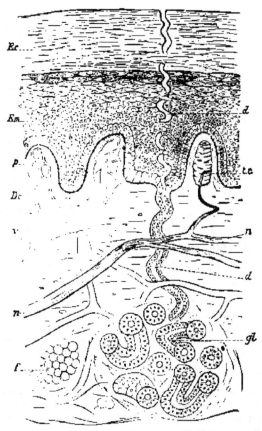

FIG. 295. How a piece of skin would look if it were sliced through and very much magnified.

The skin is about a tenth of an inch thick (of different thicknesses in different parts of the body). On the outside of it is *cuticle* or horny skin—*Ec* in the picture. This layer is dead and is continually being worn away. Underneath it is a layer, *Em*, of live cells from which new outer skin is continually being built up. All the rest is the *dermis*—true skin. It is full of veins carrying blood—*v* in the picture (trace out the veins in the picture with a pin). It is full of nerves, too—*nn* in the picture. Trace out the course of this nerve and you see it branches into a little coil *tc*. It is by little coils like this, joined to nerves, that you are able to feel when you touch anything; *gl* is one of the *sweat-glands* in your skin and it is connected with the outer parts by a tube, *dd* (trace it out).

The Organs of Touch. — Throughout the skin there are little coils joined to the nerves (*tc*, in the last picture). When the skin above one of these is touched, the nerve telegraphs to the brain " I am touched." If you take a pencil in your hand it touches a long row of such coils . . . . . . Each one of the row telegraphs to the brain and your brain (somehow) knows the shape of the pencil even when your eyes are shut. (Try it.)

If you press a postage stamp on your hand it touches a lot of coils arranged this way :

. . . . . . each one of these coils tele- . . . . . . graphs to the brain " I am touched,". . . . . . and the brain (somehow) knows the shape of the thing that is touching. Not only does the brain know the *shape* in this way, but it learns something about the *hardness*. A copper cent feels differently from a round piece of cardboard of the same size (try it with your eyes shut). A warm cent feels differently from a cold one, too. The brain learns something about the *temperature* in this way, also.

Some Parts of Your Body are More Sensitive than Others.— Take two lead pencils sharpened to dull points and hold them

close together, side by side. Have one of your companions
close his eyes and do you touch the back of his hand or the top
of his tongue gently with both points at once. He will tell you
that two things are touching him. Now touch him with both
points on the back of his arm, or on his shoulder-blade. He
will tell you that only one point is touching him. (Try this experiment and others of the same kind, using sometimes one
point, sometimes two; and putting the points sometimes close
together, sometimes an inch or more apart.) Some parts of the
body have a great many sensitive spots on every square inch
(the tongue, the cheeks, the hands); some have only a few (the
backs of the arms, the shoulders, the feet). The more of the
spots there are, the more sensitive the body is to touch.

Sweat-glands.—Just as the leaf of a tree is full
of pores, so the skin is full of little holes through
which sweat, or perspiration, escapes. See Fig.
295, *gl* and *dd*. There are about 3,000 such
sweat-glands to every square inch of the palm of
your hand and about two millions and a half
(2,500,000) in the whole body. Look at the palm
of your hand with a common magnifying glass and
you can see the holes at the ends of the sweat-gland
tubes. The little tubes leading to the glands are
about ¼ of an inch long, so that in the whole body
there are about ten miles of them.

*The Chief Use of the Sweat-glands is to Keep
the Body at the Right Temperature.*—It is a fact
that the temperature of the body of a healthy man
is about 98° Fahrenheit, no matter whether he is in
the cold arctic regions, or in the burning deserts of
Arizona. If his temperature falls a few degrees
he dies; if it rises a few degrees he dies. The
sweat-glands regulate his temperature. When the

body is very cold there is almost no sweat; when it is very hot there is abundance of perspiration which collects in drops on the skin. There it evaporates into the air as (invisible) water-vapor and in evaporating it makes the body cooler. (All evaporation cools the air.) It is in damp weather, when the perspiration evaporates very slowly (because the air is already full of water-vapor) that you feel the hottest. Hot, dry weather is far less trying. If the whole body is kept clean by daily baths the sweat-glands will work well and will be healthy.

The Complexion.—Deep down in the little cells that make the *dermis* there are grains of coloring matter like a paint. In blonde persons there is only a little of it and we say they have pale faces. Brunettes have more, and we say their complexions are dark. Negroes have a great deal. When the skin is much exposed to sunlight more of this coloring matter is formed and the skin is "tanned," as we say. If the true skin is burned by a deep burn the coloring matter is all destroyed, no more grows and therefore scars, even on negroes, are white.

Blushing.—Sometimes there is a rush of blood to the *dermis* underlying the cheeks that brings a blush. It is curious that our arms or shoulders do not blush. They are usually covered, and blushing there would not be a sign to others that we were ashamed or angry. Blushes come to the cheeks where they can be seen, just as flowers have gay petals in the places where they are of some use.

Finger-nails and toe-nails are made from the outer layer of the skin, but they are fed by the true skin (*dermis*) at their roots.   The claws of animals correspond to our finger and toe-nails.

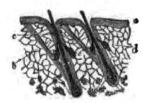

FIG. 296. A slice of the skin—much magnified—showing the way hairs grow on the body : *a* is the outer layer of horny skin ; *d* is the inner layer of skin.   Two hairs are shown growing in two little sheaths.   The oil that makes the hair glossy comes from two *oil-glands* (*e*) half way up the root of each hair.   The roots of the hairs are close to nerves.   When a hair is pulled out you feel a little pain.   When anything touches the end of a hair you know it, just as a cat knows when anything touches the ends of her whiskers.   (Try touching the hairs on the back of your hand.)

Hairs.—The bodies of many animals are covered with thick fur.   Our bodies — except the palms of the hands and the soles of the feet — are covered with a scanty growth of fine hairs (look at the back of your hand) and long and thick hair grows on our heads.

Food and How it is Used in the Body. — The body is a machine for doing work, somewhat as the steam-engine is a machine for doing work.   In the steam-engine we must have fuel that is burned and from the burning we get power.   In the body we must have food that is oxidized (that is burned) and from the food our bodies get power.[1]   When a steam-engine gets out of order, it cannot mend itself, but our bodies can and do mend themselves

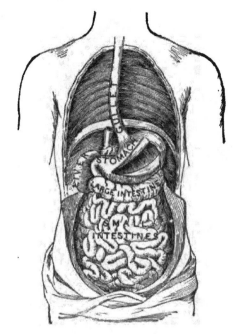

FIG. 297. The stomach and intestines.   In the picture the stomach is slit open to show its interior.

[1] The work that a man's body does is partly external, partly internal. The external work can be measured in foot-pounds (the energy required to lift one pound one foot is a foot-pound). A healthy man can do about 2,000,000 foot-pounds of external work per day, that is he can lift about 2,000,000 pounds one foot high, lifting a few pounds at a time and keeping at it. His internal work keeps his heart beating, his lungs breathing, his body at its temperature of 98° Fahr., etc., and amounts to about 5,000,000 foot-pounds daily.

in many cases. ˙For instance, if your arm is badly burned and loses its power, your blood will bring the food necessary to make it well and strong again.

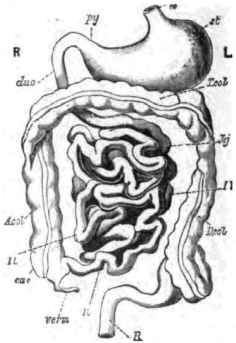

FIG. 298. The stomach, the large intestine, the small intestine (seen from the front) : *st* is the stomach; *Il*, the small intestine; *A col, T col, D col*, the large intestine; *verm* is the appendix.

˙ Food taken into the mouth is chewed and then swallowed. It goes through the gullet into the stomach. There it is dissolved by the *gastric-juice* and made into a soft mass, like very thick soup, called *chyme*. This is mixed with *bile* from the liver, and with other fluids, and passes into the small intestine where it is turned into a cream-like liquid called *chyle*.

Now at last the food is ready to be taken into the blood. The undigested and useless parts are passed along the bowels and finally ejected.

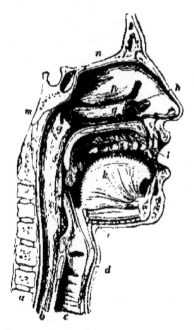

FIG. 299. The throat sliced down the middle : *b* is the gullet ; *l*, the roof of the mouth ; *c*, the windpipe ; *k*, the tongue ; *e* is a little lid which shuts down over the windpipe when you swallow so that food cannot go down " the wrong way." Put your fingers on the Adam's apple of the throat, outside, and pretend to swallow. You can feel how the little lid closes the windpipe.

Digestion in the Mouth.—If the food is well chewed there is a good supply of *saliva* (spittle) in the mouth. The mouth and gullet are lined with a soft red skin called the *mucous membrane*. (You can see part of it by standing in front of a mirror with your mouth wide open). The *saliva* moistens the food and gets it ready to be swallowed. You could not swallow a cracker—which would be mere dust—unless it were first moistened.

The smell of food, or even the thought of it, makes the *saliva* flow. "It makes your mouth water," we say.

Food Passes Down the Gullet Slowly.—It does not fall down as a brick falls down a chimney. The gullet is a small tube full of rings of muscle which seize the bits of food and move them along from ring to ring. Horses drink with their heads lower than their stomachs by this means. The water they drink is made to flow up-hill.

Gastric Juice.—The moment food enters the stomach gastric juice trickles out, somewhat as sweat on the skin, and begins to digest the food.

A Canadian hunter was accidentally shot so that the bullet left a hole from his abdomen into the stomach. His doctor was able to see exactly how digestion went on by experiments made through this wound.

After a time, sometimes one hour, sometimes as much as four hours, the *chyme* of the stomach begins to move into the small intestine. Usually the stomach is entirely emptied about three or four hours after a meal.

Digestion in the Stomach.

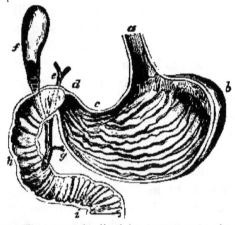

FIG. 300. The stomach sliced in two so as to show: *a*, the lower end of the gullet ; *d*, the opening into the small intestine ; *e*, the tube through which *bile* comes from the liver. The stomach is large enough to hold about four pints. Its walls are stout and muscular. Inside it is covered with a *mucous membrane* full of thousands of small glands that give out *gastric juice*.

Digestion in the Small Intestine.—The small intestine is coiled up in folds which, if extended, would be about 20 feet long. (See Fig. 298.) It takes up the *chyme* and passes it along by its rings of muscle. At the same time the *chyme* is changed into *chyle*—which is very nutritious and looks like cream. As the *chyle* passes along it is absorbed, sucked up, by thousands of small tubes. From some of these tubes the *chyle* goes into the blood at once. Other tubes take part of it, mix it with *lymph* and pour it into a large blood-vessel, ready for use in making new blood.

21

Digestion.—Water taken into the mouth is ready to mix with the blood at once. Things like sugar and salt are ready to mix with the blood as soon as they are dissolved. Starchy foods, the lean part of meat, etc., have to be changed by the gastric juice into *chyme* and then again changed into *chyle*, before they are fit for food.

Absorption. — Some of the nutritive food is absorbed by the blood-vessels of the stomach and thus passes into the blood. Much more of it is sucked up from the blood-vessels of the small intestine; still more by its *lymph-vessels*. All the useful parts of the food finally get into the blood, are carried by the blood to the heart, and from the heart this rich blood is pumped all through the body. New blood is continually being made in this way, and old blood is continually being made richer. All parts of the body are continually fed with blood. Good blood and plenty of it is what keeps us alive and well.

The Circulation of the Blood.—The blood circulates. It moves through the body in every direction. The heart is a hollow muscle filled with blood. It beats, that is it contracts like the bulb of a syringe, and squeezes its blood outwards into the *arteries*. The arteries go all through the body. You cannot put the point of a fine needle into your flesh anywhere without touching an *artery* and drawing blood. From the fine ends of the arteries the blood goes into still finer tubes called the *capil-*

lary (hair-like) *tubes*. The flesh, everywhere, is nourished and fed by arterial blood (it is bright scarlet in color). Other *capillaries* are joined on to the *veins*. The arterial blood from which the rich nourishment has been taken is sucked in by

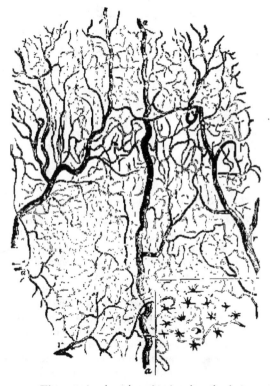

FIG. 301. The arteries (*a, a*) and veins (*v, v*) of the web between the toes of a frog, much magnified. The arrows (➡➤) show which way the blood runs. All the smaller lines stand for the capillaries.

the capillaries, passed on to the veins (where it becomes dark red) and back to the heart again.   In
its course the blood passes through the lungs, too.
Here it sucks in the *oxygen gas* of the air we have
breathed.   This oxygen makes the blood rich and
nourishing again (and scarlet in color), and so the
circulation goes on as long as you live.

Scarlet blood goes through the arteries and
nourishes all parts of the body.   After it has lost
its oxygen it is of no use as food and must return to
the lungs and to the heart to be made rich again.

There are so many thousand arteries, veins and capillaries
that your whole body is made up of countless little islands,
where no blood is, surrounded by rivers of blood flowing past
them and making them rich and fertile (the arteries) or else taking away from them food that has been once used and is now
useless (the veins).

The Heart.—(See Fig. 303.)

The Course of the Flow of Blood.—The blood starts from the
left ventricle and flows into a large artery which soon divides
into branches that lead all over the body.   These branches end
in the fine capillaries and when the rich blood has reached them
it has done its work.   It has brought nourishment to every part
of the body.   It has lost its oxygen and changed in color from
scarlet to dull red.   The fine network of veins collects the blood
from the capillaries and draws it through larger and larger vein
branches and finally pours it into the right auricle.   From there
it is pumped into the right ventricle and from there it goes to
the lungs.   Here it is again made rich by the oxygen of the air
and is returned to the left auricle.   From there it flows to the
left ventricle and begins its circulation once more, and so on as
long as you are alive.   The blood flows through the whole body;
this is the *systemic circulation.*   It also flows through the lungs;
this is the *pulmonary circulation.*

Experiment.—Bare your arm to above the elbow and let it hang down for half a minute. Its veins will be filled with blood. Now tie a bandage tight just above the elbow. The blood cannot get back to the heart fast enough and the veins will swell so that you can easily see where they are. (Try it—but do not keep the bandage on too long.)

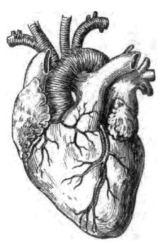

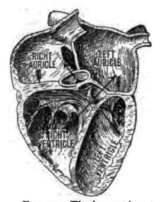

FIG. 302. The human heart, seen from the front. Your heart is about as large as your fist. See Fig. 279, page 293, which shows how it lies under the ribs.

FIG. 303. The human heart sliced up and down to show its four cavities: (1)right auricle; (2) right ventricle; (3) left auricle; (4) left ventricle. The blood flows in the direction of the arrows because the valves of the heart (like trapdoors that will only open in one way) will not allow it to flow in any other directions.

Beating of the Heart; the Pulse. — The heart *beats* about 70 times a minute. Put your fingers on your wrist and count the number of beats in a minute.

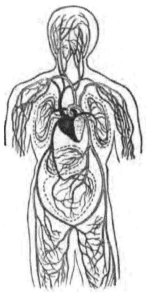

FIG. 304. The plan of the arteries and veins of the front part of the body. The arteries are black; the veins are drawn in dotted lines. (Trace out the arteries and veins with a pin for a pointer.) In the arteries the blood flows about 16 inches every second, and in the larger veins about 4 inches.

FIG. 305. An experiment to show the beating of the heart (the *pulse*) to a class. Bare the wrist and press a bit of looking-glass about half an inch square upon the wrist and hold it there steadily with one finger. Every time the pulse beats the mirror will move slightly. Let the direct rays of the sun fall on the mirror and be reflected to make a spot of light on the ceiling or wall. The motion of this spot will show the beat of the pulse, much magnified. (The teacher should show the scholars how to make this instructive experiment.)

The Blood.—The blood in a man's body weighs about twelve pounds. Blood, to the eye, looks like a red liquid. When it is seen through a microscope we find it to be a colorless liquid (the *blood-plasma*) in which float thousands of little solid particles. These are the *blood-corpuscles*. Most of them are red, but many are white.

Blood Corpuscles.—

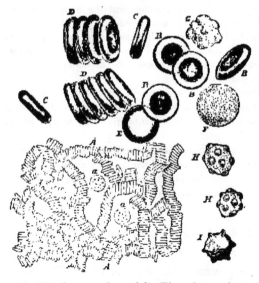

Fig. 306. Blood-corpuscles. (*A*) The picture between the letters *A* and *A* is not very much magnified. It shows the red corpuscles lying in strings like piles of copper cents, and two white corpuscles *a, a.* *B* shows two red corpuscles, much magnified, seen flatwise. *C* is a red corpuscle seen edgewise. *D* is a string of red corpuscles.

The red corpuscles are about $\frac{1}{5000}$ of an inch in diameter and about $\frac{1}{12000}$ of an inch thick.   Ten millions of them will lie on a square inch, and the body is full of them. *The red corpuscles carry oxygen with them to all parts of the body, and keep it alive.* The white corpuscles of the blood are in form and in character like the single-celled animals called *Amœbæ*. When they meet a particle of blood that has no right to be there, they flow around it and absorb it, just as the Amœba flows around and absorbs its own food. As long as the red corpuscles of the blood are healthy they are not attacked, but the moment a red corpuscle is diseased, it is treated like an enemy. *Bacteria* (vegetable germs of some diseases—*microbes*, so called) are devoured by the white corpuscles, and the body protected from harm. During an illness due to poisoning of the blood by microbes—malaria, for instance—there are countless battles between the hostile microbes and the white corpuscles. If the latter win the fight the patient recovers. If the white corpuscles are defeated the patient dies.

Without Blood We Cannot Live.—If an artery is cut by an accident, the man will bleed to death. If blood from another person, or from a dog, is pumped into his veins he can be revived—made to live again.

Blood gets its nourishing food from digested food. It gets oxygen from the air we breath. (Air is a mixture of oxygen and nitrogen gas.) As the blood passes through the lungs it gives out carbonic acid gas and this is breathed out by the lungs at each breath.

We Speak by Air Forced Through the Glottis, and different sounds are heard according as the opening of the glottis is large or narrow.   By much practice the muscles have learned just how wide to open the glottis to make the sound of A, or B, etc. Babies learning to speak have to think about the words they are going to say.   We have said them so often that our muscles have learned their habits and work almost like machines, without much thinking from us.

The Air-Passages.—

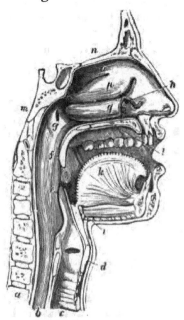

FIG. 307. The head sliced downward, nearly through the middle: *a* is the spine, *b* the gullet, *c* the *windpipe* (*trachea*) which carries air to the lungs. The *air-passages* are the *pharynx* (*g, f, e*) and the *larynx* (*d*) (the part of the same tube below *e*). The "Adam's apple" is at *d*; *e* is the *epiglottis*, a little lid or trap-door, which closes the windpipe when food is swallowed but leaves it open when you are speaking; *d* is a box of gristle in which there is a slit called the *glottis*. The air passes through this slit when we speak, and we can make the slit wide or narrow, as we choose. When we breathe it is wide open. When we are speaking it is sometimes wide, sometimes narrow.

Take a hollow tube, like a piece of a bamboo fishing rod, about a foot long and cut the top of it sloping like a Λ. Wrap a piece of thin sheet rubber (such as dentists use) round the top so as to leave a narrow slit at the very top of the Λ, to stand for the opening of the *glottis*. Tie the rubber on with a string. Now blow through the lower end of the tube and you will get a sound. Touch the vibrating rubber at different points with the sharp end of a pencil and you will get different sounds. (Try it.)

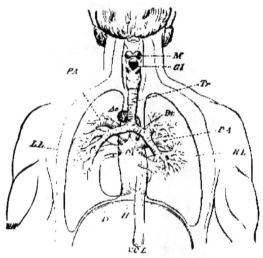

FIG. 308. Back view of the windpipe and lungs. In the picture the backbone is not shown. *M* is the mouth (seen from behind, as if the body were transparent); *Gl* is the *glottis* (part of the windpipe); *Tr* is the windpipe; *LL* is the left lung; *RL* is the right lung; *Br* (on both sides) are the *bronchial tubes* (the ends of the windpipe); *H* is the heart. (Point these parts out with a pin for a pointer.)

Breathing (*Respiration*). — We breathe air (which is a mixture of oxygen gas and nitrogen gas). It goes into the lungs through the *bronchial tubes* and mixes with the blood which takes out all the oxygen it needs. The used-up matters in the blood (mostly carbon) combine with some of the supply of oxygen and make carbonic acid gas. This poisonous gas we breathe *out* about 18 or 20 times a minute (oftener for children).

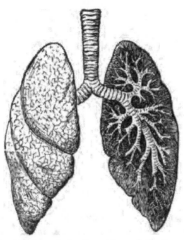

FIG. 309. The lungs and the branches of the bronchial tubes.

Experiment.—Take a very small piece of *quick lime* and drop it into a little water at the bottom of a good-sized jar. It will bubble fiercely and become hot (the water is combining with the lime). When it is cool filter a clear solution—lime-water—into a tumbler. Now let one of the pupils breathe into the lime-water through a clean glass tube. The water will become turbid. Why? Because the carbonic acid gas of the breath has combined chemically with the lime to form carbonate of lime which is insoluble in water. Let the water settle. Pour off the surplus liquid, leaving only the semi-solid mass. Add vinegar. It will displace the carbonic acid gas which will go off in bubbles.

Movements of the Chest in Breathing.—

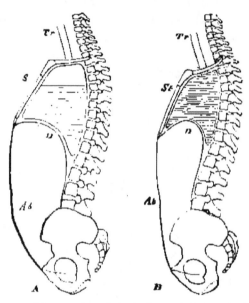

FIG. 310. *A* is a section of the body as air is breathed *in.* *B*, as air is breathed *out.* *Tr* is the windpipe, *D* is the diaphragm, *Ab* the muscular walls of the abdomen. The chest, abdomen, breastbone (*St*) and ribs move when you breathe.

Plenty of Fresh Air is Necessary to Life. — If there is not enough fresh air, the blood will not get enough oxygen and the body will starve. Many headaches come from lack of fresh air. Go out of doors and they will disappear.

Good ventilation is supplying plenty of air to the rooms in which we live—study-rooms, living-rooms, sleeping-rooms. Always have fresh air and plenty

of it, and arrange the doors and windows so as not
to make "draughts" of air blowing directly on
you.

Sneezing and Coughing.—Draw a deep breath and fill the
lungs, and then force out the air through your nose. (Try it.)
Now let some one tickle the inside of your nostril with the fine
end of a feather. You sneeze; you *have* to sneeze; you cannot
help it. Filling the lungs full and then forcing the air through
the nose, *when you cannot help doing so*, is sneezing. Coughing
is forcing the air out through the mouth.

*Breathe Through Your Nose, Not Through Your
Mouth.*—Keep your mouth shut when you breathe,
even when you are running. Air that gets to the
lungs should be warmed by passing through the
passages of the nose, not taken in directly through
the mouth, in which case it is likely to be too cold.
The little hairs inside the nostril act as strainers,
and catch dust that ought not to get into the lungs.

The nervous system consists of the Brain, the
Spinal cord (or marrow) and a set of *nerves* spreading all over the body.

The brain is a complicated mass of very sensitive
matter that fills the upper part of the skull. It
weighs about 4 pounds. (A butcher will show you
a sheep's brain if you ask him.) It has three main
parts: the *cere'brum*, or large brain (in this part all
the most important things we do are decided); the
cer'ebel'lum, or lesser brain (this part arranges our
motions so that our muscles work together in har-
mony). If this part is removed from a bird's skull
it can still see, hear, eat and fly—but it cannot fly

straight nor balance itself) ; the *medul'la* (this part tells the lungs when to breathe, the heart when to beat, the mouth when to swallow or to cough, etc. It manages the *involuntary muscles* (see page 309).

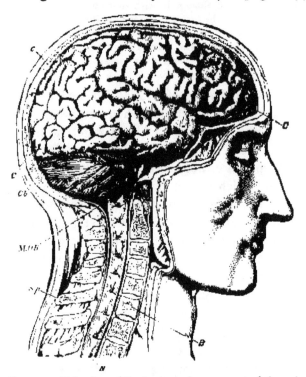

FIG. 311. Side view of the brain and upper part of the spinal cord. *CCC*, is the furrowed *cere'brum* or larger brain ; *Cb*, the *cer'ebel'lum* or lesser brain ; *M, Ob*, the *medulla oblongata*, a complex nerve-center ; *N*, the *spinal cord* and its nerves.

The brain — somehow, no one knows exactly how — remembers what you have seen and heard,

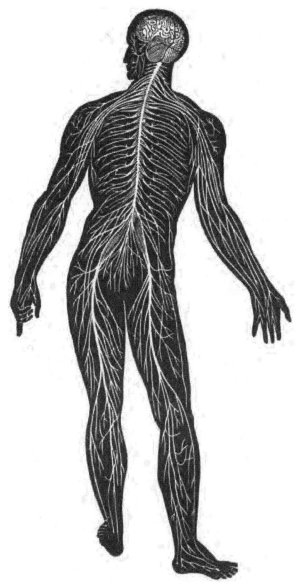

FIG. 312. The brain, the spinal cord, the nerves. (p. 335)

knows what you are seeing and hearing now, decides what is best to do now, and sends out orders
through the *nerves* for the muscles to do it — and
they obey.

The brain is connected with the spinal marrow, and nerves
branch off in every direction (very many more than are drawn in
the picture).

The nerves are fine hollow tubes filled with
something like clear jelly. They run all over the
body as telegraph wires run from a central office.

*The Nerves Carry Messages To and From the
Brain.*—The brain acts as if it were a central telegraph station. Some nerves, like telegraph wires,
carry messages *inwards* to the brain, and others
carry messages *outwards* from the brain. Suppose
some one pricks your finger with a pin. The pin
touches a nerve. This nerve carries a message to
the brain and says "I am touched." The brain
sends a message to the muscle of your finger along
another nerve and says "move away." The muscle shortens and the finger moves away from the
pin. All the most important bodily actions of men
and animals are decided in this way.

This can be proved. We know exactly which nerve takes the
message from the finger to the brain, and which nerve brings the
order out. We can cut them with a knife, if we choose.

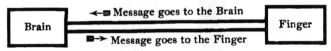

Suppose we cut the top nerve, and then prick the finger.
The finger cannot send any message to the brain because its

nerve is cut. The brain will know nothing about the pin-prick because it has received no message. It will send out no order. Or, suppose we leave the top nerve whole, and cut the lower one. Now prick the finger. The finger will send a message to the brain and say "I am touched." The brain will know it. It will try to send out a message "move away," but as the nerve is cut the message cannot go that way.

Paralysis.—All the nerves that are in the leg unite near the hip into three or four large cords which join the spinal cord near its lower end. If these nerves are accidentally broken at the ankle, the foot is *paralyzed;* it cannot feel or move. But the rest of the leg is all right. If these nerves are broken at the knee, the lower leg is paralyzed ; the upper leg can still feel and move. If they are broken at the hip, the whole leg is paralyzed. If the nerves of the leg are not injured, but the spinal cord is wounded, all the body below the wound is paralyzed,

Spinal Cord	Hip	Knee	Foot
Omaha	Chicago	Albany	Boston

If a telegraph line from Omaha to Boston is cut beyond Albany, then Boston can get no messages ; if it is cut beyond Chicago, then Albany and Boston suffer ; if it is cut between Omaha and Chicago, then no messages can be sent to any part of the line beyond the break.

N. B.—We do not purposely cut nerves to try such experiments, but men sometimes meet with accidents that cut their nerves in two. In all such cases the doctors have noticed just what has been described.

If the whole cerebrum is cut out of an animal, a frog for instance, all its intelligence and will goes. It remains alive, but it is a mere machine that breathes, whose heart beats, etc. It can no longer *choose* what it *likes* to do. If the frog's legs are touched it moves them (not because it wants to do so, but because it cannot help it—just as you cannot help sneezing when the inside of your nose is tickled).

Such movements are made when messages are sent out from the nerve-centers in the spinal-cord, which control the beating of the heart, breathing, coughing, sneezing and all actions that

22

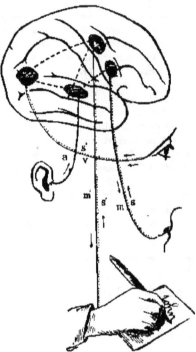

Fig. 313. A sketch to show how one set of nerves takes messages *to* certain centers in the brain, and how another set of
nerves carries orders *from* these brain-centers *to* the mouth, the
hand, etc. *V* (in the back part of the brain) is the center for
seeing; *A* (connected with ear) is the center for hearing; *E* is
the center for speaking; *W* is the center for moving the muscles
of the hand in writing. If a sound comes to the ear a message
is sent *in* to *A*. If a picture is seen by the eye a message is sent
in to *V*. If you wish to speak a message is sent *out* from *E* to
the lips. If you wish to write a message is sent *out* from *W* to
the hand. It is as if the brain were the central telegraph office in
which there are many operators at *V*, *W*, *A*, *E*, etc. When one of
them receives a message coming *in* he tells the others what messages to send *out*. The messages are sent *out* and the hand or the leg
or the lips obey the messages they receive. The messages come
in along the nerves *s*, *s'*; they go *out* along the nerves *m*, *m'*. ·

must be done whether you will or no—*reflex-actions* as they are called. The *involuntary muscles* are controlled by centers in the spinal-cord.

Reflex-Action.—Experiment: Sit on a chair and cross your right leg over your left one. Now take a book and tap your right leg with it gently, just below the knee-cap. A short time after the tap your right leg will kick out, whether you will to do so or not. A set of nerves of the knee takes a message to the spinal cord (not to the brain), "I am struck." The spinal cord telegraphs back, "Kick then." The spinal-cord does all the work. The time between the tap on the knee and the kick is taken up by the two messages travelling two ways and by the action of the muscles of the leg. (Try it.)

Nerve Centers.—The nerve centers that control such movements as sneezing, etc., are in the spinal cord. Other parts of the brain are centers for seeing, centers for hearing, for speaking, for moving the hand, for moving the leg, for remembering, etc.

The different centers were discovered by noticing what happened when men's brains were injured by accident. If one part was injured, the man could not speak, though he could hear, see and move. If another part was injured, he could not move, though he could see, hear and speak. In this way it has been found that in certain tracts of the brain the powers of memory, of sight, of hearing, etc., reside.

How a particular spot in the brain makes us remember no one knows; but it is certainly so, for if this part of the brain is injured we cannot remember anything; as long as it is not injured, we can.

Sleep. — Plenty of sound sleep is necessary to give the brain rest. Children need about ten hours sleep. Seven or eight are needed by grown-up persons. During sleep the muscles rest as well as the brain, the heart beats more slowly, the breathing is more quiet, the temperature of the body is lower.   The whole of your body does not go to sleep at one and the same time.   First the eyes go to sleep, then the smell, then the taste, then the hearing, and last of all, the touch.   When you wake your touch wakes first, then your hearing, taste, smell and sight in that order.

Death.—Parts of our bodies are dying all the time ; the outer skin, for instance. It dies and is rubbed off. Parts are dying all the time and being revived all the time ; the blood-corpuscles, for instance. They lose their oxygen, which is their life, but get new oxygen from the lungs. A very bad burn kills the arm and it may wither and die, though the rest of the body lives on very well without it. The whole body dies a natural death when the heart stops sending good blood, or when the lungs stop breathing. So long as the heart and lungs are doing their work the body is alive. When they stop, either through disease or as the result of some injury or violence, the body dies.

Decomposition.—The body is built up of chemical elements. So long as it is alive the *life* within us (whatever that may be— no one knows) has the wonderful power of making each element do some useful work in building up bone, muscle, fat, in making blood or tissue. When the *life* is gone, when the body is dead, the chemical substances of which it is made go back to form parts of the earth from which they originally came. Atoms that once formed part of Julius Cæsar's body were taken into the soil and may now be part of the clay of some vase in a collection of Roman pottery, or they may stop a hole in some workman's cabin to keep the wind away as Shakspeare has said :

" Imperious Cæsar, dead and turned to clay
    Might stop a hole to keep the wind away :
    Oh, that that earth, which kept the world in awe,
    Should patch a wall to expel the winter's flaw."

The Senses.—" The five senses " are sight, hearing, smell, taste, touch.   There is at least one more

—the temperature-sense. You can tell whether a piece of iron is hotter than your hand without touching it and with your eyes shut. It is possible that birds and fish have special senses that men do not have. They seem to know their way home in cases where men would be quite lost.

We Know the Outside World Through Our Senses. — Things in the external world are known to us only through our senses. We see, hear and touch them. If we are blind or deaf we know much less than we otherwise should know. The nerves of sight, hearing, touch, bring messages from things in the world to our brain. Our brain thinks about these messages and decides what is to be done. If anything is to be done it sends messages to the muscles and they do it.

We often make wrong judgments about the messages that our senses send to the brain, as is proved by the experiments on page 346. It is not certain, then, that we always know the outside world correctly. Any one of us is much more certain about anything he hears or sees if he knows that some one else sees or hears it in the same way. The things in the outside world that we are most certain about are the ones that a very great number of people have seen and described a very great number of times.

Personality. — There is one thing that we know without asking anyone's help. Each one of us knows that he exists; that he is a person. So long as his mind and brain go on thinking, and reflecting about his thoughts, he is sure that *he* exists, any way.   No other animal but man thinks about his own thoughts.   A dog *may* notice that snow is white, besides being cold; that chalk is white, besides being hard; that milk is white, besides being good to drink.   It is possible, though not likely, that when he is thinking of milk to drink he may remember that milk is white.   But no dog ever imagined such a thing as *whiteness*, nor thought that milk, chalk and snow, different as they are in most respects, at least are alike in this one respect — namely of whiteness.   Most animals are, in a large degree, machines—they act without thinking about their acts.   Men also do many acts in a machine-like way.   For instance if some one pretends to aim a blow at your eye, you wink — you cannot help doing it — although you know very well you are not going to be hit.   If the inside lining of your nose is tickled with a feather you *have* to sneeze.   You cannot help it any more than a locomotive can help going when the steam is turned on.   When the *stimulus* (the exciting feather-touch) comes the action *must* follow.   If an insect-eating plant is touched, even by a stick, it shuts its leaves with a snap.   If an oyster feels anything floating over its open shell it shuts up whether the thing is good for food or not.   If a fly lights on your forehead you brush it off even when you are asleep. You are like the lower animals in this machine-like response to a stimulus. But you are very different from them in your power to think, to remember your thoughts and to reflect about them; in your power to know what is honorable, what is good, and what is right. That kind of knowledge makes you a person, and it makes you *responsible*. If you have such powers it is your duty to use them rightly.

Cells. — If we keep on dividing any part of the body of an animal (or a plant) as long as possible we find, at last, that it is made of *cells*. A cell is a little box with walls, filled on the inside with living *protoplasm* (something like the white of egg). The bones, the tissues, the muscles, the blood, the nerves are made of small cells. The smallest are about $\frac{1}{3500}$ of an inch in diameter. Even the largest are very small. Each cell is alive, that is, the protoplasm inside it is alive. Many cells (as the white corpuscles of your blood — see page 327) can move and do grow by division just as the single-celled animal, the *Amœba*, moves and grows.[1] Every such cell grows; divides over and over again to make others; by and by decays; and finally dies. While it is alive it does work of some kind and takes food. If it is a muscle-cell it helps to build up muscle. If it a tissue-cell it builds up tissue. Sometimes, in case of need, a cell will take up work not its own. If, for instance, a muscle is injured, tissue cells will help to build it up.

The Human Body is a Colony of Cells. — The human body is something like a great colony or

[1] See Book VI, Zoölogy, page 188.

ant-hill of different kinds of cells each one working
to help the colony to live and prosper. Some cells
make food, others carry it where it is needed (the
blood-cells), others build up bones and muscles,
others transmit messages (the nerve-cells). In the
spinal-cord there are committees of cells (nerve-
centers) that manage all matters like breathing,
sneezing, etc., without troubling the brain with such
little things; and finally in the brain there are
higher committees of cells (nerve-centers) each at-
tending to its own work. One brain-committee
attends to hearing, another to seeing, another to
touching, and other committees help us to remember, to make judgments, to be affectionate or angry.
A tree is something like a colony of coral animals.[1]
The body of a man is a much more complicated
colony — something like a great city with all kinds
of persons in it, each kind doing one sort of useful
work, and all working together to make the whole
body healthy and strong.

The Human Will Governs the Body. — Back of
all this there is your personality; the thing, whatever it is, that makes you *you* and not someone else.
This can decide what is right, and *will* to do it. It
can wish to do right. It can try, and if it fails one
time, it can keep on trying. Your body, with all
its wonderful arrangements, is, after all, of no
special good unless it is directed by a will that
means to do right — to be true, brave and kind. It

[1] See Book VII, Botany, page 246.

is *your* business to have that kind of a will : it is the business of your body to do what *you* tell it to do.

Seeing: The Eye.—

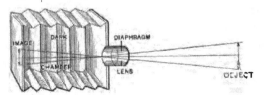

FIG. 314. How the image of an object is seen on the ground glass of a photographic camera. Rays of light from the arrow **➡→** pass through the lens of the camera, through the dark chamber, and make an *image* (see Book I., Astronomy, p. 12) on the ground glass.

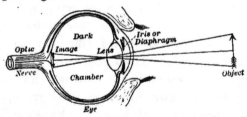

FIG. 315. How the image of an object is seen on the back part of the eye (on the *retina*). Rays of light from the arrow **➡→** pass through the lens of the eye, through the dark chamber of the eye and make an image on the *retina*. The retina is covered with nerves and these send messages to the brain "I am touched by light—by light of such a brightness and of such a color." The brain receives all these messages and makes up its mind what sort of a thing is seen. *It is the brain that does the real seeing, not the eye.* The eye only forms the image. The brain decides what it is.

Experiments.—Wipe the tongue dry and put a bit of sugar on the tip. It will not taste sweet till the sugar is dissolved.

Take two one-pound weights from a grocer's scales (both iron or both lead and of the same size). Heat one of them and leave the other one cold. The cold weight will seem the heavier.

Smell: the Nose.—The mucous membrane that lines the nostrils is the organ of smell. Nerves from each nostril run to the brain. A piece of camphor is all the while giving off little particles. Some of these touch the ends of small nerves in the nostrils and other nerves carry the news to the brain. *It is really the brain that does the smelling, not the nose.*

Taste: the Tongue. — The upper side of the tongue is covered with thousands of little elevations under which are nerves — sometimes nerves of touch, sometimes nerves of taste. When sugar is put on the tongue these nerves telegraph to the brain. *It is really the brain that tastes, not the tongue.* What we call tastes (flavors) are often not tastes but smells. Hold your nostrils tight and chew a piece of cinnamon. You will have a hot sensation but no *taste* till the nostrils are opened. (Try it.) Remember this when you have medicines to take. Hold your nostrils tight shut, and in most cases you can not taste what you are swallowing.

BOOK IX: THE EARLY HISTORY OF MANKIND.[1]

BOOK VIII, *The Human Body*, tells how the body of a man is made, what work it does, and how his mind directs his body what to do. It gives an account of one man—of any man taken by himself.

[1] Note to Teachers: The young reader commencing this book knows very well the customs and beliefs of his own time and of his own country. He does not know, however, that each and every one of them is rooted in the remote past. It is here sought to give, so far as space allows, a picture of society which will suggest to him the origins of human customs, arts, governments, religions, and to trace their developments up to the historic period. In other books he will, hereafter, read the written history to which these pages are introductory. In some few cases it has seemed wise to treat of matters well within the historical period. It is of the first importance that the pupil should connect what is given here with what is already familiar to him. It will assist him to understand human progress if he sees, side by side, the boats of barbarous peoples and a modern steamship; or the fetish of African negroes and a modern cathedral. Many illustrations of this sort are given. Occasionally, however, stress has been purposely laid on the unfamiliar—and for the reason that abstract ideas are often best illustrated by examples quite out of one's daily experience. One can understand the religious beliefs of savages far better if they are compared with those of Moslems or Buddhists than if the comparison is made with Christianity. The endeavor has been to choose the form of presentation that gives the simplest notion both of the methods of ethnology and of its results.

349

But men do not live by themselves. Savage men live in little bands somewhat as animals do; barbarians live in tribes and clans; civilized men are gathered together in nations — the German, the English, the American, for instance.

FIG. 319. A Sioux (Dakota) chief in full dress; eagle feathers in his hair, his dress embroidered with beads.

Ethnology is the science that treats of men living in companies—in small companies like the family, in larger companies like the tribe, in great companies like nations. Men are social creatures; ethnology describes how they live in societies, what laws they make, how they live in peace and war, how they invent tools and weapons, what kind of family life they lead, what sort of government they have, what kind of religion they believe in, and so on.

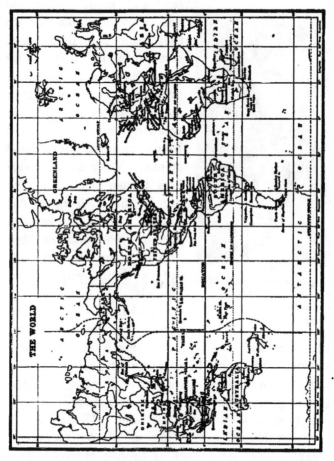

FIG. 320. A map of the World. When a place is spoken about in this book turn to this map and see if you know where the place is; if it is not given here find it on some larger map.

Savages live by eating wild plants and animals, and usually roam from place to place in

search of food. They do
not cultivate plants nor do
they tame animals (except
sometimes the dog). The
Australians are savages,
and there are many other
such peoples.   Their
weapons are clubs, spears,
bows and arrows, and
stones. They do not know
how to use metals. They
are in the *stone-age*. All
human beings know the
use of *fire* and in this
and in many other things,

FIG. 321. An Australian
savage with a kangaroo that
he has killed with his boomerang.

are a long way above
animals.

Barbarians cultivate
plants for food — wheat,
maize or barley — and store it up until the next
season. They live in huts or tents, usually in villages. They often have herds of cattle, horses,
sheep, goats, camels, and so they generally have a
supply of milk and meat at hand. Most tribes of
this sort know how to use metals for tools and
weapons — either copper or bronze or iron. The
North American Indians, four hundred years ago,
were all barbarians, some of them in the stone-age,

some in the metal-age, some living in tents, some in Pueblo villages.

Half-Civilized Peoples.—Peoples that are more intelligent than barbarians are called civilized. Some of them, like the peasants of Eastern Russia may be only half-civilized and others like the inhabitants of Europe and the United States wholly so. There is a long step between the barbarian and the civilized man, between the wild tribes of African negroes and the Egyptians who built great temples and pyramids, cultivated farms, kept written accounts, manufactured glass, fine pottery, jewelry and so on. A tribe that knows how

FIG. 322. An African negro woman doing field work. In most barbarous tribes the women cultivate the ground while the men engage in war or hunting.

to read and write is civilized. They canno: know how to write without, at the same time, knowing a great many other things as well.

The Stone-Age.—Men are said to be in the stone-age when their best weapons and tools are made of stone ; in the *bronze-age*, when their best weapons

23

and tools are made of bronze ; in the *iron-age* when
their best weapons are made of iron.   The Hawaiians, for instance, were in the stone-age until the
English gave them iron.   The Red Indians of Lake
Superior were in the stone-age until they discovered

FIG. 323. A group of Hindus (India). They are intelligent
and educated after their own fashion, refined, polite, gentle.

copper-mines, and in the copper-age till the white
men came to America and gave them iron weapons
and tools.

Men have lived on the Earth at least a hundred
thousand years.   At first they were hunters and

fishers. Their weapons were of wood, bone or
stone. At least ten thousand years ago some men
(the Egyptians, for instance) cultivated farms,
raised flax, grapes, and grain. The men of the
bronze-age, at least five thousand years ago, had
axes, chisels, sickles, knives, spears, etc., made of
bronze, which is an alloy of copper and tin. Before
that time some men had weapons and tools of copper.

FIG. 324. People of Eastern Europe, etc. Counting from the
left, Nos. 1 and 2 are from Georgia (find it on the map of
Europe); No. 4 is an Albanian; No. 5 is a woman from Iceland
(a Dane by descent); No. 6 is Russian; No. 7 a Roumanian;
Nos. 8 and 9 a Polish man and woman.

These early men made necklaces, rings, buttons,
and bracelets out of metals — copper, gold and silver.
Some nations knew how to write, then. Some men
began to work in iron about the same time.

Progress of Mankind. — All the people now on the globe are either savage, barbarous or civilized. The progress (improvement) of mankind is through these three states, or steps. So far as we know every tribe or people was once (it may be very long ago) savage; most tribes or peoples have progressed (improved) until they have made the first step from savage life to barbarian life; many tribes and peoples have progressed until they have made another step, too, from barbarism to civilization.

FIG. 325. Savages in the Philippine Islands hunting with bows and arrows.

For instance, there are now very few *savages* in the world, very few tribes that live by eating wild plants and animals and that have no houses or villages. Yet there are some; the Australian savages, the Veddahs of Ceylon, some South American Indians, etc., are like that.

FIG. 326. Eskimo family from Labrador.

There are a great many *barbarians* in the world even to-day, that is people who have cattle, houses, villages, but who have no idea of civilized life, of an alphabet, of reading and writing and so forth. The negro tribes in the interior of Africa, the Eskimo, some Indians of South America, some of the Red Indians of North America and many other tribes are barbarians. Usually a tribe becomes more civilized as time goes on. It improves. There are some cases, however, when the " progress" is backward, when the tribe becomes *less*

civilized.   Nearly all the people you will see in
your lifetime are civilized, or at least half-civilized.

FIG. 327. Filipino family—Island of Luzon.   An upland farm
and its buildings belonging to the Igorrotes in the island of
Luzon, Philippines.   Notice the warrior in the foreground with
his spear and shield.   He is ready to fight to protect his property.

There are about 1500 millions of people in the
whole world to-day and about 200,000,000 of them
are savages or barbarians — about three times as
many barbarians as there are inhabitants in the
United States.

Origin of Mankind.—We do not know anything for certain
about the first men ; they have left no records.   But it is probable that the first men lived on the Eastern Continent, and came
into America through Alaska which was, long ago, connected
with Asia.   We may guess that there were men on the Earth
something like 300,000 years ago and that our own Continent

was peopled by men of Mongolian stock—by men not very
unlike the Mongols—about the time of the Glacial epoch—perhaps 100,000 years ago.

FIG. 328. An educated Filipino native.

*So far as we know every Tribe in the World was
once Savage.* — When Julius Cæsar (a civilized
Roman) landed in England, B.C. 55 — nearly two
thousand years ago — the inhabitants were barbarians. They were called Britons by the Romans
and their country was called Britannia. The ancestors of the Britons were the Celts, and they
were savages.

The ancestors of the now civilized Frenchmen
were savage tribes called *Gauls*. The ancestors of

the civilized Germans were savage tribes — *Teutons* and others. The ancestors of the civilized Hungarians were savage tribes from Asia, called *Huns*. The ancestors of the civilized Egyptians of 6,000 years ago were half-civilized people who lived in cities at least 10,000 years ago. Before them were barbarians, and before them savages. Every tribe and nation in the world was once savage.

The Celts of England were still savage when the Egyptians had become civilized. The North American Indians were barbarians when Columbus landed (A.D., 1492). The Inca Indians of Peru were civilized when they were conquered by the Spaniards under Pizarro (A.D., 1524). They were in the bronze age, they did not know the use of iron, to be sure, but in many ways they were as civilized as the Spaniards themselves.

Cannibals.—Savages in many parts of the world have the notion that they can acquire bravery by eating the hearts of ferocious animals—tigers, etc.; swiftness by eating the legs of swift animals—deer and antelopes—and so on. Hindu drivers put the eyes of owls in the food of their elephants to make them see well at night. Some wild tribes eat part of the bodies of the men, especially of the brave men, that they have captured in battle, or else their priests and chiefs eat for the whole tribe. The famous English explorer, Captain Cook, was killed by the natives of Hawaii in 1779; they admired his bravery, and the Hawaiian high priest, whose name was *Ii*, ate a part of Captain Cook's heart in order that the whole nation might thus become brave and wise.

How we can tell the Previous Conditions of a People.—In a hundred thousand years from now the city of New York may be a heap of ruins covered by the soil, just as some great cities of Egypt now are. If a man in the year A.D. 100,000 digs in the soil where New York now is he will find all kinds of things buried there which

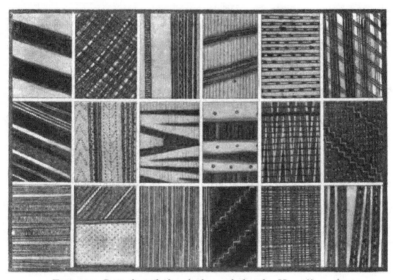

FIG. 329. Samples of the cloth made by the Hawaiians from the inner bark of trees. It is very soft and flexible, woven in beautiful patterns and of soft brown and red colors.

will tell him what sort of people we were. He will find iron and steel tools and machines — steam engines, pieces of fine glass and china, brass tablets with writing on them, columns from great buildings, parts of pianos and organs, leaves out of printed books, fragments of marble statues and so forth.

Can you imagine a man who never died but always wandered to and fro on the Earth? A French poet tells what such a man saw every time he visited a certain spot. The man says:

When I first arrived in this place, riding in my chariot, I saw a great city, with its walls, workshops and palaces. Men were running to and fro. I asked one of them how long that city had been in that spot. He answered with pride: It has always been here. It is my country.

Five thousand years passed by,
Again I visited that spot.

Walls, palaces, temples—all were gone. The sun shone down on green meadows where a single shepherd was tending his sheep. I asked him how long these meadows had been there. He answered: They have been here forever and always.

Five thousand years passed by,
Again I visited that spot.

A vast forest covered the plain; great trees and vines grew in the silence and sheltered packs of wild beasts. I asked a solitary hunter how long the forest had been there. He answered: These oaks are centuries old; the forest has been here forever and always.

Five thousand years passed by,
Again I visited that spot.

It was an ocean now. On its waves a fisherman was riding in his little boat. I asked him how long since the forest had been covered by the sea. He answered: The sea is the oldest thing in the world; it has always been here.

Five thousand years passed by,
Again I visited that spot.

It was a desert now. Waves of sand were where the ocean waves had been. The desert stretched further than the eye could reach. I asked a camel-driver in the caravan how long the desert had been there. He answered: The desert is eternal; it has been here forever and always.

Five thousand years passed by,
Again I visited that spot.

There was another city in that spot! Walls, workshops, palaces. Once more I asked the busy merchants how long that city had been there. They answered: It has always been here; it is our country.

And I laughed in the faces
Of my Aryan forefathers.

FIG. 330. Pottery made by North American Indians in former times. The three pieces at the top were made by the Zuñis of New Mexico; the other three by Indians who once lived in Georgia and Indiana. These Indians had leisure to think of something else than merely getting enough food to eat, and they used their leisure in making pottery of good shapes and in painting it in patterns that they thought beautiful. The idea of beauty had been born in them.

Excavations.—If we dig at almost any place in Egypt or Greece we find something that tells us

that men used to live there.[1]   The same thing is
true for nearly every part of the world.   We know
almost as much about it now, as its people knew,
then.   If we find fish hooks made of bone, axes and
clubs and arrow heads made of stone, but no metal,
no pottery, we can say that the people who made
those things lived in the stone-age; that they were
savages.   If we find weapons and tools of copper or
bronze or iron we can say they lived in the copper
age, the bronze age, the iron age.   If there are
charred bones of oxen, we can say that the people
used cattle for food and understood how to make a
fire.   Such excavations (diggings) nearly always
show some human remains, especially in Europe
and Asia where men have lived a long time.

Archæology is the science that treats of the relics and remains
that man has left upon the earth, particularly the remains that
were left by men who lived in ancient times before there was
any written or printed history.   An *archæologist* is a man that
studies such things, just as an *antiquary* is a man that studies
the relics of men who lived in early times after history began to
be written.   Men that lived in the days before written history
begins—thousands of years ago—are called *pre-historic men*.

How to Measure Time in the Ancient History of Mankind.—
We can make a good guess in many cases how long ago the men
lived who made and used the tools we find.   For instance, in
Denmark, the forests are now mostly beech trees.   Underneath
the peat-bogs[2] there are still to be found many stems and roots
of oak trees and deeper down there are many stems and roots of
pine trees.   For thousands of years Denmark has been covered
by beech forests; for thousands of years before that, it was cov-

[1] We now know almost as much about Pompeii (see page 163)
as the Romans did when they were living in it.
[2] See page 170.

ered with oak forests; for thousands of years before that it was covered with forests of pine.

Now-a-days the Danes cut down their beech trees with steel axes; among the oak tree stumps bronze axes are very often found; among the pine stumps stone axes are very often found. Geologists and botanists can tell us pretty nearly how old each of the forests is; therefore we know about how long ago the Danes lived who used bronze axes (they were in the Bronze Age); and how long ago the Danes lived who used stone axes (they were in the Stone Age).

The stone axes that are found in the very lowest depths are rude and badly made; the stone axes found in higher levels are much more neatly fashioned; the bronze axes improve in shape and workmanship as you go upwards. This proves that the people themselves were learning all through these thousands and thousands of years.

Along with stone axes and the stumps of fir trees we find the bones of the mammoth, the rhinoceros, the hippopotamus, the lion. That proves that in those ancient days all those wild animals were found in Denmark. There are no living mammoths now. And there are no lions nearer than Africa and Asia. But in that old time they were plentiful in Denmark, in France and in England. There were many grizzly-bears and musk-oxen in England then. Now there are none nearer than the Rocky Mountains and Athabasca.

Cave-men. — Savages that lived in very ancient days—about the time of the Glacial Epoch [1] (perhaps 100,000 years ago) often used caves for houses. Many of their caves have been discovered and searched. The dirt on the floor contained rude stone hatchets, bone spear-heads, awls, arrow-heads, along with the bones of the reindeer, the bear, the tiger, etc. The bones are often split open lengthwise so as to get the marrow from them, and black-

[1] See pages 147, 178.

ened in the fire.   Even the *cave-dwellers* had fire, then.

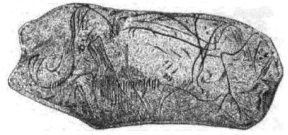

FIG. 331. A drawing of a mammoth scratched on a mammoth's tusk by a pre-historic man.

Pictures of Animals Drawn by Pre-Historic Men.
In these very caves there have been found rude carvings of animals scratched by the cave-dwellers

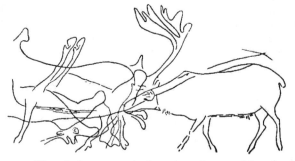

FIG. 332. The reindeer : scratched on a bone by a pre-historic man.

on ivory or stone.   These are the very oldest pictures in the world, thousands and thousands of years older than any pictures yet found in Egypt.   The men that made them were living almost like wild

animals—hid in caves, clothed in skins, in terror of
ferocious beasts, often hungry—but they were very
far above even the wisest animal. They could
make a fire; they could draw pictures of the beasts
they hunted. The strange thing — the important
thing—is that they wished to do it.

Pre-historic men are those that lived before
written history began. We learn what kind of men
they were by the remains that they have left. There
is no other way.

Remains of Ancient Peoples.—In order to understand how much we can learn from the remains
left by an ancient people it is worth while to study a
particular case; and therefore a little is set down
here about the ancient history of the Egyptians.

FIG. 333. One of the pyramids near Cairo in Egypt. It was
built about B. C. 2,000, four thousand years ago, as a tomb for
the King. It took 100,000 men 30 years to build this tomb.

Early History of the Egyptians.—We know more about the early history of the Egyptians than about that of any other people. At least 10,000 years ago the Egyptians near the mouth of the Nile lived in great cities. At least 7,000 years ago the fertile valley of the Nile was filled with a nation under one king. Memphis — the capital city—was protected from the yearly floods of the river by a huge stone dyke built so strongly that part of it still exists.

We begin to know a great deal about the Egyptians of B. C. 2,000—about 4,000 years ago.

The pyramids, built by three kings of Egypt, are still standing near Cairo, as solid as ever. The largest pyramid is nearly 500 feet high and was built for King Cheops. The covering stones were so nicely jointed that a hair could hardly be put between two blocks. Inside of the huge mass there was a long passage way leading to a few little rooms. All the rest was solid. One of these little rooms was the tomb of the king and the whole pyramid was his monument. The passageway within the pyramid pointed exactly at the North Star.[1]

The Egyptian priests of 4000 years ago were skilled astronomers as well as good architects.

Near the pyramids is the *Sphinx*, a huge statue as high as a five-story house, made from a single stone. It was an idol, or image, of one of the gods whom the Egyptians worshipped — the god of the Rising Sun ; and the Sphinx is older than the pyra-

[1] See Book I, Astronomy, page 7.

mids. The Egyptian records say that it was in need of repairs 4000 years ago. These are only a sample of the wonderful buildings with which Egypt was filled. The inner walls of tombs were covered with spirited paintings and the outer walls of temples with carvings and statues.

FIG. 334. The Sphinx and one of the Pyramids of Egypt. They were built more than 4,000 years ago. The Sphinx is carved from a single stone and is older than the pyramids.

The fertility of Egypt depends upon supplying its farm lands with water. Near Memphis one of the kings built great dams 50 yards thick to make reservoirs for storing the needed water. On the

24

frontiers he built fortresses to keep back the hostile Nubians, and across the Isthmus of Suez a wall for

FIG. 335. A part of the great wall in the northern part of China. It is 1,500 miles long—as far as from New York to Galveston, as Omaha from San Francisco—and was built to keep out the Tartars about 200 B. C., 2,100 years ago. It goes over mountains and valleys along the boundary line.

defense, just as the Chinese built a wall to keep out the Tartars.

Life of the Egyptians. — The Egyptians, more than 4,000 years ago, were civilized. Their pictures and statues tell us everything about their daily life, just as a set of photographs might do. The rich

men lived in houses of several stories and had great
farms cultivated by peasants, or by slaves.

FIG. 336. Copy of a painting in bright colors on the walls of
a tomb in Thebes, in Egypt. The work was done about 1380
B. C., more than 3,000 years ago. It shows Nubian chiefs bringing presents of wine, fruits, cattle, a giraffe, etc., to the King of
Egypt (Pharaoh). Notice the hieroglyphic writing in different
parts of the picture. (See page 372.)

They ploughed their land with oxen dragging a
hooked plow. The seed was trodden in by the feet
of men. Wheat was thrashed by oxen who
trampled it out. The vine was cultivated and wine
was plenty. There were carpenters, masons,
makers of pottery, glass-makers, weavers, paper-
makers, and all kinds of mechanics who used tools
of stone and metal.

Rich men had libraries of books (manuscripts)
and librarians to take care of them. Some of their

books on geometry, medicine and religion have come down to us. Their religious poetry is very like the poetical parts of our Bible.

Egyptian Writing.—The oldest Egyptians that we know anything about could write. Their writing was, at first, *picture-writing*. When they wanted to say " man," they drew a sketch of a man; when they wanted to say " army," they made a picture of an army; when they wanted to say " tool," they drew the likeness of a tool. By and by, they changed their way of writing. They still used pictures; but a picture of a man no longer stood for *man*, but for its first sound *m*. A picture of an *army* stood for *a*; of a *tool* stood for *t*, and so on. Now they had a way of spelling new words. Three pictures—man, army, tool—spelled *mat*, and so on. They had an alphabet. Such pictures were called *hieroglyphics*. By and by they invented new ways by which they could write much faster. They used pens made out of split reeds, and they made writing paper out of the *papy'rus* plant.

The King.—The king (Pharaoh) was worshipped as a god on earth. He was absolute master of all his people. When he wanted a pyramid built they were obliged to work for him as long as necessary.

The Priests. — Egypt was full of temples, and thousands of priests directed the worship of the different gods (for there were many).

The Scribes (learned men).—There was another class of well-educated men who were bookkeepers,

clerks, engineers, architects, government officers.
They superintended the public works, were secretaries to governors, etc. Learning was the road to
power and riches in Egypt, just as it is in China
to-day.

The Army.—The king kept a large army—sometimes 400,000 men. Some were foot-soldiers
(infantry), some horse-soldiers (cavalry), and some
who drove the war chariots. Egypt was a rich
country surrounded by savage tribes, and had many
wars, therefore.

The People.—The Egyptian people were mostly
small farmers. They were gentle, merry, gay,
like children (and they still are so). Each man
paid a tax of part of his harvest every year, and
was obliged to work for the king in making roads,
building temples, and so forth, whenever he was
called upon.

Egyptian Commerce.—The Egyptians understood how to work in metals—iron, copper, gold,
silver. They wove fine linen and dyed it in
bright colors, made cups and plates of glass, fine
pottery, bronze and silver vases, jewelry, paper
and so forth. They sold these things to traders who
brought back gold from South Africa, ivory, copper,
wood from other countries. They were not sailors
themselves, nor travelers.

Religion of the Egyptians.—The Greek traveler
Herod'otus, who visited Egypt between 460 and 454
B. C. described them as the most religious of men.

Their principal god was the Sun.   There were many other gods and goddesses — some that were believed to make good harvests, some that brought the water in the Nile.   Each city had a god of its own, beside. Some of the gods were kind to men, they said, and some were cruel.   All of them were worshipped, good and bad alike.   They thanked the kind gods for their goodness, and prayed to the cruel gods for mercy.

Sacred Animals. — The lion, the crocodile, the bull, the cat, the beetle, and others beside, were sacred animals.   It was a crime to kill them, and they were worshipped like gods.

Mummies. — The Egyptians believed that when the body of a man died something in him—his soul, his spirit, his ghost — continued to live.   They thought the soul would be happier after death if the man's body were preserved, and so they embalmed the dead body and put it in a spacious tomb with food, water, clothing, etc., which, somehow, would be useful, they thought.

At first they believed that the soul, after death, stayed near the dead body.   Afterwards they came to think that souls went to some kingdom underground, near the sunset, and that each soul was judged before admission.   The actions that a man did during his lifetime were weighed in scales, they said, the good actions in one scale, the bad ones in another.   If the good actions weighed the most the man was admitted to an eternal, happy life.   If the man had been bad during his life the soul was punished and tortured, bitten by scorpions and serpents, and finally perished altogether.

How we Have Been Taught by Ancient Nations. The Egyptians and the people of Chaldea (a country whose chief city was Babylon) were very closely connected. The Jews who were captives in Egypt in the time of Moses, and in Babylon, were much influenced by the learning and beliefs of their masters. The account of the Deluge in the Bible is largely copied from the Chaldean records; Moses "was skilled in the learning of the Egyptians." Through the Bible of the Jews—the Old Testament —we, to-day, are influenced by the beliefs and traditions of Egypt and Chaldea. The early Greek philosophers and scientific men studied in Egypt, and Greek philosophy and science is the foundation of that of all Europe. Greek art is founded on the art of Egypt and the West of Asia, and our art is mostly derived from that of Greece.

An American boy may not have a drop of any blood in his veins except English. For a thousand generations his ancestors may have been Englishmen. Yet in his beliefs he is influenced by Asiatic or Egyptian peoples. His religion comes from Asia, the laws of his country are Roman and English and depend upon ideas of justice and right that were first invented in the Orient. His science is built upon Greek foundations, and the Greeks learned their science in Egypt. Our arts of life—farming, manufacturing, glass-making, metal-working—are developed from those of ancient peoples. If we follow the history of Egypt forwards it leads us to our own time and country and civilization.

FIG. 337. War dance of the Sioux (Dakota) Indians. Notice that one warrior is flourishing a stone war club while others have guns. Their faces are covered with war paint.

How to Study the History of Mankind.—If there were room enough in this little book, we might study the history of each nation separately. We might set down in order everything that is known about the English, the Americans, the Germans, the cultivated Greeks, Romans and Persians, the barbarous Tartars, the savage Australian natives, and so on. But there is not room, and we have to take another way.

Pictures that Show how each Nation Lives.—If we wish to know, for instance, what kind of people the Egyptians were there is no quicker way than to look at pictures that show the people of Egypt plowing, weaving, building; that show the statues and temples and pyramids they set up; their buildings; and the dress and manners of their men and women. The pictures speak for themselves more

FIG. 338. A Chinese mandarin or officer of the government. He is well educated. None but educated men can become officials in China.

plainly than words. You have only to think what they mean.

In this book, then, a great many pictures are given, and under each picture a few words to help you to understand what the pictures mean. For instance, Fig. 388 gives a picture of a Chinese junk—one of the vessels that they built at least two

FIG. 339. King Lunalilo of Hawaii (died 1874). He was the last pure-blooded Hawaiian King.

thousand years ago, in which they made long voyages to India. Clearly, the Chinese of that time were civilized.

Again Fig. 321 is a picture of an Australian savage. He certainly lives very much like a wild animal, but he has invented a curious throwing stick, a boomerang, with which he kills wild animals. He knows how to cook his food with fire. The apes of South Africa fight by throwing cocoanuts at their enemies; but no animal knows how to light or to use a fire. The Australian savage, low as he is, is a very long way above any animal.

The pictures in this book have been chosen to explain the way in which all kinds of people live, but especially to show the life of America and its dependencies and neighbors, Hawaii, the Philippines, the West Indian Islands; and also especially to show the life of those nations of the Old World that have given us the most important ideas—Egypt, Greece, Italy, England, Germany.

Races of Mankind.—If you were to see a Chinaman, a Negro, an Hawaiian, a North American

Indian, an Englishman, all dressed alike and standing side by side, you would notice in a moment how different they are one from another. They belong to different *races of men* just as a Newfoundland, a Scotch terrier, a greyhound, belong to different races of dogs. When the five men are standing side by side it is easy to tell them apart.

Color of the Skin.—The Chinaman has a yellow skin, the Negro is black, the Hawaiian is brown, the Indian is red, the Englishman is white. The color of the skin is one mark of race.

Fig. 340. Negro and two negro women from the Loango Coast, Africa. Notice that all three are tattooed.

The color of the eyes corresponds, in a general way, to the color of the skin. Fair-skinned people usually have blue or gray eyes; dark brown people usually have brown eyes. Two thousand years ago the Romans described the Germans as people having tawny hair and blue eyes, and Germans are like that to-day.   Egyptian paintings of 4,000 years ago represent certain races very much as they are to-day (see Fig. 336).

FIG. 341. A cowboy of the western plains (United States).

The Shape of the Skull.—If you look directly downwards at the skulls of different races you will find that some are long and narrow (like the skulls of most Negroes); some are wide and thick (like the skulls of most Eskimos); and some are about half way between the two (like the skulls of most Europeans).   The jaws of most Negroes project much further forward than those of Europeans.   The shape of the skull is another sign of race.   People of the same race usually have skulls that are very much alike.

Shape of the Nose, Eyes, Lips.—Negros usually have a flat nose and thick lips; Eskimos have a

FIG. 342. An Eskimo boy from Baffin's Land.

flat nose; Chinese and Japanese have eyes set slantingly in the face.

The Hair.—The hair of the North American Indians is black, coarse, straight, and grows very long. The Negro's hair is curly like wool. The hair of an Englishman is generally rather wavy.

FIG. 343. A negro girl (Africa).

FIG. 344. An Australian savage.   Notice the tattooed scars
on his arm.

If a single hair is cut crosswise and looked at by the microscope you find that the hair of a Japanese is *round*, of a German *oval*, of a Negro a very long oval, and so on for other races. The hair is one of the very best marks of race.

Climate.—If you take a map of the world and write on it the names of the races that inhabit the different countries, you will see that race has something to do with climate. The natives of the tropical regions of the world in Asia, Africa and America are all dark skinned. Think of Africa, for instance.

FIG. 345. Indians of South America.

Along the equator and on both sides of it are Negroes — black people. Further south are the

Hottentot-Bushmen people. They have a narrow skull and frizzy hair, but their color is brown, not black.

FIG. 346. Japanese girls.

The brown people of the world generally live outside of the tropics. The yellow people live in China, Siam, etc. The white people are natives of temperate climates, though they travel everywhere. In the tropics it is easy to get enough to live on; there are plenty of fruits. Tropical races are lazy and idle. In the polar regions it is so very hard to live that when a man has once got enough to eat he has no spirit left to do anything else. In the tem-

FIG. 347. Bushmen from Cape Colony, Africa, dressed in white men's clothes.

perate zones it is sufficiently difficult to get enough to live on to keep men's energies wide awake; and not so difficult but that a man may have leisure. It

25

is the races of the temperate zones that have done the great things in the world's history. The Romans have made our laws; the Greeks have taught us science, and produced the greatest works of art; the Hindus, Persians, Egyptians, Jews have given us great ideas of religion and philosophy.

FIG. 348. Three Zulu warriors (Africa) with English guns.

Language.—Each nation has its own spoken language. All Germans speak the same language. The Dutch language, spoken in the Netherlands, is not unlike the German and not so very unlike English. The Dutchman says, *Hoe is het weder?* where we say *How is the weather?* He says *ik ben zeer koud*, where the Germans say *ich bin sehr kalt* (which would be, in English, *I be sore cold*).

These and many other words, in three languages, are so much alike that they prove some kind of cousinship between the Germans, the Dutch and ourselves. And, in fact, we know that the Dutch and Germans are both descendants of barbarian tribes of the north of Europe and that other descen-

Fig. 349. A German country girl spinning, just as our great grandmothers did, before spinning was done by machinery.

dants of the same tribes — the Angles and the Saxons — conquered parts of England in the fifth century. We know this from written history. Even if there were no such history the languages would prove that they are all related, and that the ancestors of Germans, Dutch and English spoke the same tongue.

The French language, the Spanish, the Portuguese, the Italian, the Roumanian are all very like the Latin language which was spoken by the ancient Romans.

When we compare the language of the people of ancient India — it is called *Sanskrit* — with Greek and Latin, we find that all three languages are alike in many ways.

Fig. 350. A man from Armenia in Turkey-in-Asia. He is white, like the Persians and like ourselves.

The Aryan People and Language.—The explanation of all this is simple. There was once, thousands of years ago a people dwelling somewhere in the southeastern parts of Europe, or in the northwestern parts of Asia, who all spoke a language called the *Aryan* language. The people are called *Aryans*. They were of fair complexion, they tilled the soil, kept flocks and herds, worked in metal, went forth in chariots to fight their enemies, made laws and obeyed them, worshipped gods who lived in the sky, in the sun, in fire, in rivers, they said; and reverenced their ancestors. Enough of their speech still remains as fossil words in modern lan-

guages to prove all this. From parts of old poems
and hymns of theirs we know what they believed.
We know that they kept oxen, horses and sheep,
that they tilled the ground and so on, because we
know the very words they used for oxen, sheep,
farming, etc.

FIG. 351. A Persian girl.

This people multiplied and at various times some
of them emigrated to new pasture lands. Some
went towards India; a branch went to Persia.
Where they went they carried their ancient laws and

customs, their habits and language with them.   In
new surroundings the language slowly changed.
The language of the Indian branch became Sanskrit.

FIG. 352. A modern Greek farmer with his gun.

The language of the Persian branch became
Persian.   Old Persian and Sanskrit are alike very
much as Dutch and English are alike.   Other parts
of the Aryan people took possession of lands in
Europe.   Some went to Greece, some to Italy,
some to Russia, some to Germany.   It took thousands of years for this scattering of the tribes and
during all this time the language of each tribe
slowly altered.   As they met new circumstances
they invented new words to describe them.   In the
new countries some new laws were needed.   But

some of the old laws and customs of the Aryans remain in modern European nations, and many of their old words and beliefs are ours even to-day.

FIG. 353. A Turkish lady in the streets of Constantinople.

Caste. — The Aryans who went to India were much fairer in complexion than the dark people who were there before them and whom they conquered. By and by all India was divided into classes called *castes* (caste means color in the Sanskrit language). The highest class were priests (Brahmins), the next class were warriors and kings, the next class were merchants, and the lowest of all — *outcasts* — did all the meanest work. In

other countries, too, there are classes of the same
sort, but they are most sharply marked in India.

FIG. 354. An Arab of the desert (Bedouin). The wild Arabs
have been very much the same for thousands of years. There
is little chance to improve when you live in a desert. Still,
they are very far above barbarians. They are religious in their
way; they care for heroic poetry; they are brave and wise in
their own fashion.

The Semitic Languages. — There is another great group of
languages which are like each other, but not like the languages
of the Aryan group. The Arabic and Hebrew languages are two
that belong to this group. The modern Arab says *salâm alaikum*
meaning " peace be upon you "; the Hebrew of Bible times said
shâlôm lâchem, " peace to you." The language of the ancient
Egyptians is a very distant cousin to the Hebrew.

Other Groups of Languages. — There are other groups of
languages, also. The Chinese languages are alike, though a
Chinaman from Canton cannot understand the speech of a
Chinaman from Peking. Our North American Indians spoke
many different languages.

In the whole world we know that there are or
have been at least 800 different languages : " dead

languages" like Sanskrit or Latin; living languages like English, French or German.

FIG. 355. Mongols; men of the Tartar races of Northern Central Asia. Many inhabitants of China, especially of Northern China, are of this race.

Sign-language. — Deaf and dumb people have an alphabet of their own, by which they can spell out words to each other. This sign-language was invented for the deaf and dumb by teachers who already understood how to read and write. But savage and barbarous people, who have no idea of reading and writing have invented another kind of sign-language by which they can talk to other wild tribes who do not understand their speech.

The red Indians of North America, for instance, were divided into tribes—the Sioux, the Chippewa, the Blackfoot, etc. Each tribe had its own language; but beside there was a language of signs that was understood by all the red Indians of the plains.

Indians make their fires in a little hole in the ground so that their enemies may not see the flames. Their sign for *a fire* was made by holding the hand vertical with the five fingers upwards, the tips of the fingers touching and by then gently opening and closing the fingers. (Try it.) This represented the gentle flickering of the tips of the flames above the hole in the ground. The sign for a man riding on a cantering pony was made by extending and joining the four fingers of the right hand, while the thumb (the rider) stood straight up. Then the hand was moved forward in a series of leaps like those of a galloping horse. (Try

FIG. 356. A Pueblo Indian (United States) carrying a painted jar.

it.) For hundreds of years they used these signs for *fire* and for a *man on horseback* and all understood what was meant. About fifty years ago white men built the first telegraph line across the plains and explained to the Indians, in words, that electricity was a kind of fire that traveled very swiftly. So the Indians made a new sign to stand for *telegraph*. They first gave the sign for *fire* and quickly added the sign for *man on horseback* going swiftly to carry a message. It is in such ways that new signs were invented as they were wanted. By several hundred signs of this kind Indians could tell long stories of fighting, hunting or adventure. They could direct each other how to make long journeys, say how many days each journey would take, tell where good water was to be

found, etc., and every Indian, no matter what language he spoke, could understand this language of signs.

We use a sign language ourselves. Suppose a boy opens the parlor door. His brother, sitting there, puts his finger on his lips as much as to say "Don't speak, you'll wake papa who is taking a nap on the sofa." Then the boy makes the sign of whittling a stick: "Where is your knife?" The brother makes other signs to say: "It is in the pocket of my coat on the hatrack," and more signs to say: "Hurry and shut the door—be

off.'' We all use signs of this sort. We shiver to show how
cold we are; frown when we are angry; make the motions of
writing to show we want a pencil, etc. You can tell quite a long
story without saying a word. (Try it.) Indians tell the whole
history of a battle in their war-dances (see Fig. 337).

FIG. 357. An Indian village (the pueblo of Taos) in New
Mexico. The houses are built of sun-dried mud (adobe) one on
another and were easily defended against enemies who had only
bows and arrows. The Pueblo Indians who were clever enough
to build houses like this were far more civilized than the wild Indians of the plains who lived in tents made of the skins of animals·
The Pueblo Indians lived always in one spot and cultivated their
farms of maize. The wild Indians roved from place to place in
search of game. The farmer is more civilized than the hunter.

The Language of Animals. — Animals have a language that
is made partly by signs, partly by sounds. Hens scratch the
ground and cluck to teach their chickens how to get food. A
dog jumps and barks to have the door opened for him. Bands
of apes set sentinels to warn them of approaching danger by
cries and by signs. But the language of animals does not go
very far. Your dog can understand what *you* say far better than
he can express what *he* has to say.

Writing. — The first writing of every nation is picture writing.

Just such pictures as this were painted by other North American Indians on buffalo robes and their history was recorded in this way.

FIG. 358. A picture-writing by Red Indians on a rock near Lake Superior. It means that a chief with five canoes and fifty-one men (count them) traveled for three days (three suns under three arches of the sky) and reached land on the other side of the lake (shown by the land-turtle). The chief of the whole party is the man on horseback (though, of course, he did not take his horse over). One of the chiefs in the first canoes was named *Kingfisher* (the bird near the large canoe). What they did on the other side of the lake is not recorded.

Chinese Writing. — The Chinese characters represent *things* or else ideas.

	SUN	MOON	MOUNTAIN	TREE	DOG
ANCIENT	○	♪	〰	朩	犬
MODERN	日	月	山	木	犬

FIG. 359. Chinese characters: The upper line is ancient; the lower modern. The older characters are rude pictures of the sun; the moon; a mountain; a tree; a dog. By and by they were changed to modern forms, more easy to make with a brush dipped in India ink.

Egyptian Writing. — The first hieroglyphics of Egypt were pictures. By and by they made a picture stand for a sound (page 372), just as if we should make a picture of a *cat* stand for *c*, a picture of an *ostrich* stand for *o*, a picture of a *bull* stand for *b*, etc.; *cat-ostrich-bull* would spell *cob* then, and any word could be spelled by sound. The Assyrians used writing at least 5000 years ago.

The Alphabet. — The Phœnicians who lived in Syria, and on the north coast of Africa (Tyre and Carthage were two of their cities) were close neighbors of the Egyptians and carried on trading with them. At least as early as 1000 B. C.—3000 years ago—they invented an alphabet, which was afterwards copied, with changes, by the Hebrews, Greeks, and Romans. The English alphabet is directly derived from those of the Greeks and Romans.

So soon as a people has learned to write it has made a great step forward. Men no longer have to remember everything which they wish to know. They can write some things down and leave their minds free for other things. They can set down words that other men can read long afterward. History can be written. Bargains between merchants can be recorded. Letters can be sent to distant friends. One king actually *tattooed* a letter on the skin of a messenger and sent him to another king, far away! In many countries it was a long time before writing was *generally* used. Scribes and secretaries and clerks did the writing and the kings and nobles signed it or sealed it. · King Richard I of England, did not know how to write his name, for instance.

Printing.—In very early times kings and merchants had their names engraved on seals (sealrings were first used in this way). The Chinese about 1,300 years ago (A. D. 593) used to engrave a whole page of a book on a block of wood and print a page at a time. In the XIV century this plan is mentioned in Arabian books that were known in Spain and in other countries of the west. Separate letters of the alphabet were engraved on little blocks of metal in Europe, about the middle of the XV century, so that the same types could be used to print many different books. Printing is one of several arts that we owe to the Chinese.

Paper was invented by the Egyptians, but most early manuscripts were written on *parchment* (goat or sheep skin) which was much tougher.

Counting.—Almost all savages can count up to five, using the fingers of one hand for counters. More than five they often call "many," without trying to say *how* many. Many barbarians use the word for hand to mean *five*. The Zulu's word for *six* is "taking the thumb." He means he has taken the left hand and a thumb besides to count with. In *writing*, but not in spelling, Roman numerals we call six: "five-one" (VI), seven: "five-two" (VII), and eight: "five-three" (VIII). Many uncivilized people use such names in speaking; six is *called* five-one; seven, five-two; just as we also call twenty and one, twenty-one. Ten is counted on the fingers of both hands, and our arithmetic is *decimal* simply because our ancesters had ten fingers. If they had had twelve we should have done all our counting by dozens instead of by tens. Up to twenty a man can count on fingers and toes together. Some Central American tribes count by twenties as we count by tens, and the French now say eighty-eleven where we say ninety-one. They are counting by twenties.

Fig. 360. Flutes made of bamboo, invented by Hawaiians. Notice that the holes are differently placed from the holes in our flutes. That shows that the Hawaiian scale of music is different from ours.

Measuring.—The first measures were the lengths of parts of a man's body. We still say a board is so many *feet* long, a horse so many *hands* high. A *pace* was a double step (*passus* in Latin), and a thousand (*mille*) of them made a *mile*. The Egyptians had pieces of wood for standard measures, just as we have foot rules. The King's chamber in the Great Pyramid is exactly 20 by 10 *cubits* (an Egyptian cubit was $20\frac{68}{100}$ English inches). Our pound and ounce, gallon and pint come from the

old Roman measures. A quart is a *quart*-er of a
gallon. The Egyptians were great farmers and
the name *geometry* is nothing but " land-survey " in
Greek. The Greeks learned the art in Egypt and
we learn it out of books written by Euklid, who
lived in Alexandria, in Egypt.

FIG. 361. Guitar and harmonica made by the Wayao negroes
of Africa.

Mathematics is nothing but the science of measuring, and begins with counting units. The first
units were the lengths of parts of a man's body as
we have seen.

Beginnings of the Sciences. — *Chemistry* began when a savage
found that a metal could be melted in a fire, or that vinegar
poured on copper would make verdegris. *Astronomy* began
when a shepherd watched the planets, or a sailor steered his little boat by the North Star. The Chinese regularly observed
eclipses thousands of years ago. The barbarians who played
on a flute made of a reed laid the foundations of the science
of sound (*acoustics*). Amber (*electron*—from which comes the
word electricity) attracts light pieces of straw and paper. The
hunter who cut up an antelope for food knew something of *anatomy* and *physiology*. *Medicine* began with the use of common
plants; ipecacuanha is in the Brazilian language *ipe-caa-goene*

which means " little-wayside-plant-emetic." Plato (died B. C. 347) compares the heart to a fountain sending the blood to nourish the body which, he says, is like a garden laid out with irrigating channels. Aristotle (died B. C. 322) knew a very great deal about *natural history* and many other kinds of science. Our knowledge has grown by small steps for thousands and thousands of years and will keep on growing.

Food. — The very first need of men is food. In tropical regions there are fruits — the banana, the bread-fruit, the cocoa-nut — sufficient for all. In the temperate zones, fruits and grains — wheat, maize, barley, oats—must be cultivated. Fish and wild animals are to be found nearly everywhere. Savage men live on such food as long as they can and move to a new place when it is necessary. The very first machinery and tools that men invented were for hunting and fishing — traps for game, fish-hooks, spears, clubs, etc. Men trained dogs for hunting many thousand years ago; leopards were so trained in India and hawks and falcons in Europe.

If you want to understand what sort of men savages are and how much they know, try to make for yourself, without any iron tools, a stone adze (like Fig. 365) or a good bow. Try to get fire without matches; make a hut in a tree (like Fig. 369). Remember you must use no iron tools.

Flocks and Herds. — The Laplander has herds of reindeer that give him milk and drag his sledge from place to place. The wild Arab has herds of camels, sheep and goats. Herds of cows are kept by many roving tribes and by nearly all that have

26

settled down to village life. So soon as a tribe owns cattle it is free from the immediate fear of hunger and it begins to have leisure and comfort. When such a tribe takes to farming it lives in one place and builds houses and barns.

Government and Laws.—Villages spring up and some kind of government is invented — usually a government of the oldest and wisest men. Laws are made and those who do not obey the laws are punished. From the very simplest beginning a company of people grows into a tribe or clan—and by and by tribes join together to make a nation. The Iroquois Indians were six North American tribes (" The Six Nations "), joined together for defence and offence. These barbarians were on the road to make a nation.

Fire.—There must have been a time when some savages did not understand the use of fire, but no tribe of men is now known that does not use it. Forest fires are often set by lightning, and fire can be had by tribes that live near volcanoes or burning oil-wells. Perhaps the first fires came in this way. Our own remote ancestors, the Aryans (see page 388) thought fire a sacred thing and worshipped it, and carried it carefully from place to place in their wanderings.

Flint and Steel.—Fire can be had by striking a hard tool against rocks and letting the sparks fall on very dry wood. The fire-drill used by the ancient Mexicans and in Australia, China, Africa and many other places was a drill of hard wood twirled between the hands on a piece of soft wood on which tinder or wood-dust is spread.

Matches.—Our common matches were invented about 1840 and it is only two generations since every kitchen fire was lighted with flint and steel!

Light.—Fire not only kept men warm in wintry weather but protected them from wild beasts, and gave them light at night.

Metal-working.—Metals were mere heavy lumps like stone till men melted them with fire to form weapons, tools, and ornaments of all kinds.

Pottery.—*Baked* earthern ware is hard and durable and as soon as it was invented a great step towards comfort and decent living was made. Meats could be cooked in pottery jars; a supply of water could be kept, etc.

FIG. 362. Ancient Egyptians making pottery.

Bricks.—Clay blocks burned in the fire make bricks for building and enable people to do without stones. The very first books were soft clay bricks on which men wrote before they baked them hard in ovens. To speak one's thoughts in language is the greatest outward difference between men and animals, but to use fire as men do is a difference almost as great.

Money. — Savage nations live by *barter;* by exchanging a spear for a knife, for instance. The man who wants a spear has to find a man who has a knife to exchange. Our way is to sell the knife for money to any one who wants it and to buy a spear from some one else with the money we get.

FIG. 363. A Mexican cart with wooden wheels. Where iron is scarce wheels are usually made like this and not with spokes and tires. The first carts and chariots in all countries were of this kind.

With fire men could obtain the metals—gold, silver, copper, iron —and work them into coin. Anything wanted could be bought with coin, because the man who took the coin knew that anything *he* wanted he could buy. The ancient Egyptians used rings of gold and silver for money. Very ancient Chinese coins were made in the shape of shirts as if to say " this coin is worth as much as a shirt." The coins of Alexander the Great (B. C. 330) are the most beautiful ever made, which is a good proof that coins were common two thousand years ago.

Salt made into bricks serves for money among the tribes of the north of Africa; tea, in bricks, in the northwest of China, little shells in other places, but gold and silver are the most convenient kinds of money.

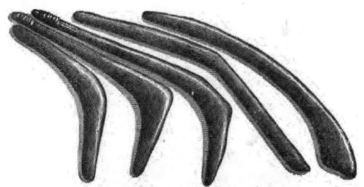

FIG. 364. Australian boomerangs. (Cut some of these shapes about five times as large out of stiff pasteboard and try them out of doors.) The Australian sticks are of hard wood, heavy enough to stun a kangaroo. Nearly every savage tribe has used weapons like these. The ancient Egyptians had bent sticks not unlike boomerangs.

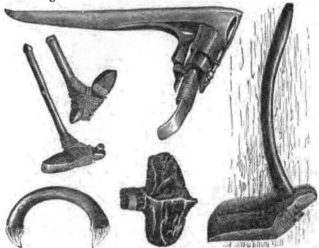

FIG. 365. Weapons and tools made by the Hawaiian and other Polynesian islanders. The lower left-hand weapon was held in the closed fist. It has two shark's teeth set in the ends. Stones or scraps of iron are lashed to wooden handles. The old Scandinavian word *hammarr* means either hammer or piece of rock.

FIG. 366. A young man of Ceylon (a Veddah) shooting with the long bow. Our English ancestors won the battles of Cressy and Agincourt from the French in the fourteenth century by shooting such bows as this. "They shot so wholly together that the air was filled with arrows as if with snow." Very likely the bow was first invented by savages who had trapped animals by a noose tied to a young tree bent over to make a *springe*. At any rate it was invented thousands of years ago — in the stone age. The arrow is nothing but a short spear. The *barb* of the arrow which keeps the head from pulling out of a wound, and the feathers on the end to make it fly straight were two great inventions.

Weapons.—The club is the oldest weapon of all. At first it was no more than the gnarled root of a tree. Next a stone was fastened at one end to make it heavy. A sharpened stone turned the club into a hatchet, and when men learned to use metal they made their metal hatchets like the early hatchets of stone. Clubs (metal *maces*) were used by the Knights of the Middle Ages, and the heavy walking sticks we carry now are nothing but handy clubs.

FIG. 367. Weapons now or lately used by the Arabs and Moors of Arabia and North Africa. The battle-axes are very much like those used by the Crusaders (Europeans) in the thirteenth and fourteenth centuries. The flint-lock guns are copies of European guns used a couple of hundred years ago. The curved swords (scimetars) are of shapes used by Arabs and Turks for centuries. The Arabs have simply copied their weapons from those of other nations.

Blow-guns.—Many savage tribes use blow-guns (long hollow tubes of reed or bamboo) to fly their arrows. A long tube makes them fly straight.

FIG. 368. Knives and swords used by the Moros (Mohamme-dans) of the Philippine Islands.

Some tribes in Africa and in South America *poison* their arrows. Centuries ago the Chinese invented gunpowder to use in fireworks. It made a puff when it exploded. A hollow tube of iron—a blowgun — with gun powder to do the blowing and a bullet instead of an arrow was the first musket.

Fig. 369. Many tribes of savages have lived in trees. The picture shows the dwellings of a tribe in Southern India. They are safe from tigers and other wild animals, and such a house is easily defended against human enemies.

Dwellings. — Savages often inhabit caves (see page 365) or build themselves rude dwellings of some sort. Those built in trees are hardly more ingenious than the nests of birds or the homes of beavers. Wooden huts covered with straw or daubed with clay are easy to make, and so are rude huts of stone. Where stone is scarce sun-dried bricks were often used. By and by hard bricks, baked

with fire, were invented. Pottery (earthen ware)
baked in ovens, was invented about the same time.

FIG. 370. A negro village in Africa. These rude huts *prove*
that the people who live in them are barbarians with few wants.

FIG. 371. A village of lake dwellers.

FIG. 372. A very old cottage of Irish peasants.

FIG. 373. A Filipino family. Notice the rude plow.

FIG. 374. A native house in Manila in the Philippines built of bamboo and straw. It is very suitable to a hot, damp climate, where the people are only half-civilized and have very few wants.

Barbarians live most of the day out of doors and use their huts chiefly to sleep in. They are " long sleepers" as the Romans said long ago of the ancestors of the Germans.

FIG. 375. An old English cottage with a thatched roof.

FIG. 376. Shakespeare's house at Stratford-on-Avon in England. Shakespeare died in 1616—four years before the Pilgrims landed at Plymouth.

FIG. 377. A log house like those built by the early settlers of America except that those had no glass windows. Chimneys were at first built of stones or clay, afterwards of brick. The first bricks in America were brought in ships from England. But as the colonists perfectly understood how to make and burn bricks it was not very long before they made all that were needed.

Lake-Dwellings.—Lake-Dwellings were built in Switzerland, in Venezuela and many other countries by barbarous tribes. They lived on wharves, near their boats, and could easily defend their homes or escape in their boats if necessary. (See page 410.) The great city of Venice began as a village of houses of this kind.

Fig. 378. A New England farmhouse. There was plenty of timber in America and so the first houses were made of logs, and the next improvement was to saw the logs into joists and boards and shingles and to build neat and cheap cottages like this.

Early stone buildings were constructed without cement or mortar. The splendid temples of Egypt and Greece had their stones fastened together by metal clamps, not by cement. The Romans were great builders and " Roman cement" is the name we give to-day to the best kind of cement. Very wide doorways could not be spanned by a single stone, and finally the *arch* was invented (see the arches all around the walls of the Colosseum, Fig. 381).

About 450 A. D. the Huns, a barbarous tribe, invaded Italy. Italians from Padua fled before the invaders and established themselves in the marshes and lagoons that now form Venice. They were

FIG. 379. Houses of the cliff-dwelling Indians in New Mexico. They lived in cliff houses for safety, and descended to the plains to cultivate their crops. When you see a cliff-house like this it proves at once that the people who lived in it were in daily danger of their lives from other barbarous tribes.

safe there and could sail away to sea if necessary, for the barbarians had no boats. Venice was a village of lake-dwellers (see Fig. 371) only it was

inhabited by very civilized people. Living near
the sea they became sailors and merchants and
controlled much of the commerce of the Mediterranean and Black Seas for a thousand years. Nearly
all the goods from the Orient came to Venice and

FIG. 380. The palace of Xerxes, King of Persia, at Persepolis.
The city was destroyed by Alexander the Great, a Greek, in the
year B. C. 330—more than two thousand years ago. The Persians of that day were rich, powerful, intelligent, civilized; this
building is itself a sufficient proof.

FIG. 381. Ruins of the Colosseum at Rome. It was built for
chariot races, fights between men and animals and public shows
of the sort about 72 A. D. nearly 2000 years ago. It is more
than 500 feet in diameter.

from thence were sent to the other countries of Europe.

"Long time she held the gorgeous East in fee and was the safeguard of the West."

FIG. 382. The palace of the Dōges (rulers of Venice) built in the fourteenth century. The splendid tower fell in ruins in 1902.

Venice would not have been founded if it had not been for the invasion of the barbarians — or at least would have had a very different history.

Boats.—The first boat was a floating log. A few logs lashed together make a raft. A log hollowed out by fire or dug out with tools, and sharpened at the ends makes a rude and strong canoe. The North American Indians made capital

27

Fig. 383. A castle on the Rhine (Germany). The towers were built in the middle ages (before the sixteenth century) for defence. Each Baron lived in his castle like a petty King, made war on his neighbors and took whatever he wanted from anyone who was not more powerful than he.

Fig. 384. A castle in Austria, built in the middle ages (before the fifteenth century). Notice its thick walls made for defence.

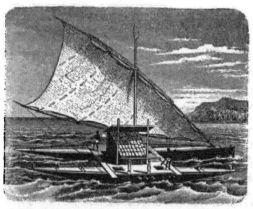

FIG. 385. A double canoe invented by the Fiji Islanders. It will not tip over, you see; and it will go either end foremost by simply shifting the sail.

canoes by covering a framework with pieces of birch-bark sewed together and made tight by a covering of gum. So soon as men had boats they

FIG. 386. A boat of the Tagals of the island of Luzon in the Philippines. Notice that the sail and the roofs of the cabins are made of bamboo. Such boats are now in use there.

learned to use oars and sails, but boats were steered
with paddles for thousands of years before rudders
were invented.

Most people that live near the sea use boats.
The Phœnicians, who lived on the north shore of
Africa (their capital city was Carthage) about four
thousand years ago, made long voyages to England

Fig. 387. A Greenland Eskimo in his boat (*Kayak*). It is a
canoe made of skins sewed together over a light framework of
wood. In this light canoe, using a harpoon, he kills seals, wal-
ruses and so forth.

to get tin from Cornwall. Tin mixed with copper
makes bronze. Bronze swords and lances are much
harder and better than copper ones and almost as
good as iron.

FIG. 388. A Chinese junk. The Chinese have used vessels
like this for a thousand years at least. Some of them are large
enough to carry 500 passengers and to make long sea voyages
to India. The Chinese Emperor sent an army of 100,000 men
in such junks to fight the Japanese about A. D. 1200 (and all the
men were lost in a storm). China has had a large coasting trade
for thousands of years.

FIG. 389. A New England fishing-smack (a schooner) driven
by sail power only. Vessels like this can and do go anywhere
in the world.

The fleet of Columbus in 1492 on his voyage to discover America consisted of small ships not so very different from the junks of the Chinese. In such ships as these Columbus had previously visited England, Iceland and most of the ports of the Mediterranean sea.

FIG. 390. A modern steel steamship. The ship is the *Kaiser Wilhelm der Grosse*, which crosses the Atlantic like a ferry boat, in less than six days, regularly. It does not wait for wind nor mind any weather.

Society.—All men join together in societies and so do most animals—ants, wasps, bees, elephants, and so forth. They help each other in a thousand ways. Some birds take care of young birds of families not their own; antelopes set sentinels to warn the herd of danger; apes take the advice of the oldest and wisest of the band. Men gather together in companies (tribes, nations) for their own pleasure and advantage; and the chief difference between a mere mob of people and a nation is that the mob looks only to the pleasure of the moment while the nation has found out—what is true—that you cannot have a happy life without law and justice. Society is a mass of men organized so as to get justice and preserve it. Every man must yield a little of his liberty for the benefit of the rest. All men must see to it that each man has justice and a fair chance. You will understand how laws should be made if you think about this sentence: *What is good for the hive is good for the bee.* What is good for men in general is good for you even in cases where it does not at once seem to be so. The motto for a civilized nation should be: *One for all—All for each one.*

Laws.—At the very first each man made his own laws to suit himself and carried them out by fighting, if necessary. If some one stole from him he arrested the thief and punished him. He was policeman, judge, jury, and jailer all in one. But just as soon as several families were joined together in one place they, the tribe, made laws to suit everybody in general, not some in particular. They made rules about hunting, rules to say how the game they killed should be divided, rules about marriage, about war, about the worship of their gods, about property. If any man had killed one of their tribe, the whole tribe hunted down the murderer and punished him. The laws were made by the wisest men. If the tribe had a chief or a king it was his particular business to see that the laws were carried out. Republics like our own are not governed by kings but by committees of wise men (Congress) who make laws that are intended

to suit everybody; by a chief (the President) who
enforces the laws; and by judges, who study the
words of the laws and say exactly what the laws
mean.

Fig. 391. The Capitol at Washington. It is about 750 feet in
length. The governors of the nation—the Congress—meet here.

It is a long way from the laws that savage men
make while they are squatting round a camp-fire
and deciding how to divide the game brought home
from the hunt, to the laws of a civilized country
that say how much tax a man shall pay for the
privilege of running a steam engine, or decide how
the business of a bank shall be conducted. But if
you will think of the customs and the laws of savages and of barbarous tribes, you will see that such
tribes have the beginning of law; that, as circumstances change they must make new laws; and
finally as they become civilized that they will have
laws very much like ours.

The Family. — The earliest group consisted of the father, the mother, and children — sons and daughters. They lived together, got food, and arranged for shelter. The man, with his sons to help, did the hunting and fishing. The woman and her daughters tended the fire and did the cooking.

FIG. 392. A negro weaving a mat with a native loom. Most barbarous nations know how to weave. First they learn how to *plait* and sew the plaits together to make mats. Next, they weave broad strips in one piece, for rugs.

We always think of the father as the head of the family, but in many tribes the mother was the head. The children took their mother's name. They belonged to her clan, not to the father's.

The Clan. — Families united to form a clan — a large family. Frequently all the persons in the clan had the same *totem*.

Totems.—Many savage tribes believe that they are descended from animals — from bears, wolves, birds, turtles, etc. A wolf painted on a man's body or part of a wolf's head carried or worn is the sign (*totem*) of the wolf clan; a turtle is the *totem* of the turtle clan; and so on. The North American Indians were divided into clans (big families) of the sort; and there were several clans in a tribe.

Fig. 393. A Zulu woman weaving a straw mat. It is a long step forward to weave a mat out of straw from merely sleeping on a heap of straw, almost like an animal. Woven mats are good for doors and curtains as well as for sleeping rugs. So soon as you have doors and curtains you begin to have privacy.

It was to the advantage of the clan to be as powerful and numerous as possible. So, among many peoples, the rule was that a young man must get his wife from a different clan and thus bring a new pair of hands to help in the work. A " wolf-man " must not marry a " wolf-girl." He must bring some girl from another clan, and he must buy her, or capture her, if necessary.

Marriage.—So in many savage tribes the young men got their wives by stealing them from other

Fig. 394. Spinning in Palestine as it is done to-day and as it has been done for three thousand years. Spinning wheels somewhat like the one in the picture were in use in America a hundred years ago. Since then spinning machines have taken their place.

tribes. In barbarous tribes wives were purchased, though sometimes, even to-day, there is a pretense of capture. The girl among the Tartars runs away on horseback and the young men chase her.

But she takes good care to be caught by the right man. It is only in civilized countries and in modern times that the woman has the right to choose her own husband.

Slaves.—Wild tribes are perpetually at war with each other; they capture wives in this way, property and prisoners. The prisoners are sometimes killed but often brought back to work as slaves. Since the world began men have enslaved each other and it is only recently that all European peoples have agreed that slavery was wrong. The negro slaves in America were freed in 1863. Africa and Asia are full of slaves to-day, especially the former. Try to think how it would be if you belonged to some one else just as his horse belonged to him; if you had to do what work you were told to do, and if the money you earned belonged not to you, but to your master.

Religious Ideas.—The very lowest savages probably had little notion of any God or Gods. The Australian savages believe that what they see and hear in dreams is as real as what they see and hear when awake. They think there are two worlds; the world of dreams and the world of waking-hours. Men live in one world; the ghosts or spirits of men in the other, they say.

African negroes think there are evil spirits that bring ill luck, good spirits that bring good fortune. Their *Fetishes* are images or idols of these good and evil spirits. The negro often prays to his *fetish* for a favor—he wants rain, for instance. If the rain does not come he beats the idol. If he does not want his *fetish* to know what is going on he wraps it in a cloth to hide its eyes.

Causes of Sickness.—The savage believes the air to be full of spirits, and he thinks that all his good luck comes through good spirits, and his bad luck from evil spirits. Bad spirits, he thinks, enter into a man's body and make him ill. To cure the patient the bad spirit must be cast out. The English word *nightmare* is the Anglo-Saxon word meaning *Evil Spirit of the Night*. The priests of barbarous tribes are doctors, too, and they pretend to cast out evil spirits by magic. Death, they think, is always caused by magic — and when a man dies they always try to find the witch who killed him. The witch-doctor usually pretends to find some one, and that entirely innocent person is killed in revenge.

Many tribes — the ancient Greeks, for instance, believed in a great number of gods. They had one god who ruled the sea,

FIG. 395. An idol (*fetish*) of African negroes. Such images made by the hands of their own priests, or sorcerers, are supposed to have magic powers —to bring rain, to give good luck in hunting, to cure diseases, keep off dangers and so on.

another who ruled the land, and gods of the plains, the hills, the groves, the mountains.

Fig. 396. Hindu temples on the Ganges River at Benares in India. In such temples as these the ancient gods of the Aryan peoples (see page 388) are worshipped by the Hindus. *Brama* created the world, they say; *Vishnu* maintains it; *Shiva* will destroy it. There were many other gods in their religion—*Agni*, the god of fire, has been worshipped from the very earliest times.

In Chaldea each city had its own patron god, and the king of the city was the chief priest of the god.

The Sky, the Sun, the Moon were once Worshipped as Gods. — The early Aryans worshipped the sky as a god. The Roman god *Jupiter* was the Heaven-Father — the father who *was* the sky.

Thunder and lightning were his doing; rain was his welcome gift to men, they said.

FIG. 397. The Parthenon—a Greek temple—at Athens. It was built B. C. 450—2300 years ago—and is one of the most beautiful buildings of the whole world. It was dedicated to the goddess Pallas, the goddess of wisdom and war, the special patron of Athens. It stands on the foundations of an older temple. The Greeks did not invent their own architecture. They took the main idea of it from Egypt and other countries but changed it and improved it with splendid results.

Names of the Days of the Week. — *Sunday* (the Sun's day) was a day once sacred to the worship of the Sun; *Monday*, to the Moon; *Tuesday* (in French it is called *Mardi*), to the worship of Mars; *Wednesday* (the day of the Anglo-Saxon god Woden—the supreme god); *Thursday* (the day of Thor—the Norse god of thunder); *Friday* (the day of Freia — the Norse goddess of fruitfulness, the Norse Venus); *Saturday* (the day of Saturnus or Saturn, the Roman god of agriculture and farming). Mars, Venus, Jupiter, and Saturn are planets and the gods were supposed to live in these stars.

Fig. 398. A temple of the ancient religion of Japan (the Shinto religion, a worship of nature—that is, sunlight, thunder, lightning, rain, trees, mountains, lakes, rivers). Many Japanese are Buddhists. (See page 433.)

Worship of the Sun and Moon.—All life on the Earth comes from the Sun (page 279), and the Sun in the sky and fire on the Earth have been worshipped from the earliest times. The Parsees of

India worship the Sun to-day, and thousands of Hindus pray to it. The Moon is useful to men in marking off the months and in giving light, and has been counted a goddess by many nations.

FIG. 399. This is a palace, or a temple, of the ancient Maya people in Central America.

Buddhism.—Buddha was born in India about 600 B. C. He was a prince. Reflecting about the cause of all the misery and sorrow in the world he saw that it was caused by desire, by self-will. He said that

28

men could not be happy or good until all self-will and desire were destroyed. By example and precept he preached a new religion which spread all over India, to Ceylon, China, Tibet and Japan. There are few Buddhists now in India, but Buddhism still

FIG. 400. A statue of Buddha.

flourishes in the other countries named, so that it is reckoned that there are at the present time 455,-000,000 Buddhists in the world.[1]

[1] There are about 500,000,000 Christians.

Jerusalem was founded nearly 2,000 years B. C. Here King Solomon built a temple to Jehovah about 1,000 B. C. It was in the hands of the Saracens (Mohammedans) after A. D. 637, and

FIG. 401. View of some Christian churches in Jerusalem.

the Crusaders — Christian soldiers — captured it in A. D. 1099, in order that the tomb of Jesus Christ should not be in the hands of unbelievers. In 1187 it was re-taken by the Saracens and since 1516 it has been held by the Turks (who are Mohammedans). They allow Christians, however, to build churches and to worship there.

Mohammed.—The Arab prophet and lawgiver was born at Mecca about A. D. 570. When he was 40 years of age he heard, he said, the voice of an angel ordering him to write down words spoken to him in a dream or trance.   This happened many times and all these words, written down, make the *Koran*, which is the Bible of the Mohammedans. The Arabs of his day worshipped idols.   He taught them to worship one god—Allah.

FIG. 402. Saint Sophia in Constantinople.   It was built for a Christian church about 500 B. C. and so used until the Turks captured the city in 1453, since which time it has been a Mohammedan mosque.

Any man who could say " There is no God but Allah—and Mohammed is the prophet of Allah " was his follower.   " All Mohammedans are brothers " was one of his sayings, and this rule is actually practised among them.   All the Arabs were converted and in time this religion spread over all the nearer East— Egypt, northern Africa, Arabia, Persia and part of India.   The Mohammedan Moors ruled Spain from 711 to 1492.   There are now about 200,000,000 Mohammedans in the world ; the "Moros " in the Philippines are Mohammedans.[1]

[1] There are about 500,000,000 Christians in the world to-day.

FIG. 403. An Arab school in the streets of Cairo in Egypt. The boys repeat the words of the *Koran* (the Mohammedan Bible) all together, as loud as they can scream; the schoolmaster has a stout stick for lazy scholars, and finally the pupils learn a large part of the *Koran* by heart.

FIG. 404. A Mohammedan mosque and royal tomb at Agra, India—the Taj Mahal. It was built about A. D., 1630 (the year in which Boston was founded), and there is no building more beautiful in the whole world. It stands on a marble platform 313 feet square near the river, and is approached on the land side through a delightful garden. In its very center are the tombs of the Mogul Emperor Shah Jehan and his wife Mumtaz-i-Mahal.

Worship of Ancestors.—Many tribes believe that the ghosts of their dead ancestors are still living in a world of spirits, in a world of dreams. The Anglo-Saxons, our own ancestors, believed that the echo of a man's voice was a spirit answering him.

FIG. 405. A church of Greek Christians in Moscow, Russia. The Greek Catholic Church separated from the Roman Catholic Church A. D. 729. The Greek Church has been the State Church of Russia for about a thousand years.

We now explain the echo in a very different way. The civilized Egyptians had beliefs of the same sort (see page 374). Many tribes also believe that their ancestors know what is going on in the real world — the world of waking thoughts — and so they pray to them asking help. The Chinese, for instance, set up tablets to their ancestors and burn incense before the tablets, telling them all their affairs and asking sympathy and assistance.

FIG. 406. The Christian cathedral at Cologne in Germany. The building was begun A. D. 1248, nearly 700 years ago, and is one of the most beautiful Gothic buildings in the whole world.

The Egyptians put little cakes and honey in tombs for the dead to use. The Russian peasant to-day puts bread on a shelf under the picture of a saint for a like reason.

No Hindu is happy until he has a son, who will some day grow up and do for *him* what he has

FIG. 407. An ancient Chinese temple in Peking. The city was founded about A. D. 1267 and the temple may be nearly as old as this. Temples of the same sort in southern China are at least two thousand years old.

piously done for his own father. Ancestors are often worshipped as if they were gods. The Roman people believed that their Emperors were divine even while they were alive and worshipped them after they had died.

Property.—Among savages the land belongs to everybody to use as he likes. He uses it only to hunt over. Barbarous tribes that keep flocks and herds use grazing land in much the same way, but when a man once plants a field of corn or builds a

FIG. 408. A Chinese Temple (Pagoda). Such old temples as this are to be found all over China.

house, that particular piece of ground belongs to him alone, just as the bow and arrow of a savage belong to him. As men became more civilized there were more and more things that could belong to a man personally—things that he alone had the right to use in his lifetime, and to give to his children when he died.

Every one in the tribe understands that the property of every other person *in the tribe* must not be taken. "Thou shalt not steal" only applies to the things that belong to one's fellow-tribesmen, at first. Civilized men know that this commandment applies to the property of strangers, as well. They have learned that it is right to treat all men as if they were their brothers. But all barbarians think that it is quite right to steal from strangers.

As a country becomes more civilized there are more and more things that it becomes the duty of the government to do, because no single person can attend to them properly.

Civilized people must see that their government provides water and light, makes good roads, keeps up good schools, a good police, takes care of the insane, and sick, and poor and so on. To do this well the government must have money — it must have property, just like a person.

Taxes are payments by the people to the government to enable it to do its work. Now-a-days we pay our taxes in money. In some countries the farmer still pays his taxes by giving hay or corn. Each man pays his taxes; the government spends the money for the benefit of all. Think for a moment what you get by living in a civilized country —your life is safe, all your wants are provided for, you have a fair chance, justice. A few dollars in taxes every year is not much to pay for all this.

Conclusion. — This little book has told a few of the many things that are known about the different races of men and about their habits, customs, laws and religions. Most of its pages describe the very early history of mankind, but you must remember, when you come to read the written history of your own country and of other countries, that every one of our habits, customs, laws and beliefs has · a starting point far back in the past, and you must try to understand that the whole history of mankind is *continuous.* You are the remote descendant of those men of ancient times and that is why it is important for you to understand what kind of people they were, and to study the early stages of our long human history.

TARR AND McMURRY'S
GEOGRAPHIES

A NEW SERIES OF GEOGRAPHIES IN THREE OR FIVE VOLUMES

BY

RALPH S. TARR, B.S., F.G.S.A.

CORNELL UNIVERSITY

AND

FRANK M. McMURRY, Ph.D.

TEACHERS COLLEGE, COLUMBIA UNIVERSITY

—————

THE THREE BOOK SERIES

FIRST BOOK (4th and 5th Years) **Home Geography and the
Earth as a Whole** . . . . . 60 Cents
SECOND BOOK (6th Year) **North America** . . 75 Cents
THIRD BOOK (7th Year) **Europe and Other Continents** . 75 Cents

THE FIVE BOOK SERIES

FIRST PART (4th Year) **Home Geography** . . 40 Cents
SECOND PART (5th Year) **The Earth as a Whole** . 40 Cents
THIRD PART (6th Year) **North America** . . 75 Cents
FOURTH PART (7th Year) **Europe, South America, Etc.** 50 Cents
FIFTH PART (8th Year) **Asia and Africa, with Review of
North America** . . . . . 40 Cents

To meet the requirements of some courses of study, the section from the Third Book, treating of South America is bound up with the Second Book, thus bringing North America and South America together in one volume.

The following Supplementary Volumes have also been prepared, and may be had separately or bound together with the Third Book of the Three Book Series, or the Fifth Part of the Five Book Series.

SUPPLEMENTARY VOLUMES

New York State, 30 Cents.   Kansas, 30 Cents.
The New England States, 30 Cents.   Ohio, 30 Cents.
Virginia, 30 Cents.   Utah, 40 Cents.

When ordering, be careful to specify the Book or Part and the Series desired, and whether with or without the State Supplement.

—————

PUBLISHED BY

THE MACMILLAN COMPANY

66 Fifth Avenue, New York

CHICAGO   BOSTON   SAN FRANCISCO   ATLANTA

CPSIA information can be obtained
at www.ICGtesting.com
Printed in the USA
BVHW071537140920
588712BV00002B/77

9 781376 453287